About the Internet Security Alliance

ISA Mission: The Internet Security Alliance seeks to integrate advanced technology with economics and public policy to create a sustained system of cybersecurity.

ISA Goals:

- Thought leadership
- Policy advocacy
- Stimulating the use of sound security standards, practices, and technologies

The ISA Board of Directors:

Chairman
Jeff Brown, Vice President and Chief Information Security Officer, **Raytheon**

First Vice Chairman
Gary McAlum, Senior Vice President and Chief Security Officer, **USAA**

Second Vice Chairman
JR Williamson, Director and Deputy Chief Information Security Officer, **Northrop Grumman**

Tim McKnight, Chief Information Security Officer, **General Electric**

■ ■ ■

For information about joining the Internet Security Alliance, please contact Larry Clinton at lclinton@isalliance.org (703-907-7028).

The Cybersecurity
Social Contract

Implementing a Market-Based Model for Cybersecurity

Internet Security Alliance
Edited by Larry Clinton and David Perera

ISBN: 0692755039
ISBN 13: 9780692755037

Acknowledgments

Ben Abrams, Northrop Grumman | Stacey Barrack, Internet Security Alliance | Robyn Bew, NACD | Jeff Brown, Raytheon | Joe Buonomo, Direct Computer Resources | Jim Connelly, Lockheed Martin | Center for Audit Quality | Andrew Cotton, Ernst and Young LLP | Daniel Crisp, BNY Mellon | Ken Daly, NACD | Scott DePasquale, Utilidata | Tanner Doucet, Deloitte | David Estlick, Starbucks | Bill Flannery, AIG | Matt Fleming, Synchrony Financial | Traci Grella, AIG | Stephen Hermanson, Vodafone | Lisa Humbert, BNY Mellon | Miheer Khona, Rising Sun Advisors | Chuck Jainchill, AIG | Gary McAlum, USAA | Tim McNulty, Carnegie Mellon University | Garin Pace, AIG | Geoffrey Peters | Dr. Michael Papay, Northrop Grumman | Brian Raymond, National Association of Manufacturers | Anthony Shapella, AIG | Richard Spearman, Vodafone | Larry Trittschuh, Synchrony Financial | Greg Vernaci, AIG | Dustin Wilcox, Centene | JR Williamson, Northrop Grumman | Dr. Robert Zandoli, Bunge

Contents

Foreword

In less than a generation, we have gone from the industrial age to the digital age. The Internet, and the digital technologies associated with it, are arguably the most influential inventions in the history of humankind. Digital technologies affect virtually every aspect of our lives from our physiology to our identity, how we develop and manage relationships, the meaning of core values such as privacy, and many of the assumptions we have long held about national issues such as economics and national defense.

Unfortunately, governance has not kept pace with the digital revolution. The digital revolution has come upon us so quickly, so easily, and in many respects, so pleasurably that we have not devoted the time and effort necessary to understand how to manage the digital world.

It's hard to underestimate the costs of failing to manage the risk of digitalization. Numerous doomsday speculations envisioning critical infrastructure going dark or defense weaponry misfiring because of cyberattack have been well chronicled elsewhere. Recent sophisticated economic modeling shows that the difference between establishing an Internet characterized by strong cybersecurity and one in which cyberattackers continue to enjoy their ability to compromise the system is a staggering loss of $90 trillion by 2030.[1]

As awareness of the cyber threat has grown, public and private policy makers have been subjected to a cacophony of ideas, prescriptions, technologies, and advice. All too often this massive information overload has led to confusion and uncertainty with a resulting paralysis of action just when we need clearheaded and decisive policy.

This book is an attempt to provide a coherent and systemic framework for collaborative action. Advanced technology needs to be integrated with practical economics and thoughtful public policy to create a sustainable system of cybersecurity. Our hope is to provide a clear path the next president and Congress can follow in collaboration with the private sector. The proposals provided build on conceptual consensus that has already been embraced by both political parties and the private sector. However, this volume moves this consensus from concepts onward to strategy and implementation.

Our goals are to crystallize the problem, recognize areas of progress, and identify gaps that need to be filled.

The book is separated into three sections. The first two chapters provide a snapshot of the current problem and brief history of US public policy, including why traditional approaches are a poor fit for this unique problem and how a new model—the Cybersecurity Social Contract—has evolved. The second chapter offers a series of high-level recommendations, many of which receive more detailed treatment as they are applied in the subsequent sections.

The second section encompasses eight chapters. Each chapter covers cybersecurity issues from the perspective of individual economic sectors and outlines pragmatic steps to improve cybersecurity in these specific sectors. Each of these chapters discusses what makes the sector unique, what challenges the authors see for the next administration and Congress, and offers a set of specific policy recommendations tailored to that specific sector. Each expert has been charged with answering the question: If you had thirty minutes with the next president of the United States to advise on cybersecurity, what would you say?

The recommendations occur at three levels of abstraction. Since one of the major impacts a new president can have is to set tone, direction, and prioritization, some recommendations focus on that higher level of abstraction (e.g., we need to act with greater urgency and spend more money).

Other recommendations are at a systemic level, such as government needs to get hold of the metastasizing bureaucracy strangling effective action and adapt to more modern approaches to supply-chain management, workforce education, and auditing. Still other recommendations are at the concrete operational policy level, such as specific recommendations to develop metrics for cybersecurity programs, to altering clearance processes, and even altering Medicare reimbursement.

The final section addresses a set of seven crosscutting issues that government and industry need to face irrespective of any unique sector. These chapters address how corporate boards understand the cyber risk, how the auditing community is adapting to the cyber risk, how organizations can structure themselves to best address the cyber risk, what role insurance can play in transferring cyber risk as well as addressing issues such as workforce development, privacy, and the best way to manage the public-private partnerships called for in the social contract.

The goal is to provide a coherent, comprehensive, credible policy framework for government and industry. The volume is comprehensive not only in the sense that it addresses issues and sectors not generally discussed in this field (such as agriculture, manufacturing, and auditing), as well as the usual suspect critical industry sectors, but also because it takes a comprehensive view of the problem, including economic, structural, and policy issues in addition to technical ones. The book is credible in that the chapter authors are individuals who do cybersecurity as their day (and often their night) job. It follows a thought-out conceptual framework—a theory—already intellectually accepted by both industry and government (bipartisan) and adapts it to the implementation level.

The reader may note some redundancies across the chapters. There are several reasons for this. One reason is that good ideas in one sector may well be good ideas in a different sector. However, more importantly, the book is designed so that it can be read in modules. With a prime audience intended to be policy makers, it is understood that readers interested in financial services may not be interested in the defense chapter even if similar ideas are proposed in each.

We are hopeful that by laying out this theory and demonstrating how it may be implemented in multiple domains of the problem, we will make it easier for government and industry to enact policies and procedures to more quickly address a growing problem of cyber insecurity.

---

1 Atlantic Council, Frederick S. Pardee Center for International Futures, and Zurich Insurance Group, *Risk Nexus: Overcome by Cyber Risks? Economic Benefits and Costs of Alternate Cyber Futures*, ed. Jason Healey, comp. Barry Hughes (Zurich: Zurich Insurance Group Ltd., 2015), Web.

Section I

A Social Contract for Cybersecurity

One

A Brief History of the Cybersecurity Problem and Policies That Have Attempted to Address It

Larry Clinton, President and CEO, Internet Security Alliance

THE PROBLEM: IT'S REALLY BAD—AND ABOUT TO GET MUCH WORSE

The Pentagon's 2015 annual report states

> The military's computer networks can be compromised by **low to middling skilled** attackers. Military systems do not have a sufficiently robust security posture to repel sustained attacks. The development of advanced cyber techniques makes it likely that a determined adversary can acquire a foothold **in most DOD systems** and be in a position to degrade DOD missions **when and if they choose**. (Emphasis added)[1]

This finding begs the question: If the most powerful and best-funded military organization in the history of the world is subject to "low to middling skilled attacks," what level of security is reasonable to expect from discount retailers (Target), movie studios (Sony), or other organizations facing these, or more sophisticated, attacks?

In February 2015 congressional testimony, James Clapper, director of national intelligence, summed up the effects of our current vulnerability:

> We must be prepared for a catastrophic large-scale cyber strike. We've been living with a constant and expanding barrage of cyberattacks for some time. This insidious trend will continue. Cyber poses a very complex set of threats, because profit-motivated criminals, ideologically motivated hackers, or extremists in variously capable nation-states, like Russia, China, North Korea, and Iran, are all potential adversaries, who, if they choose, can do great harm.[2]

Unfortunately, that is not the bad news.

The bad news is that our situation is likely going to get worse—much worse.

THE SYSTEM ITSELF IS GETTING TECHNOLOGICALLY WEAKER

The Internet was designed in the '70s and '80s to be an "open" system, not a secure system.[3] The core protocols that the Internet is based on are insecure by design. In addition, new software services and applications tend to be built on these core protocols (virtually no one builds from scratch), and so modern innovative products inherit the original vulnerabilities.[4]

To make matters worse, the attack community, sustained by the incredible profits cybercrime is generating for them, is reinvesting in its business to find new vulnerabilities. This includes going back through the core Internet protocols and finding new vulnerabilities heretofore not considered. ("Heartbleed" is an example of this core-protocol review process.)[5]

The explosion in the use of mobile devices further weakens the system's vulnerability. We will go from five billion mobile devices in use now to twenty-five billion in five years.[6] Business practices such as *bring your device to work* lead to intermingling insecure personal devices with corporate systems, vastly increasing vulnerability.

This trend will be exacerbated by the Internet of Things. The IoT refers to the ubiquitous digital interconnection of consumer devices, such as cars, security cameras, refrigerators, with the Internet. This development will bring increased consumer utility and benefit, while vastly complicating our cybersecurity issues.

THE ATTACK COMMUNITY IS GROWING MUCH MORE SOPHISTICATED

Nearly a decade ago, the National Security Agency coined the term "advanced persistent threat." APT was originally used to describe the ultra-sophisticated, multistaged cyberattacks we had begun to see between nation-states and the defense establishment. A critical characteristic of APT attacks was that they routinely circumvented all traditional perimeter-based cyber defenses, such as firewalls or intrusion-detection systems, and inevitably breached targeted systems.

We are now seeing these same sorts of attacks being launched throughout the cyber ecosystem. Not just the traditionally defined critical infrastructure, such as energy, defense, or financial services, but also manufacturing, retail, entertainment, and others now suffer from these sorts of attacks.

The advanced persistent threat has now become the *average* persistent threat.

We are long past the day when our primary concerns were with rogue individuals and "script kiddies" (although these still remain problems). Today's attackers tend to be sophisticated, well- funded and organized, and often state supported. Whereas a few years ago there were only a few nation-states engaging in cyberattacks, now there are over a hundred such countries. FireEye CEO Kevin Mandia has asserted that up to 90 percent of the attacks he works on involve state actors.[7]

These attackers often have at their disposal thousands of custom versions of malware. A large company with a sophisticated detection system may be subject to two million attacks a year, a quarter of which may be using designer malware specifically created for attacking that particular company.[8] The attackers escalate sophistication to respond to defenses. They maintain their presence in targeted systems, periodically calling home with stolen information. More insidiously, attackers are not just stealing data but also corrupting or manipulating these data, which could undermine basic faith in critical databases. Even the threat of corrupting or disabling data access has led to an epidemic of "ransomware" attacks where targets are forced to pay attackers to free their data from outside control.

Policy makers and the media often overlook the persistent element of modern attacks. Too often when a high-profile attack is discovered, media will seize on the one element of compromise and suggest, "If only the victim had used *xyz* well-known practice, the attack would have been thwarted." This overly simplified analysis fails to appreciate that if that particular pathway had been blocked, the attackers would most likely have continued to probe until they found a hole in the dike. In reality, the target would not have had to block the one compromised pathway to their system but all pathways. The notion of creating perimeter defense to keep the bad guys out of an information system is as outmoded as moots are to defend cities.

This is why even most defense systems are vulnerable to even low-skilled attacks, and why sophisticated cyber defenders understand that we need to move past the era of simple defenses like passwords, antivirus, and intrusion-detection systems and evolve a more sophisticated, affirmative multitiered, collaborative, and—frankly—more costly strategy.

ALL THE ECONOMIC INCENTIVES IN CYBERSECURITY FAVOR THE ATTACKERS

Cybersecurity discussions typically focus on technological standards, hardware and software vulnerabilities, and the like. Naturally, these issues are critically important. However, far too little of the cybersecurity analysis focuses on the economics of cybersecurity.

Technology is the pathway for cyberattacks. Technology describes *how* cyberattacks occur. However, in order to adequately address the issue, we also need to analyze *why* the attacks occur. From a private-sector perspective, the *why* is predominantly economic.

A wide range of independent research from sources including PricewaterhouseCoopers/CIO magazine,[9] CSIS/McAfee,[10] and even President Barack Obama's signature policy paper on the subject, "Cyberspace Policy Review,"[11] have found that a major factor, often the principal problem, in cybersecurity is not technology but economics.

When one considers the economic balance—the cost benefits of cybersecurity—it quickly becomes apparent that the economic balance overwhelmingly favors the attackers.

Cyberattack methods are cheap and easy to get access to. They are available via the Internet for surprisingly little investment and can even be outsourced. Even highly sophisticated cyberattacks, when compared to other military or criminal operations of similar scope and effect, are comparatively cheap to launch, especially in relation to the enormous profits they can generate.

And cyberattacks are very profitable. Estimates of the worldwide profit from cyberattacks range from the hundreds of billions of dollars to up to a trillion dollars a year, and climbing dramatically.[12]

Cybercriminals also have an extremely attractive business model. Unlike many traditional illicit enterprises that require the use of a large, unreliable workforce and long supply chains, cyberattacks require comparatively small workforces that can be safely located far from disruptive civil forces. In addition, the same cyberattack product can be used over and over again against literally millions of different targets.

On the other side of the equation, cyber defenders must overcome multiple disadvantages. Attackers generally have first-mover advantage in deciding who, when, and how to attack, often on the basis of stealthy reconnaissance. Defense is historically a generation behind the attacker (although that may be changing). Stealthy attacks are typically not discovered until months after they have been launched. Defenders must devise how to respond to an attack that may be using unique designer malware, while the attack is already long underway.

Although the costs to an enterprise of successful cyberattacks can be substantial, generating adequate investment in cybersecurity is still difficult. Modern management leans toward investment decisions on the basis of cost-benefit analysis driven by available metrics. It's hard to show return on investment on what you prevent. Absent solid metrics on the actual costs to a company for cyber losses and given the difficulty in protecting one's own enterprise when vulnerabilities in an enterprise you may be interconnected with could be the cause of your problem (e.g., Target). Gauging adequate expenditure is difficult. Moreover, the long criticized, but still prevalent, tendency to judge corporate investments on a quarter-to-quarter rather than a long-term basis further complicates the cyber-investment conundrum.

The inherent reality, for both the private sector and public sector, is that there are no unlimited funds for cyber defense.

Complicating the economic imbalance, many of the technologies and business practices that are required for enterprises to operate successfully in a worldwide competitive market tend to undermine cybersecurity.

Technological innovations such as Voice over Internet Protocol and cloud computing as well as business practices, such as the use of long international supply chains and bring your own device, are practical necessities for many businesses. However, these innovations can also vastly complicate cybersecurity. There are methods to mitigate and even improve security using these information technology innovations, but these come with added cost, placing economic viability at odds with cybersecurity.

It is infeasible, and unwise, to curb these innovations. However, it is necessary to fold these broader systematic business finance issues into the calculation of systemic cyber risk. We need to develop policies that mitigate cyber risks while still achieving the broader social goals of growth, profitability, innovation, international competitiveness, and job creation. All these issues need to be part of the same discussion.

WHY TRADITIONAL MECHANISMS ARE FAILING TO PROVIDE SECURITY

THEY WERE DESIGNED FOR A DIFFERENT TYPE OF PROBLEM

Cybersecurity is a unique twenty-first-century problem. Traditional mechanisms such as independent regulatory agencies, consumer lawsuits, and government regulation are proving ineffective in adequately bolstering our security in light of the modern threats.

The reasons these industrial-age methods are proving ineffective is largely because they were designed to address fundamentally different types of problems than we face today.

Much of our traditional regulatory processes and judicial enforcement are designed to address malfeasance. However, the core problem with cybersecurity is not that the technology is poorly constructed or companies are unwilling to invest in reasonable security. It's that the technology is under attack. And the technology is under attack because there are overwhelming incentives to attack it.

In instances such as the Enron and WorldCom scandals of the 1990s, the independent agencies, and then regulators, properly took the side of consumers fighting against corporate malfeasance. However, in today's cybersecurity environment, the government, consumers, and industry are on the same side. The opponents are vast criminal syndicates and increasingly nation-states and their surrogates.

GOVERNMENT DOESN'T HAVE THE CREDIBILITY NEEDED TO REGULATE FOR CYBERSECURITY

The foundational assumption of government regulating the private sector is that government knows what to do; all that is needed is to compel a recalcitrant private sector to follow government mandates. There is no evidence that government has attained that degree of expertise in cybersecurity. In fact, the data suggest the opposite.

A 2015 study by Veracode found computer-security incidents in federal agencies have increased 1,100 percent since 2006.[13] The study also compared civilian federal agencies (not DoD or the intelligence community) to the private sector and found the federal agencies ranked dead last in fixing security problems in software they build and buy. Federal agencies failed to comply with security standards 76 percent of the time.

Greg Wilshusen, director for info security at the Government Accountability Office, explained in congressional testimony some of the reasons the federal government didn't stack up against the private sector on cybersecurity:

Agencies rarely have adequate procedures for testing for security. When we evaluate agencies we tend to find that their evaluations are only interviews with people…they don't actually test the systems. We constantly find vulnerabilities that we identify as part of our testing and audit procedures that are not being found and fixed by the agencies.

Government agencies follow what IT pros call a policy-based approach to cybersecurity where agencies check off a list of requirements set by lawmakers and regulators that they have to follow.

Private companies typically do the same thing (because they have to). But, they also add to their mix a risk-based approach. With a risk-based approach you look at what the attackers might want and what's in place to stop them.[14]

Although the Veracode study focused on the federal government, available research suggests that even our best-resourced and most sophisticated state governments fare no better.

An August 2015 report from the California State Auditor found Golden State agencies did not "provide adequate oversight or guidance...Seventy-seven of the reporting entities indicated that they almost universally lack of compliance or had not achieved full compliance with information security standards."[15]

GOVERNMENT IS NOT PROPERLY STRUCTURED TO DEAL WITH THE DIGITAL AGE

Consistent with the finding that government procedures to protect information security are inadequate is the finding the government is not structured to manage or effectively govern for cybersecurity.

A Bank of America Merrill Lynch 2015 report found that "The U.S. government is still in the process of determining who will have jurisdiction in cyberspace. As the Department of Defense, DHS, and their subordinate organizations like the Air Force, Navy, Army, Defense Agencies and Commands battle for jurisdiction and funding. The result is a fragmented system muddled with a political agenda which hinders the development of a more secure system."[16]

Government's lack of clarity leads to confusion redundancy and inefficiency for the private sector, complicating an already daunting problem.

EVEN IF GOVERNMENT WERE UP TO THE TASK, THE REGULATORY MODEL DOESN'T FIT THE PROBLEM

The expert agency regulatory model, wherein an elected body empowers a regulatory agency to specify requirements for the private sector, was born to deal with the hot technology of two centuries ago—railroads—with formation of the Interstate Commerce Commission. The model has been replicated repeatedly throughout the industrial age with the Securities and Exchange Commission, the Federal Trade Commission, and the Federal Communications Commission, and so on.

Cybersecurity is not like consumer-product safety regulated through the Consumer Product Safety Commission. These models essentially attempt to locate a static standard that assures safety wherever producers are in compliance. While this process has served democracies well for many years, it is poorly suited to address the unique issues raised by digital technology in the twenty-first century. While there is clearly a need, as we will discuss later, to upgrade "cyber hygiene" on a systemic basis, following existing cybersecurity practices and standards is not the answer to sophisticated or persistent threats.

There is a role for regulation in certain spaces, such as requirements to notify citizens when their personal data have been compromised, or in industries where the core economics of the industry are already intimately involved in regulation, such as municipal water services. But traditional regulation is generally falls short as an effective, sustaining private-sector cybersecurity, due to the nature of government and the nature of the problem itself.

Technology and attack methods change constantly and quickly. The traditional regulatory process cannot keep up with the evolution of what constitutes the required cybersecurity at any given time. The regulatory process, imbedded with time-consuming reviews, comments, and often litigation, is inherently cumbersome.

Moreover, regulations create a "floor" of required minimums. While this may be effective with static issues, cyber is not static. Attackers routinely assess the status of target's defenses and design new methods to circumvent existing defenses. What is required is a more dynamic system that motivates continued, cost-effective, improvement.

The obvious effect of the regulatory process is that the regulations may well be out of date and ineffective before they take effect. But there is an even larger problem with trying to apply the outdated regulatory process to the modern cyber problem. Complying with regulations takes time and resources. When scarce security resources are sucked up by compliance costs, it means less time and money for actual security. Mandating compliance with outdated regulations is ineffective and counterproductive.

It is also essential to consider cyber regulations from a broader systems perspective. Policy makers need to understand the effects a plodding pace of regulation will have on investment, innovation, and job creation. Cybersecurity in major organizations is a complicated, complex, and costly undertaking. Uncertainty about regulatory compliance, especially if backed by significant penalties, will delay investment. Companies can't afford to make substantial investments not knowing if their configuration will be deemed as compliant.

Delays will not apply just to cybersecurity solutions but to investments in innovative products and services. This is exactly the opposite investment environment to what we want.

Finally, the regulatory process is not comprehensive enough to generate a sustainably secure system. Cybersecurity is an international problem. Nation-states don't have adequate jurisdiction, and international entities do not have enough consensus to substantively address the issue. Even if the United States were able to divine a perfect regulatory system, it would only apply domestically. If, as would almost certainly be the case, there were added costs for US companies, that would leave American companies at a competitive disadvantage. Extensive cyber regulations would provide an incentive for companies to move operations overseas, especially to Asia, seeking more competitive operational environments—all to the detriment of the US worker and economy.

OTHER INDUSTRIAL-AGE CONTROL MECHANISMS ARE NOT WORKING, ARE INAPPROPRIATE, AND MAY BE COUNTERPRODUCTIVE

Disclosure Models Don't Fit the Digital Age

One proposal that has received traction with some regulators is to apply twentieth-century disclosure models to cybersecurity. This "naming and shaming" is often justified with assertions that such disclosure protects investors and, by triggering negative stock performances, they will motivate improved security.

While citizens have an obvious right to know if their personal data have been compromised (as virtually every state now demands), disclosure as a motivator for improved security is too blunt an instrument to achieve our broader goals.

In an era when virtually all organizations, including the military, are subject to successful cyberattacks, simply identifying which vulnerability was exploited is not a reasonable standard of malfeasance. Absent clear data on cost-effective solutions to prevent these attacks, ex post facto enforcement actions amount to blaming the victims of the attack when we need to be helping them.

As John Carlin, assistant attorney general for national security, recently pointed out, blaming companies for sophisticated breaches by nation-states is akin to blaming a pedestrian who gets stabbed by a stranger for simply making eye contact beforehand. Officials need to work with the press to ensure media coverage is not focusing on blaming the victim.[17]

Not only does the blame and shame approach betray a misunderstanding of the current threat environment but it is also ineffective and counterproductive.

A review of stock performance for companies that have suffered high-profile breaches shows a clear pattern of short-term price reductions followed by mid- and longer-term recovery. Target's stock was up 30 percent a year after its highly publicized breach. Sony's stock was up 40 percent six months after its breach.

These are not isolated instances. The academic literature shows that in general, when stock prices do fall from public embarrassments, the typical effect is an initial drop of about 7 percent, only to typically rebound back up 13 percent from the initial drop.[18]

Moreover, modern attacks tend to be stealthy and difficult to discover. We need to be motivating corporations to be investing in, sometimes expensive, discovery techniques. Getting funding for such good practice will be harder if the reward for such diligence is an SEC or FTC enforcement action.

Finally, these solutions again fail to take into account the broader negative systemic effects they can have. If, for example, an attacker knows that a successful breach will result in disclosure and negative stock effects, they may intentionally launch the attack after shorting the stock. Thus, the attackers can profit both from the spoils of the attack and the supposed remedy. Ironically, if the SEC launched such a program, it might well be incentivizing sophisticated stock manipulation in direct conflict with their core mission.

Court Action Is Proving Ineffective

Notwithstanding the hype from the plaintiff's bar, the predicted (for ten years) avalanche of lawsuits by consumers harmed by cyberattacks and the resulting improvements in security to avoid such suits have not materialized. One of the main reasons for this mechanism's failure to promote the needed security upgrades is that the suits are usually unsuccessful.

While it's quite easy to put out a press release in the wake of a cyber breach, actually succeeding in court is more daunting. Was the attack from a nation-state that could not be prevented? Was it the result of an insider or unaffiliated interconnection in another system? Is the cause faulty hardware? Software? Are there real damages?

A May 2015 study by *BankInfoSecurity* found that the reality was that most of these cases were being dismissed:

> The vast majority of consumers' data breach lawsuits get dismissed after judges rule that the "plaintiffs' bar" has failed to prove the defendants suffered actual or threatened injury.[19]

We need a twenty-first-century systems approach to address the cybersecurity issue. The new model needs a much more dynamic motivator than backward-looking regulations and potential enforcement. Since 90 percent of the cyber infrastructure is owned and operated by the private sector and the principal problem with cybersecurity is economic, the best model to promote a forward-thinking risk-management approach to cybersecurity would be injecting positive economic incentives into continual upgrading and management of private cyber systems.

THE PATH FORWARD: THE CYBERSECURITY SOCIAL CONTRACT

The concept of the social contract was popularized in the eighteenth and nineteenth centuries through the writings of Jean-Jacques Rousseau, John Locke, Thomas Hobbes, and others. It initially focused on the relationship between the individual and the state and what each would exchange with the other in order to achieve broader social order and benefit for the community.

In the early twentieth century, the social contract was adapted to the exchange between corporations and the state in order to achieve mutual and greater benefit for the social order.

At the time, the hot technologies were telecommunications (phones) and distributed electricity. Initially these services were provided where the economies justified them: urban and affluent areas. The policy makers of the era not only understood that universal service of these technologies would have broad social benefit but also realized government couldn't accomplish this on its own. Moreover, compelling the private sector to provide the services without adequate compensation would be an unsustainable model.

So, a "social contract"—essentially an economic deal—was developed. Private companies agreed to provide universal service at regulated rates. In exchange, the government agreed to guarantee a substantial rate of return on their investments. Thus was born rate-of-return regulation, and the private-investor-owned public utility.

Critical to understanding the social contract as applied to infrastructure development in the United States is the realization that not only did it enhance the greater public good but there was also an economic exchange in return for this societal benefit.

And it worked. The broader systemic benefits of the social contract were enormous. The electric and telecommunications infrastructures were deployed at an accelerated pace compared with other nations that chose a government-centric model. Moreover, the infrastructures, adequately supported by the economic incentives imbedded in the contract, were continually made more sophisticated and innovative. The rapid development of these infrastructures provided the foundation for accelerated industrialization, job creation, and innovation. These systemic effects were essential to turning the United States from a second-rate world presence at the turn of the twentieth century into the world's leading superpower in a little more than a generation.

In publications printed in 2008 and 2009, ISA argued that a similar situation exists today with respect to cybersecurity.[20] For example, although there are substantial pockets in both the public and private sectors that are doing an admirable job funding and applying strong cyber defenses, because of the interconnection of the system, we need a universal solution.

Neither companies nor government operating on their own can adequately secure themselves. A new system needs to be developed. That new system needs not just standards and practices but also economic support for their universal application and continued rapid innovation and adjustment in the face of the ever-evolving cyber threat.

We noted that there already existed standards and practices that, if deployed universally, could substantially improve our nation's cybersecurity. ISA called for these standards and practices to be identified in a public-private partnership. Industry's role would be continuing to develop and deploy these techniques. Government's role would be to support and encourage this development and adoption by providing a menu of incentives tailored to the unique needs of industry sectors.

In the ensuing years, we have seen substantial progress at the conceptual level as the private sector and both political parties have gravitated toward embracing the cybersecurity social contract model. Initially, policy makers from both parties proposed variations of a traditional regulatory approach to cybersecurity. From 2004 through 2012, regulatory proposals were circulated by Senators Jay Rockefeller, Olympia Snowe, Joe Lieberman, and Susan Collins and House members including Representatives Adam Putnam, Tom Davis, and Bennie Thompson. As these proposals were floated and analyzed, the inadequacy of the approach became apparent, and an alternative approach was sought.

Following the publication of the social contract model, a broad coalition of industry trade associations and privacy groups, including the Chamber of Commerce, TechAmerica, the Business Software Alliance, the Center for Democracy and Technology, and ISA, produced in 2010 a detailed white paper that embraced the principles in the cybersecurity social contract.[21]

In 2011, then House Speaker John Boehner appointed a GOP Cybersecurity Task Force chaired by Rep. Mac Thornberry. The task force became the first government entity to appreciate the economic dynamics of cybersecurity and craft an alternative approach. It embraced social contract principles and made the deployment of a menu of market incentives to motivate voluntary adoption of sound standards and practices its number-one recommendation.[22]

President Obama's signature policy paper on cybersecurity, "Cyberspace Policy Review," authored by Melissa Hathaway, made ISA's 2008 "Cyber Security Social Contract" publication it's first and most frequently cited reference.[23] In 2013, the president issued an executive order on cybersecurity that also embraced the principles of a cybersecurity social contract.[24] The president abandoned the traditional regulatory approach and instructed the National Institute of Standards and Technology to identify the appropriate standards and practices that ought to be voluntarily adopted by the private sector and reinforced by the development of market incentives.

Although we have now developed a broad consensus on the conceptual approach, we need to stimulate progress on implementation. As we turn to a new administration and Congress, there is still a great deal of work to be done, at both the macro- and microlevel, to build on the consensus that has been developed and implement a secure cyber system that is both technologically responsive to the evolving threat and economically sustainable.

---

1 US Department of Defense, Office of the Secretary of Defense, *Annual Report to Congress: Military and Security Developments Involving the People's Republic of China 2015* (Washington, DC: Department of Defense, 2015), Web.

2 *Opening Statement to Worldwide Threat Assessment Hearing: Senate Armed Services Committee*, 114th Cong. (2015) (testimony of the Honorable James R. Clapper, director of National Intelligence), Web.

3 Craig Timberg, "A Flaw in the Design: The Internet's Founders Saw Its Promise but Didn't Foresee Users Attacking One Another," *Washington Post*, Mar. 30, 2015, Web.

4 Symantec Corporation, *ISTR20: Internet Security Threat Report*, vol. 20 (Mountain View: Symantec Corporation, Apr. 2015).

5 Ibid.

6 Gartner, *Gartner Says 4.9 Billion Connected "Things" Will Be in Use in 2015* (Gartner Newsroom, Nov. 11, 2014), Web.

7 Tara Seals, "Kevin Mandia: Nation-State Cyber Espionage Becomes the Norm," *InfoSecurityMagazine*, Oct. 13, 2015, Web.

8 PricewaterhouseCoopers (PWC), *Managing Cyber Risks in an Interconnected World: Key Findings from the Global State of Information Security Survey 2015* (PWC, 2014), Web.

9 PricewaterhouseCoopers. *The Global State of Information Security* (PWC, 2008).

10 Center for Strategic and International Studies and McAfee, *Net Losses: Estimating the Global Cost of Cybercrime* (Intel Security, June 2014), Web.

11 Executive Office of the President of the United States, "Cyberspace Policy Review: Assuring a Trusted and Resilient Information and Communications Infrastructure," *WhiteHouse.gov*, 2009, Web.

12 Ibid.

13 Veracode, *State of Software Security Report, Volume 6: Focus on Industry Verticals* (Veracode, June 2015), Web.

14 *Enhancing Cybersecurity of Third-Party Contractors and Vendors*, 114th Cong. (2015) (testimony of Gregory C. Wilshusen, director of Information Security Issues, US Government Accountability Office), Web.

15 Elaine M. Howle, *High Risk Update—Information Security: Many State Entities' Information Assets Are Potentially Vulnerable to Attack or Disruption* (Sacramento, CA: California State Auditor, Aug. 2015), Web.

16 Sarbjit Nahal, Beijia Ma, and Felix Tran, *Thematic Investing: You've Been Hacked!—Global Cybersecurity Primer* (Bank of America Merrill Lynch, Sept. 3, 2015), Web.

17 John P. Carlin, "Acting Assistant Attorney General for National Security John P. Carlin Delivers Remarks at the American University Business Law Review 2014 Symposium,"

American University Business Law Review 2014 Symposium, Department of Justice, American University, Washington, DC, Mar. 28, 2014, Web.

18 Andrea Bonime-Blanc, *The Reputation Risk Handbook: Surviving and Thriving in the Age of Hyper-Transparency* (Oxford: Do Sustainability, 2014).

19 Matthew J. Schwartz, "Why So Many Data Breach Lawsuits Fail," *BankInfoSecurity*, May 11, 2015, Web.

20 Internet Security Alliance, *The Cybersecurity Social Contract: Policy Recommendations for the Obama Administration and 111th Congress* (Washington, DC: Internet Security Alliance, 2008); Internet Security Alliance, *Social Contract 2.0: A 21st Century Program for Effective Cybersecurity* (Washington, DC: Internet Security Alliance, 2009).

21 Internet Security Alliance, Business Software Alliance, Center for Democracy & Technology, TechAmerica, and US Chamber of Commerce, *Improving Our Nation's Cybersecurity through the Public–Private Partnership*, white paper (Washington, DC, Mar. 8, 2011), Web.

22 US Cong. H., House Republican Cybersecurity Task Force, *Recommendations of the House Republican Cybersecurity Task Force*, 112th sess., H. Rep., Washington, DC, Oct. 2011, Web.

23 Executive Office of the President of the United States, "Cyberspace Policy Review: Assuring a Trusted and Resilient Information and Communications Infrastructure," *WhiteHouse.gov*, 2009, Web.

24 Exec. Order No. 13636, 3 C.F.R. Section 7(a) (2013), Web.

Two

A Twelve-Step Program
for Implementing the
Cybersecurity Social Contract

Larry Clinton, President and CEO, Internet Security Alliance

A new president and Congress must set the tone and priorities for cybersecurity as well as enact specific legislative and policy changes to implement the priorities. If I had thirty minutes with the president, I would recommend the following program.

1. WE NEED TO ATTACK THE CYBERSECURITY PROBLEM WITH GREATER URGENCY

Many of the structural, strategic, and operational problems that are discussed here and in later chapters have been well known for years, and a broad consensus has been reached on the basic policy framework—the social contract model. However, implementation is where the rubber meets the road, and we have been driving in second gear for far too long.

The most obvious characteristic of the digital age is speed. Technologies (and security issues) are created, modified, and implemented at rates far exceeding historical norms. Yet governments with their bureaucratic processes and constant turf battles have been noticeably slow in comprehensively addressing the cybersecurity problem.

Compared to the speed with which our information technology systems are being compromised, federal policy making has moved at a glacier pace.

While the United States has been a leader compared to other governments in terms of recognizing the issue and developing an enlightened approach to it, even here our progress has been too slow.

It has taken nearly a decade to finally get a full component devoted to cyber proposed in Department of Homeland Security reorganization. It took us four years just to get an assistant secretary for cybersecurity named. It took us six years to enact a modest information-sharing bill, and there are virtually no other bills to implement the incentives called for in the Executive Order 13636 and recommendations of the House Republican Cybersecurity Task Force. Most damningly, critical measures called for by the executive order—such as determining how to cost-effectively implement the NIST Cybersecurity Framework—are ignored. Three years after its creation, there is still no systematic effort underway to document what, if any, impact the framework has actually made on private-sector cybersecurity.

There are countless other examples, many detailed below. The point is that if cybersecurity is as large a threat to both our economy and our national security as we are often told, then we need to be far more aggressive in addressing the problem. A new president can do a lot to set the proper aggressive tone to the issue. Cybersecurity needs to figure prominently in the new president's first hundred-day agenda.

2. GOVERNMENT NEEDS TO RECOGNIZE THE IMPORTANCE OF ECONOMICS IN CYBERSECURITY

A great deal is written about the asymmetric nature of the cyber threat. Much less is done to tackle the asymmetric nature of cyber economics and the impact that imbalance has on mitigating the threat.

The critical factor for addressing cyber risk is cost.[1]

Economics is the driving force for much human, and most private-sector, behavior. Yet, as detailed in chapter 1, in cybersecurity virtually all the economic incentives favor the attacker. Moreover, firms competing in a world market many times find it a competitive necessity to use business practices and technologies that undermine security.

PricewaterhouseCoopers has independently substantiated that the approach taken by the National Association of Corporate Directors in training the private sector to better understand the cyber threat has been successful.[2] Core to that strategy is the notion that boards of directors need to stop thinking about cybersecurity as an "IT issue" and instead integrate cybersecurity into all their business decisions.

Government, too, must integrate cybersecurity into its broader infrastructure programs. As detailed in the chapters on healthcare and utilities, government has appropriated billions of dollars for innovative digital programs such as smart grid and electronic medical records without properly apportioning funds to assure these new digital systems are secure.

While this scenario is true for all enterprises, it is especially true with respect to smaller companies. Virtually all small companies want the same thing—to become big companies (or be bought by one). Small companies, especially, want to spend their money on sales and marketing. So, for a smaller company, the question is not "Should I spend on security?" but "Where to spend the few marginal dollars I have to upgrade my security?" To provide smaller companies with nothing more than a superstore of options like the NIST framework and tell them to go research the cost benefits is unrealistic and ineffective on a large scale.

Despite the fact that cybersecurity is arguably more an economic issue than an IT issue, government policy virtually ignores economics. Although Executive Order 13636 and the House GOP Task Force's report on cybersecurity both recommend the development of a menu of market incentives, there has not been a single legislative proposal apart from provisions of the Cybersecurity Information Sharing Act for market incentives to receive even committee-level consideration. On the rare occasion when a congressional committee holds a hearing on the economics of cybersecurity, it tends to focus on the economic impact of cyber events, which serve more to hype the issue than solve the problem. DHS has hundreds of IT professionals working on cybersecurity and only two economists. Government programs to assist the private sector are not tested for their cost effectiveness, leaving the private sector in the dark about where to best spend its limited dollars on security.

The United States is a capitalistic economy. The IT systems we rely on for national and economic security are intertwined. The new administration must integrate a more comprehensive understanding of cybersecurity by embracing the role of economics. Absent the integration of practical economics into public policy, we will never achieve a sustainably secure system. Congress and the administration need to expand the focus on cybersecurity beyond the IT silo and embrace the broader nature of the problem and the need to rebalance the economic-incentive structure in cybersecurity.

3. GOVERNMENT NEEDS TO DRAMATICALLY INCREASE FUNDING FOR CYBERSECURITY

Perhaps the most concrete evidence of the inadequacy of government efforts on cybersecurity is the lack of adequate funding, especially in light of the criticality of digital systems and the threat against them.

Virtually every government function and service depends on cyberspace but its systems contain inherent vulnerabilities and are under constant attack. The attacks are growing more common and severe and are likely to get worse, for reasons outlined in chapter 1. Vastly increasing the funding priority for securing these systems seems very appropriate. Government funding needs to increase not just for federal systems but also to improve security for the entire country, including the private sector.

The inescapable fact is that improving cybersecurity will cost money.

Someone will need to pay for the needed improvements in security. If the government isn't going to pay for the needed improvements, it will likely mean consumers are asked to pay for it. The National Infrastructure Protection Plan acknowledges a difference between commercial security, which industry naturally needs to fund, and national security, which is a government responsibility.[3] In a digital environment where systems are shared, government must partner with industry, even spending public monies to support private systems whenever the latter are vital to the national interest.

A policy façade sometimes proffered is that corporate shareholders should foot the bill. However, shifting costs to "the shareholders" is a chimera, since the real bill payers will be consumers, whether through higher prices, reduced shareholder value and concomitant lower 401(k) portfolios, and less innovation and job creation.

In fact, private-sector spending on cybersecurity is already substantial and outpacing government spending. Total private-sector spending on cybersecurity (not just technology) is currently estimated at approximately $120 billion a year.[4] PWC's annual *Global State of Information Security Survey* has reported private-sector spending is increasing at 24 percent, more than twice the rate of government increases.[5] In comparison, DHS's entire budget for everything—immigration, airport security, Secret Service, and so on—is approximately $60 billion. The private sector is spending twice that on cybersecurity alone.

Although accurately assessing the costs of cyberattacks is difficult, there is consensus that the price tag is staggering and going up. In his 2009 paper "Cyberspace Policy Review," President Barack Obama said the costs from cyberattacks were approximately a trillion dollars a year.[6]

Eight years later, total federal spending on cybersecurity is less than $14 billion annually, and about half the federal spending goes to the Pentagon, leaving less than $10 billion to help protect the rest of vast government enterprise.[7] Homeland Security gets a bit more than $1 billion for cybersecurity. To contextualize that spending, two banks annual cyber budget for 2016 is $1.25 billion for cybersecurity. That means two bank's budget for cybersecurity is nearly a quarter more than what DHS gets to protect the entire civilian sectors of the economy and coordinate cybersecurity for all the civilian federal agencies.

Cybersecurity spending in the rest of the civilian federal government is even more minuscule. DHS is the only civilian federal agency to spend as much as 3 percent of its budget on cybersecurity. Eleven federal agencies spend less than 1 percent of their budget on cybersecurity including the Social Security Administration, NASA and the Department of State. The Office of Personnel Management spent the lowest percentage on cybersecurity of all federal departments, which is interesting since it suffered the biggest federal agency breach to date.[8] In an October 2015 letter to the Senate Finance Committee, IRS commissioner John Koskinen compares his agency's cybersecurity spending to the private sector where spending has grown in double-digit increments in recent years. "Our IT budget has actually decreased in recent years, despite the fact that we maintain sensitive data of millions of American taxpayers," Koskinen wrote.[9]

With government estimating the costs of poor security at $1 trillion and economic modeling suggesting the costs to be several hundred times that number by 2030, the need for the government to invest substantially more on cybersecurity is obvious.

Streamlining government structures might generate some savings that can be more efficiently used. However, structural efficiency will not be enough to reverse the trend to less security. Some additional resources can be generated via partnership programs with the private sector as discussed below, but government also needs to take a sincere look at legacy spending that can no longer be afforded in the digital age.

4. GOVERNMENT NEEDS TO BE ORGANIZED TO REFLECT THE CURRENT DIGITAL REALITIES

Government's credibility in educating, let alone regulating and mandating, cybersecurity in the private sector is clearly undermined by its lack of demonstrated ability to manage its own house.

The chaotic and disorganized governmental structures are not just inefficient but they also have serious downstream negative implications for the private sector and the citizens. Several years ago, the administration added a position of White House cybersecurity coordinator. But the position lacks the authority to command the resources needed to truly rationalize the federal cybersecurity policy and processes. As discussed in more depth in chapter 7, the position might need to be significantly upgraded to at or near cabinet level.

Much of government's organizational problem emanates from the lack of responsiveness to the digital age. Speaking at the Council on Foreign Relations in June 2016, CIA director John Brennan says laws haven't "adequately adapted to the emergence of this new digital frontier. Most worrisome…is that there is still no political or national consensus on the appropriate role of the government, law enforcement, homeland security and intelligence agencies" in safeguarding the online domain.[10]

Moreover, government needs to inject systemic rigor into managing its own programs, and the budgeting process, at least for IT spending. The budget cycle is two or three orders of magnitude slower than the threat we face.

No less authority than current White House cybersecurity coordinator Michael Daniel has made this case.[11] "We've got architectures in various places (in the federal government) and hardware and software that is indefensible…We tend to treat these computer systems as these gigantic capital investments like buildings rather than an investment that you need to continually refresh and treat more like a revolving fund or a management budget," Daniel, also a former OMB official, remarked.[12]

Today, getting funding for cybersecurity often requires the chief information security officer to convince his or her boss, usually a career bureaucrat chief information officer. That CIO, in turn, must persuade the political appointees of the project's importance, especially when compared to spending directed to the agency's primary mission. The funding proposal goes to the Office of Management and Budget, which evaluates it in terms of dollars, rather than risk. The White House may yet step in to change it for purely political reasons. Only then does it go to Congress. There, the proposal is examined by multiple committees whose staffs may have little real experience with cybersecurity. Maybe the proposal gets in the spending bill, unless there is a continuing resolution that merely extends the previous year's budget with little or no modification.

This outlines a process that takes twelve to twenty-four months. But even with the money in hand, federal agencies must go through the cumbersome federal acquisition process. If the proposal results in a big contract, it almost inevitably will be hung up with a protest filed by a losing company. If everything goes exactly right, it could be at least two years from the time the CISO identifies a need to the time a solution is actually available. It should be no surprise that federal agencies have problems buying the technology they need.

Daniel's idea of building a refresh mechanism into the process is a good one. Agencies should not have to go through the entire congressional budgeting process to get the funds to upgrade from Windows 7 to Windows 10. The case for major IT systems is not as clear but more important. Major automated information systems such as those the DOD requires are increasingly reliant on commercial-off-the-shelf solutions to save money. That's a good thing except the money to upgrade them in five or ten years never materializes. That's why contractors have to maintain outdated Windows 95 and XP in their environment to support the systems they provide to the government.

The one aspect of federal budgeting that needs to be carried over to the IT side is with respect to cyber insurance. When the government builds a physical infrastructure, it routinely requires the contractor to have insurance, but it doesn't apply that same best practice to digital infrastructure. Doing so is sound risk management and could stimulate the cyber insurance market for the private sector, which is already a federal goal.

In addition, all current and future government cybersecurity programs ought to have clear objectives that are subject to a cost-benefit analysis. Programs need to be periodically evaluated, and if cost benefit cannot be demonstrated, then program needs to be reformed or canceled. If a reformed program still fails, the cost-benefit-analysis-test responsibility for the program should be shifted. If the program still cannot pass the analysis, it should be canceled.

Perhaps the most intrinsic factor complicating government's ability to adapt to the digital age is its unwillingness to manage itself. It is only slightly hyperbolic to note that the most powerful force on Capitol Hill is not policy, or partisanship, or even money—it's turf. Today there are seventy-eight congressional committees and subcommittees that have jurisdiction over DHS. Yet some areas of critical infrastructure receive no concentrated cybersecurity attention (see chapter 11 on the food and agriculture sector).

Congress itself is structured on an industrial-age model with its sector-specific committees and subcommittees (banking, energy telecommunications, etc.) These structures are in place not because they make sense for effective governing but because they make sense to the members who sit on them. A new president and a new Congress should seize the opportunity to reorganize government for the digital age.

Finally, government needs to more fully integrate the private sector into its cybersecurity planning and operations.

While there has been lip service paid to the need for partnership for over a decade, the actual degree of partnership on cyber issues has been, at best, sporadic. The National Infrastructure Protection Plan lays out a useful model for how the partnership is supposed to work. Each critical sector has created a privately run sector coordinating council, and each lead government agency has a corresponding government coordinating council.

Some sectors operate better than others, but in the main, the exact roles for the various councils are ill defined, and actual projects tend to be run by various staff who are left on their own to define what the partnership process means. Too often this translates into little, if any, coordination and what coordination there exists is little more than pro forma consultation with the sector council.

Government needs to clarify the roles of the various councils and senior government officials and to train staff on how to operate a partnership process. Since industry is by far the dominant player when it comes to owning, operating, and defending cyber infrastructure, government need to treat industry as a full partner, not merely as one of many stakeholders.

Chapter 17 reports on a set of successful partnership programs and a mutual industry-government analysis of what constitutes best practices for success in managing partnership programs. These best practices ought to be officially recognized by government agencies and used as part of the employee evaluation system for officials charged with operating partnership programs.

5. FOCUS MORE ON CYBERSECURITY FROM A LAW-ENFORCEMENT PERSPECTIVE

Estimates on the impact of cybercrime vary widely but all suggest tremendous annual losses often between a half and a full trillion dollars a year. Long-term impacts reach astronomical levels.

Yet our law-enforcement efforts are minimal. Best estimates are that we successfully prosecute less than 2 percent of cybercriminals.

This is not to say our law-enforcement agents are not doing a good job. They are. However, they are vastly overmatched in terms of the scope of the problem compared to their resources. Moreover, the legal structure, particularly internationally, has not been adapted to deal with modern cybercrime.

Even domestically, there is uncertainty about who and how victims of cybercrimes report them, and what rules will be applied to the victims (if and when they do seek law-enforcement assistance).

The lack of clarity about the ramifications of brining law enforcement into a cyber incident, coupled with the uncertainty of the impact it will have on the criminals, often undermines corporate interest in cooperating with law enforcement.

The new administration should engage in a multitiered program to bolster cyber law enforcement. Assuming the agencies themselves are clear on their roles in terms of public interaction (should victims call the FBI? DHS? Local police? A regulatory agency?), public awareness program specific to this topic needs to be launched. Private-industry business associations should be heavily leveraged to assist in communicating this message.

More broadly, a review of legacy law-enforcement spending with an eye toward properly resourcing efforts to stop cybercrime is needed. Government needs to be much more creative in terms of integrating, leveraging, and sharing information and resources more broadly among the full law-enforcement community.

Finally, a concerted effort to create a functional international legal structure to address cybercrime is needed. This process will be difficult for many reasons including widely varying understandings of what constitutes cybercrime as well as related Internet issues. Given this complexity, an intellectual triage of cyber issues ought to be conducted with intensive focus on areas of greatest consensus such as protections of intellectual property and preventing cyber disruption of critical infrastructure.

During the Cold War, people like myself literally hid underneath school desks in fear of Soviet missiles, yet our policy makers were still able to enact nuclear test–ban treaties, nonproliferation pacts, and inspection systems. We should be able to do at least as well with the major international cyber powers, many of whom also happen to be our business partners, to create a practical operational international legal structure to ameliorate cybercrime.

6. TEST PILOT THE NIST CYBERSECURITY FRAMEWORK

One of the most positive and popular cybersecurity initiatives of the Obama administration was the creation of the NIST Cybersecurity Framework in 2013. This framework was the result of Executive Order 13636. Both the process used to devise the framework and the framework itself have been justifiably praised.

Unfortunately, unlike the private sector, which would follow up design of a new service with testing and then promotion, the government went directly from design to promotion. As a result, now, nearly three years after the framework's completion, we have no objective data about its effectiveness. In fact, we don't even have any hard data on its actual use—or even what would constitute "framework usage."

Absent a definition of what "use" of the framework means, or the effects such use might have engendered, it is impossible to empirically testify to its effectiveness.

The independent research that has been done does not suggest most companies are using, let alone adopting, the NIST framework (although results are more positive when subjects are questioned about their use of frameworks in general). For example, although the telecommunications industry has been widely, and justifiably, praised for its ardent advocacy for the framework, a recent PricewaterhouseCoopers study showed only about one-third of telecommunication companies have implemented the framework.[13]

A broader PWC study found that less than 10 percent of companies had even discussed the framework, and that number slipped to roughly 1 percent when companies with market caps below $500 million were analyzed.[14]

These numbers are even more discouraging when considering that research prior to the framework's development suggested that as much as

40 percent of private-sector companies used industry best practices, which are the essence of the framework.[15]

Despite concerted efforts by the government to tout the framework, independent assessments have suggested that the Framework in its current state will do little to change behavior or increase security. One 2016 review found that "security experts were quoted left and right saying there was nothing to be seen in the much hyped framework."[16] The *New York Times* asked if the framework would change anyone's behavior and came to the conclusion that there was little difference between the framework and the security checklists typically used at most major companies.[17] The *Wall Street Journal* agreed the framework wouldn't do much in the real world.[18]

In short, although this author believes the NIST framework has been helpful, there is little or no hard evidence that it has generated any significant behavior change or that use of the framework actually improves an entity's cybersecurity. We need to move beyond the use of personal testimonials and begin to develop some hard data.

With a small amount of money, the new administration and Congress could vastly leverage the excellent work that has been done to generate much wider and more productive use of the framework.

Again, a model that would access the partnership model enshrined in the National Infrastructure Protection Plan has been available in the public domain for some time, but has not been implemented.

Similarly, research on framework use could be modeled to demonstrate cost effectiveness—something called for by Executive Order 13636. Being able to define what elements of the framework are cost effective for defined industry segments would provide a major boost for the voluntary nature of the framework. Companies will naturally deploy cost-effective measures. Being able to demonstrate such is in the public interest.

Finally, such research could identify framework elements that are effective in enhancing security but are perhaps not *cost* effective. These too would be valuable data as they would provide the president and Congress with an empirical guide for what needs to be incentivized (as is also called for in Executive Order 13636) and how strong the incentive must be to achieve implementation of proven successful security practice.

Some in the private sector have argued that generating data on effectiveness is a pathway to regulation (which ISA clearly opposes). We believe the opposite. In the face of continued effective cyberattacks, the absence of hard evidence of the framework's effectiveness will eventually be used as evidence that the social contract voluntary model is ineffective. The reality is that it and the executive order have not yet been implemented.

Sound corporate investment decisions are not based on rhetorical or emotional appeals; they are based on data. To promote a program that may well be, but hasn't empirically been shown to be, effective will lead to less voluntary use and eventually to policy regression back toward an inappropriate regulatory model.

7. GOVERNMENT PRIORITY FOR WORKING WITH THE PRIVATE SECTOR SHOULD BE REVERSED TO EMPHASIZE SMALLER COMPANIES INSTEAD OF LARGE ONES

One of the primary tenants of risk management is to direct resources to the greatest need.

A primary tenant of marketing is to segment your audience and direct resources toward the top targets.

Small businesses qualify as both: an area of greatest need and a top target for cybersecurity outreach.

"Small businesses play an indispensable role in providing the federal government with products and services," House Small Business Committee chairman Steve Chabot recently noted. "They are integral links in the government supply chain but are often ill equipped to combat against sophisticated foreign cyberattacks. This makes them a prime target for state sponsors of cyber terrorism who wish to undermine America's commerce and security."[19]

As is repeatedly observed in other chapters of this book, smaller companies are more vulnerable than larger ones, understand the issue less, are investing less, and are probably the segment that most needs government help.

Moreover, we have learned that smaller companies are now being used as access points to launch sophisticated attacks on larger firms including, but not exclusively, those designated as critical infrastructure. Target famously was attacked through their HVAC contractor, and a recent *New York Times* story reported that an otherwise secure large energy facility was successfully compromised when attackers loaded malware on the online menu of a local Chinese restaurant the energy facilities employees used to order lunch.[20]

The preponderance of private-sector interaction with the government on cybersecurity, and the concomitant policy development, has historically been with larger companies. While that may have made sense in the early days, we now know that we cannot develop a sustainably secure system by focusing on large businesses. Government initiatives occasionally touch smaller firms, but the preponderance of interaction and programs are geared to larger companies.

Government efforts to address this situation have ranged from meager to counterproductive. For example, the Improving Small Business Cybersecurity Act of 2016 currently working through Congress authorizes a paltry $1 million for DHS and the Small Business Administration to conduct studies and develop a strategy to improve small-business security over the next five years.[21] This miniscule step is a clear illustration of both the fact that government is not acting with sufficient urgency and is not willing to make adequate investment in cybersecurity.

In contrast, DHS has allocated ten times that amount over the next five years to create a standards body for information sharing and analysis organizations in what many hoped would be an effort to better address small-company needs for information sharing. However, less than a year into that project, multiple private-sector organizations including the IT and communication sector councils, the IT Information Sharing and Analysis Center, and the National Council of ISACS have felt the need to go on record urging the ISAO standards body to redirect its emphasis away from sharing methods appropriate only for large companies and devote greater attention to small-company needs.[22]

Chapter 3 in this volume clearly defines the unintended evolution of a two-tiered industry sector consisting of major suppliers and smaller ones operating under differing economic models and requiring differing strategies for cybersecurity. New rules established by General Services Administration and the Pentagon in May 2016, which adopt the outmoded traditional regulatory model by establishing "baseline" rules for cybersecurity for government contractors who handle or store or transmit unclassified or sensitive government information, are exacerbating this unfortunate trend adding new costs, hindering small companies from competing, and creating less effective government systems without improving security.[23]

Already evidence is accumulating from small businesses who have testified that the new regulatory requirements are keeping small businesses from competing.[24] Independent researchers are validating these observations: "the government is missing out on great opportunities to improve its cybersecurity posture due to burdensome cybersecurity regulations hindering small businesses from gaining entry into the marketplace."[25]

Naturally government needs to continue work with larger companies, but a vastly increased priority needs to be placed on the smaller companies who are less able to defend themselves. In an interconnected system of systems, the weak links need priority attention.

One simple and pragmatic step in this direction would be to follow through on Executive Order 13636 and determine what are the most cost-effective measures of the NIST Cybersecurity Framework.

As helpful as the framework is, it was largely designed by and for larger companies. Its multiple tiers and ninety-plus subcategories make it unsuitable for the vast majority of small companies. This is not to say the NIST Framework can't be used by smaller companies (some do). However, the multiple assessments smaller firms would have to undertake to locate what parts of the framework offer the most cost-effective way and spend their next marginal dollar on cybersecurity is too great a burden for small firms operating on thin margins.

If we want small companies to become more secure, we need to make cybersecurity easier and cheaper for them.

They want something as easy as Norton AntiVirus. They just want to know what button to press and then get back to business. Making our national cybersecurity apparatus more user friendly for smaller companies ought to be a high priority for the next administration.

It is possible, and comparatively inexpensive, to do the targeted research required to prioritize the framework by industry sector and identify the best places for classes of smaller corporations and nonprofits to spend their marginal dollar on cybersecurity. Since many smaller firms have common security characteristics that transcend industry sector, the research may well be quite generalizable. Expecting small companies to fund this research on their own is impractical.

Once a research-based prioritized list of actions is developed from the NIST framework, multiple industry trade associations are ready, willing, and able to partner with government on outreach. Government should be using these private-sector organizations as their primary leverage vehicle for small-company outreach as opposed to setting up and running their own programs.

It has long been noted that good cyber hygiene—adherence to basic best practices and standards and technologies—can stop most common attacks. While good cyber hygiene remains a goal, simply adopting standards and practices will not be enough to create sustainable security.

The expanded threat environment also poses increased risk for smaller firms. Whereas once smaller entities might have practiced reasonable security with fairly inexpensive perimeter defenses like firewalls and antivirus protection, the expansion of APT-style attacks means even smaller firms need more sophisticated, and costly, defensive strategies.[26] A June 2016 Ponemon Institute study reported that half of smaller companies suffered breaches in 2015, 76 percent of them had their antivirus compromised, and nearly 60 percent had their intrusion-detection system evaded.[27]

Smaller companies will also need to learn to fight off more sophisticated threats and do so in a cost-effective fashion. Research in this space1 is also needed.

In 2013, the ISA in conjunction with the National Association of Manufacturers conducted such a study.[28] The study broke down small companies into three tiers on the basis of the size of their information technology departments and then identified a dozen best practices that would be most cost effective for companies within these segments to use when combating advanced threats.

The research was then condensed into an easy-to-read booklet that briefly explained what to do and how to do it (see online isalliance.org/publications/common-sense-for-small businesses.pdf). This is the sort of product smaller companies need. Combating sophisticated threats may outstrip smaller firm's economics, and hence government incentives, including tax credits for small companies, may be required. Consistent with recommendations made in chapters 4 and 6 (about the utilities and healthcare sectors, respectively), embedding cybersecurity funding in programs such as small-business loans ought also to be considered.

Government information-sharing programs are also structured largely for large companies who can access and process large amounts of technical data. Government should restructure these programs to make them more user friendly to smaller firms. In addition to simply sharing the technical information, government, working collaboratively with larger enterprises, needs to place a higher priority on making this information actionable. This generally means simplifying it or making it "passive." Again, models for such a program have existed for years but have not been implemented.[29]

Partnerships between industry and government will need to be intensified. However, government policies that simply seek to pass the buck to the private sector are unlikely to be satisfactory. Oversimplified strategies such as requiring larger firms to demand and police enhanced security for the smaller firms they partner or interconnect with fail to take into account the difficulty and cost for the larger providers to accomplish these goals. Smaller firms may also choose not to go along with such demands, depriving the larger firms and the government of access to innovative companies and niche providers they need for specialized services.

These proposals also fail to appreciate the negative effects these mandates could have on the smaller operators unable to meet the higher requirements and so lose out on business, even if they are the preferred, or only, supplier for a desired product or service.

The new administration should fundamentally reprioritize the targeting of its cybersecurity programs in keeping with sound risk-management practice and focus much greater attention on the areas of greatest current need.

8. WORKFORCE DEVELOPMENT: AWARENESS YIELDS TO UNDERSTANDING AND MAKES CYBERSECURITY COOL

The deficiencies in the cyber workforce are not only troubling but also vexing. There is an apparent market failure wherein we have an exciting, modern field with lots of high paying jobs that we can't fill, and this deficit is expected to continue for some time.

The new administration must aggressively move away from antiquated development models based on single-month programs, school curriculum development, and TV spots. The reality is the average fifth grader probably knows more about technology than the average fifth-grade teacher. Teachers will tell you they don't have time to teach civics or geography, so adding cybersecurity to the mix is unlikely to have an impact.

Standard management best practice is to begin initiative with clear goals. While a decade ago there may have been a need for a cybersecurity awareness program, we are well past the awareness stage. We now need a program focused not on awareness but on understanding the issue. We need a second targeted set of programs focused on recruiting people to help fill the cybersecurity workforce void, which like the issue itself, goes beyond technical expertise and runs to overall risk management.

The antiquated notion of October being the "Cyber Awareness Month" is illustrated by its slogan, "Stop, Think, Connect," which hails from the dial-up era. Virtually everyone is now connected twenty-four seven, and cyber awareness needs to equally practiced all the time.

Instead we need an integrated, multifaceted, and targeted program with research-based messaging, just as the private sector would do when marketing any product or service.

We need to reach kids where they are and integrate cybersecurity into what they want to do, not teach them what they ought to do. One neglected vehicle is the gaming community. Much as the government has reached out to IT companies in Silicon Valley, a similar collaboration should commence with game developers. Cybersecurity principles and techniques could be integrated into an activity young people easily gravitate toward.

Gaming events can encompass hundreds of thousands of online players and spectators. If cybersecurity could be integrated into these events, it might be a pathway to reach tech-interested youths, which could be complimented by camps and contests where the notion of developing a career doing what they already like could be planted.

A few young cyber stars might put a face on the activity that others could relate to. It might also be possible to leverage television. Just as ESPN turned niche activities like poker and fantasy football into extremely popular portions of their lineup, the same could be done with gaming with a cyber component.

At another level there ought to be highly targeted outreach to opinion makers. It is critical that diverse populations of young people are recruited to be part of helping design the outreach effort toward diverse audiences. Attractive, young adult cyber professionals can be recruited to use social media like forums, blogs, Snapchat, Instagram, and YouTube to build followings talking about how interesting, lucrative—and fun—the career path can be. Again an emphasis on developing "stars" that can put diverse faces on the field need to be cultivated.

Career influencers, including high-school guidance counsels (who are generally unaware of the profession), at community colleges and universities need to be reached with messaging targeted to these particular audiences at this particular stage of their lives.

Industry, which is already operating a multitude of one-off outreach programs, should be urged to collaborate so that consistent messaging reaches as broad a population as possible in an effort to secure the ecosystem as opposed to a particular company.

Given limited resources, the new administration ought to make government's primary mission to coordinate with the private sector on its programs, as opposed to developing independent government programs (apart from government recruitment as discussed in later chapters). Government can open doors, facilitate partnership, and allow the private sector to be the major creators and operators of the workforce-development program.

One high-value area wherein government can take a direct role is doing a better job educating itself. A higher-value target for cyber education than K–12 might well be the House and Senate. Most senior government officials are digital immigrants not born into the digital world they inhabit—but nonetheless charged with establishing governance over systems they understand poorly.

Senior government officials (members of Congress, cabinet secretaries, and agency heads) can aptly compare to corporate board members in terms of status, responsibility, and cramped schedules. Senior government officials have for years campaigned to have corporate boards become more educated about cybersecurity so they could better manage it.

As detailed in chapter 12, the National Association of Corporate Directors has over the past few years taken up that challenge and developed a very well received handbook and education program.[30] PricewaterhouseCoopers in its 2016 *Global State of Information Security* has documented that this effort has yielded significant real worked effect including increasing budgets for cybersecurity by 24 percent, fostering better risk management, creating a culture of security, and engendering better communication about these issues within the enterprise.[31]

Clearly the federal government could use this kind of assistance. We ought to do the same thing for the government equivalents of corporate board members as we are already doing for our commercial directors.

The new president should insist that all senior government officials (not the IT people—they already get it) take a cybersecurity-training program based on the NACD model. Congressional leaders and independent agencies should follow suit.

9. MODERNIZE AND STREAMLINE REGULATION

Awareness about the cybersecurity problem is now so widespread that virtually every government agency seems to want to have its own cybersecurity program.

This explosion of regulations has occurred notwithstanding the avowed policy of following a voluntary model epitomized by the NIST Cybersecurity Framework. These mandates are also largely implemented without the benefit of adequate assessment by the regulators as to the effectiveness, let alone cost effectiveness, of the programs. Companies now often face multiple inconsistent regulatory and quasiregulatory systems that aren't improving security.

Regulation also interacts with the workforce-shortage issue. Without adequate cybersecurity staffing, organization's cybersecurity personnel are routinely diverted from security issues to deal with compliance requirements. Not only are cybersecurity regulations of dubious intrinsic value but they're also counterproductive since they drain scarce security resources to achieve compliance.

Although superficial promises of regulatory reviews lead to a streamlining regulatory process, interagency turf battles and bureaucratic inertia have stymied any significant movement.

The new president ought to charge the Office of Information and Regulatory Affairs with developing a cross-government program for streamlining regulations. Congress should aggressively require federal agencies to reduce duplicative regulations and eliminate those that have not been proven to be cost effective as a condition of their annual appropriations.

While independent agencies are not under the president's authority, they are subject to congressional appropriations. As part of the oversight and appropriation process, independent agencies should be urged by their authorizing and appropriating committees to review their cybersecurity programs and eliminate regulations that are duplicative or not cost effective. Money saved by these reductions can be rechanneled into future cost-benefit analysis of cybersecurity regulations so that funding from the agency perspective will be neutral.

10. DEVELOP MARKET INCENTIVES TO PROMOTE SOUND CYBERSECURITY BEHAVIOR

Multiple independent studies have pointed to economics, not technology, as the principal barrier to enhancing cybersecurity. Although Executive Order 13636 and the House GOP Task Force report on cybersecurity have come to the conclusion that we need to develop incentives to promote greater cybersecurity, there is still no substantial progress in this area.

One problem may be that policy makers have not thought through the incentive discussion in as broad and creative fashion as is required. Most policy makers think of incentives in terms of taxes. While there may be a limited role for tax incentives, such as to induce small companies to make otherwise uneconomic investments, taxes are a far too limited perspective. To make matters worse, some cybersecurity policies may actually incentivize innovation by the attack community and provide disincentives for corporations to improve their cybersecurity.

Just as a hundred years ago when policy makers creatively developed the social contract incentive model that stimulated power-grid development, policy makers today need to be more creative. For example, simply altering the assessment and compliance process by moving it away from the "pass-fail" audit model to a more useful maturity model can create incentives without any demonstrable increase in government spending. And if incentives do require increased funds, the government needs to realistically assess whether it is more appropriate to spend taxpayer money to promote the common cyber defense as opposed to hiding and off-loading costs on consumers.

There is adequate precedent for an incentive approach. We have market incentives deployed in multiple industry sectors—agriculture, aviation, ground transport, environment, and even physical security—to assist the private sector in reaching public-policy goals. We simply need to apply this creativity and will to cybersecurity.

For the incentives to be of value, they must be targeted to specific goals as economic models differ substantially from sector to sector. Incentives must also be powerful enough to affect investment decisions. This is another reason why the research such as pilot testing the NIST framework to develop metrics cost-effectiveness data advocated above are so important. Although there may be some useful generic incentives (e.g., liability benefits or insurance discounts), a menu of incentives also needs to be developed as different incentives will be attractive to different industry sectors.

The private sector has offered multiple proposals for consideration including liability incentives, procurement incentives, insurance incentives, and good actor benefits such as streamlined regulation, patent or trademark preferences, forbearance, and streamlined auditing. Successive chapters will discuss specific ideas related to various industry sectors.

11. ARTICULATE CLEARLY THE ROLE FOR GOVERNMENT WHEN INDUSTRY FACES A NATION-STATE ATTACK

It is now common knowledge that many cyberattacks are affiliated with nation-state actors. FireEye CEO Kevin Mandia, has said that roughly 90 percent of the cyberattack cases he deals with are the result of nation-state activity.[32]

For whatever many faults Sony Pictures Entertainment may have had in its cyber defense, at the end of the day, it probably didn't matter since its attacker was the North Korean government. Virtually no private institution can adequately defend itself from a concentrated nation-state attack.

The fact that private entities are not responsible for securing themselves from nation-state activity has legal precedent going back decades in the nuclear industry by virtue of the design-basis-threat theory, which has been part of nuclear-plant policy for decades. Design basis threat states that while nuclear plants are responsible for commercial security, attacks from nation-states are the responsibility of the federal government.

Yet despite the reality of the nation-state problem, there is no clear policy or systemic assistance private companies can expect from the federal government.

At a minimum, the federal government ought to offer (on request) equivalent federal assistance to a private company that suffers a cyberattack by a nation-state that it would if the attack were physical in nature.

It could be argued that providing this degree of assistance might prove quite costly to the federal government. However, such expense is more appropriately born by the government—constitutionally charged with providing the common defense—than the private sector. Additionally, the prospect of having to provide such assistance might prove a substantial incentive for the government to expedite their activity with respect to overall cybersecurity.

12. GOVERNMENT AND INDUSTRY NEED TO PARTNER TO RETHINK THE CYBERSECURITY COMPLIANCE MODEL

The traditional regulatory model is ill-suited for cybersecurity. Technology and attack methods change too rapidly for traditional regulations to keep up. The international nature of the problem is inconsistent with traditional regulatory process, and the layering of local regulations on top of national and international systems drives up costs while retarding efficiency and innovation.

Moreover, the fundamental assumptions of the traditional compliance model are ill-suited to cyberspace. This includes the backward-looking-standards-based criteria and the pass-fail system that classifies companies into two categories: in or out of compliance. Also inappropriate is the punitive nature of compliance, which assigns blame to the victim of a cyberattack. Assigning blame simply for being breached is inappropriate in a world of nation-state attackers and private-company defenders.

This is not to say that there should be no accountability in the private sector. What is needed is for us to evolve a new system of digital accountability.

Several chapters in this volume, notably chapter 3 (from the defense sector) and chapter 13 (by the Center for Audit Quality), offer directions for this new system to evolve. Instead of a backward-looking, finance-based pass-fail model, we need to create a forward-looking risk-management model powered by growth and incentives not penalties and compliance.

The next administration should not create this new model. Rather, the recommendations are that it work collaboratively with the private sector to develop this model. Chapter 17, on the operations of public-private partnerships, offers a specific set of research-based best practices to guide this development process.

Hopefully this new administration will jointly develop a sustainable, collaborative model that rebalances the economic incentives for cybersecurity, is grounded in metrics of success, and reaches all participants in a manner appropriate to their place in the cyber ecosystem.

---

1 Center for Strategic and International Studies, *Net Losses: Estimating the Global Cost of Cybercrime. Economic Impact of Cybercrime II* (McAfee, June 2014), Web.

2 PricewaterhouseCoopers (PWC), *Turnaround and Transformation in Cybersecurity: Key Findings from the Global State of Information Security Survey 2016* (PWC, 2015), Web.

3 "National Infrastructure Protection Plan," Department of Homeland Security, 2013, Web, July 6, 2016.

4   Ponemon Institute, *IT Security Tracking Study* (Ponemon Institute, 2006 to 2014).

5   PWC, *Managing Cyber Risks in an Interconnected World: Key Findings from the Global State of Information Security Survey 2015* (PWC, Sept. 30, 2014), Web.

6   Executive Office of the President of the United States, "Cyberspace Policy Review: Assuring a Trusted and Resilient Information and Communications Infrastructure," *WhiteHouse.gov*, 2009, Web.

7   *Annual Report to Congress: Federal Information Security Modernization Act*, Office of Management and Budget, Executive Office of the President of the United States, the White House, Mar. 18, 2016, Web.

8   Jaikumar Vijayan, "Despite Billions Spent, US Federal Agencies Struggle with Cybersecurity," *The Christian Science Monitor*, Passcode, June 10, 2015, Web.

9   John A. Koskinen, "Wyden Response Letter," letter to the Honorable Ron Wyden, Ranking Member, Committee on Finance, United States Senate, Department of the Treasury, Internal Revenue Service, Oct. 7, 2015, Web.

10   John O. Brennan, "Remarks as Prepared for Delivery by Central Intelligence Agency Director John O. Brennan at the Council on Foreign Relations, Washington, DC," Council on Foreign Relations, Washington, DC, *Central Intelligence Agency Speeches & Testimony* (Central Intelligence Agency, June 29, 2016), Web.

11   Jack Moore, "Some Legacy IT in Government Is So Old, It's 'Indefensible,' Official Says," *Nextgov.*, Sept. 22, 2015, Web.

12   Ibid.

13   Thomas Tandetzki and Mark Lobel, *Communications Review: As Telcos Go Digital, Cybersecurity Risks Intensify* (PWC, July 2015), Web.

14   PWC, *Managing Cyber Risks in an Interconnected World: Key Findings from the Global State of Information Security Survey 2015* (PWC, Sept. 30, 2014), Web.

15   PWC, *The Global State of Information Security* (PWC, 2008).

16   Charlie Mitchell, *Hacked: The Inside Story of America's Struggle to Secure Cyberspace.* (Lanham, Maryland: Rowman & Littlefield Publishers, 2016), pp. 72-73.

17   Ibid, ibid.

18   Ibid, Ibid.

19   Tim Starks, "Cybersecurity Fallout from the FBI Decision on Clinton," *Politico Morning Cybersecurity*, Politico, July 6, 2016, Web.

20   Nicole Perlroth, "Hackers Lurking in Vents and Soda Machines," *New York Times*, Apr. 7, 2014, Web.

21 "CBO: Small Business Cyber Bill to Cost $1 Million between 2017–2021," *Inside Cybersecurity*, July 8, 2016, n.p., Web, July 8, 2016; Joshua Higgins, "Small Business Leaders Cite Hurdles from New Cyber Rules for Government Contractors," *Inside Cybersecurity*, July 7, 2016, Web, July 8, 2016.

22 Rick Weber, "IT Industry Warns against Emphasis on Automated Sharing by ISAO Standards Body," *Inside Cybersecurity*, July 7, 2016, Web.

23 Joshua Higgins, "Small Business Leaders Cite Hurdles from New Cyber Rules for Government Contractors," *Inside Cybersecurity*, July 7, 2016, Web.

24 Ibid.

25 Ibid.

26 Ponemon Institute, *2016 State of Cybersecurity in Small & Medium-Sized Businesses (SMB)* (Ponemon Institute and Keeper Security, June 2016), Web.

27 Ibid.

28 Internet Security Alliance, *The Advanced Persistent Threat: Practical Controls That Small and Medium-Sized Business Leaders Should Consider Implementing* (Internet Security Alliance, 2013), Web.

29 Jeff Brown, "Disrupting Attacker Command and Control Channels: A New Model for Information Sharing," *Social Contract 2.0: A 21st Century Program for Effective Cybersecurity* (Washington, DC: Internet Security Alliance, 2009), 21–31.

30 Larry Clinton, AIG, and NACD, *Cyber-Risk Oversight: Director's Handbook Series* (National Association of Corporate Directors, 2014), Web.

31 PWC, *Turnaround and Transformation in Cybersecurity: Key Findings from the Global State of Information Security Survey 2016* (PWC, 2015), Web.

32 Tara Seals, "Kevin Mandia: Nation-State Cyber Espionage Becomes the Norm," *Info Security Magazine*, Oct. 13, 2015, Web.

Cybersecurity in Industry Sectors

Three

Cybersecurity in the Defense Industrial Base

Jeff Brown, Vice President and Chief Information
Security Officer, Raytheon
JR Williamson, Director and Deputy Chief Information
Security Officer, Northrop Grumman

INTRODUCTION

The Department of Defense and its industrial partners have been at the forefront of cyber defense for almost two decades, first with Moonlight Maze and more publically with the 2003 Titan Rain intrusions, precursors to the ongoing focus on the advanced persistent threat.[1]

Throughout that period, DoD and prime contractors have enjoyed a successful collaboration formalized in 2009 with the Defense Industrial Base Framework Agreement. The unprecedented agreement fostered information sharing in both directions and set the climate for cooperation and consultations across a wide spectrum of cyber issues.

While that cooperation continues today, the environment has significantly changed since 2009. The maturity of the department's and of prime contractors' defensive efforts has in recent years resulted in reduced attack volume, while the number of attacks on the primes' supply chains increased. Add to that mix the emergence of destructive attacks from North Korea on Sony Pictures Entertainment and from Iran on Saudi Aramco, and the result is a very different threat environment that demands we revisit our strategies.

The government's reaction to the changing environment has been to move from a collaborative strategy to a regulatory strategy in an attempt to force small- and medium-sized defense companies to make investments they would not otherwise make. This shift will have a profound impact on the defense industrial sector.

WHAT MAKES THE DIB SECTOR UNIQUE

The case for investing in cybersecurity in the defense industry is not a function of traditional economic-risk-management calculations. The Department of Defense won't go elsewhere if rivals steal our technology.

In most industries, the loss of intellectual property from a cyberattack hurts the bottom line. Without the need to conduct research and development or recoup R&D costs, products produced with stolen technology appear quickly in the marketplace at lower prices. Damage to the victim's profitability is predictable and rapid.

The defense industry has a different economic model. Top-tier defense companies predominantly sell to national governments that have few alternatives. Cost is a factor, but the Pentagon is unlikely to opt for a lower cost product from a rival nation, especially should the design suspiciously resemble American-made technology. The "cost" of a breach in the defense industry is seldom measured in dollars. It is more likely measured in the margin of our military superiority and our warriors' safety.

Despite the relative lack of traditional economic balance-sheet incentives to invest in cybersecurity, the defense industry still invests out of a fundamentally patriotic sense of their responsibility to our warfighters as well as for the more pragmatic reason that strong data and network security are essential to brand credibility when doing business with the military. A recent FireEye survey found that typical industry sectors suffered breach rates of 96 percent, while the defense industrial base had a breach rate of "only" 76 percent.[2]

But the weight of patriotic and reputational factors gets weaker further down the supply chain where companies' mix of defense and commercial business shifts. Small- and medium-sized businesses doing subcontract work for major defense primes have a larger proportion of commercial business. The greater the commercial component of a business, the more the traditional economic risk-assessment calculations predominate. Financial conditions facing SMBs do not afford them the luxury of uneconomic investments in cybersecurity. Indeed, as large system integrators have assessed their supply chains over the last two years, it has become obvious the effectiveness of suppliers' cybersecurity is directly proportional to size of their information technology budget. For them, the cost of security outweighs their economic risk.

This difference in incentive structures has created a two-tiered defense ecosystem. One tier features large, well-funded system integrators. The other contains everybody else. Into this mix, the Department of Defense has introduced new compliance requirements in a bid to artificially influence traditional economic-based risk-management calculations. It remains to be seen if that attempt will succeed, and there's good reason to be doubtful.

CHALLENGES FACING THE NEW ADMINISTRATION

THE RISE OF DESTRUCTIVE ATTACKS
Early cyber conflicts, such as in Estonia and Georgia, clearly show that civilians and industry may well be on the front lines of cyber conflict. Add in precedent of the destructive attacks on Saudi Aramco and Sony, and you have the potential for the information age equivalent of World War II's strategic bombing campaign targeting our ability to sustain and replenish our nation's combat power. As much as the Defense Department has enthusiastically worked with industry to combat intellectual property theft, it now needs to partner with industry equally enthusiastically to address the threat of production interruptions previously associated only with physical attacks.

CYBER ESPIONAGE
The threat of cyber espionage has been recognized by the defense industry in general and the large primes in particular for more than a decade. The battle is not new—but it requires a different sort of public-private

partnership between DoD and industry. The adversary, perceiving the improved cyber defenses of larger companies, has migrated to the defense supply chain.

Those most threatened now are small- and medium-sized companies that are least able to make investments to defend themselves. The highly successful cybersecurity collaboration between DoD and the defense industrial base needs to be revamped to make it more effective for companies without deep pockets.

As the Defense Information Systems Agency director, Lieutenant General Alan Lynn, noted during a recent cybersecurity conference, "We are fighting a two-front war cyber war right now with challenges fending off millions of attacks on our defense networks and the slow burn of economic espionage."[3] He was exactly right, but the battle has engulfed a far broader swath of the defense industry than current processes can support.

SUPPLY CHAIN

Threats from asymmetric actors in cyberspace are heightened by the potential for surreptitiously attacks against the supply chain. Modern weapon systems are built via a supply chain hundreds of companies long that spans multiple countries. There's little visibility into suppliers' manufacturing process. A logic bomb embedded into the hardware of a weapon system somewhere along this long and oblique supply chain would be extremely difficult to detect until the weapon is fired.[4] A sophisticated adversary capable of infiltrating the supply chain to make a malicious modification of an integrated circuit knows enough not to affect system performance until the embedded malware is triggered.

It's not only weapon systems that are risk. Commercial networking and computing technology destined for use by defense companies can be intercepted and corrupted with malware, whether for gleaning commercial secrets or as a means of gaining a foothold to reach government systems.[5] Already the list of commercial products shipped with malware unbeknownst to the manufacturer grows every year, and it's not just third-tier manufacturers. Dell, Hewlett Packard, Olympus, and Samsung have all been victims.[6]

INCREASED FOCUS ON REGULATION AND COMPLIANCE

In the last eight years, there have been twelve executive orders on government contracting resulting in sixteen new regulatory mandates. This has significantly increased the costs of doing business with the government in exchange for a minimal impact on real cybersecurity. According to one estimate, nearly thirty cents of every federal contracting dollar goes toward compliance with unique government regulations.[7]

The incentives discussion sparked by Executive Order 13636 that held out so much promise has largely disappeared in the wake of high-profile breaches that reversed the discussion into one of compliance with standards. Defense contractors are now contractually obligated to comply with specific cybersecurity controls devised by the National Institute of Standards and Technology.[8]

The defense industry now more resembles the highly regulated finance industry. While compliance standards are good for setting a basic foundation for security, it is critical not to confuse compliance with security.

Compliance is about what you do. Security is about how well you do it.

Breaches happen even to perfectly compliant organizations. It is a safe bet that every single compromised company or government organization was compliant with a cybersecurity standard. True security requires aggressive and consistent operational processes built on top of a solid foundation. The difference between those who are quietly successful and those who end up on the front page is not investment or compliance level but rather the degree to which internal operations foster a culture of curiosity rather than a culture of compliance.

The unintended consequences of the new compliance environment may be most evident in the rate at which resources have been diverted into compliance assessment and documentation. Speaking from firsthand experience, the number of personnel needed just to assess and document compliance eats up 15 to 20 percent of major defense corporations' cybersecurity personnel. That is a huge tax on resources with minimal payback for the large primes, whose defenses are already largely well beyond what the compliance standards mandate.

The focus on compliance extracts other negative consequences, besides unwarranted confidence in cybersecurity performance. The new contractual cybersecurity requirements apply to companies that come in contact with "covered defense information." Most small businesses find them impossible to implement.

Taken individually, each control isn't difficult to implement, but their cumulative cost dwarfs the information technology budget of the vast majority of small businesses. Companies for which the defense business is a small portion of revenue may simply opt out. In other cases, they may not be able to hire enough skilled personnel to assure compliance. The demand for cybersecurity professionals is so high that the finite talent pool is depleted quickly at entry and midcareer levels. Even major companies with deep pockets find themselves in a hiring predicament.

The net result is that some portion of small- and medium-sized defense companies may never be able to reach compliance. Although we don't expect to see the true impact until after the December 2017 compliance date, we think it very likely their inability to comply will reduce the share of small defense contractors available to the prime contractors and, more importantly, deny the government the innovative and unique technology many of the small businesses provide.

POLICIES AND PROCESSES ASSUME A MONOLITHIC DEFENSE INDUSTRY

When the Obama administration took office, the defense community was in the midst of establishing a framework for two-way information sharing, what became known as the DIB Cybersecurity and Information Assurance program. At the time, the effort was limited to the dozen or so largest defense contractors. This dynamic led to a very successful collaborative environment between industry and the defense department that was naturally tailored to the largest companies.

However, the collaborative process codified in the agreement assumed the existence of a well-trained and well-funded cyber staff in the large defense companies. It relied on predominantly manual processes for information sharing among highly skilled and dedicated individuals either via a portal or periodic face-to-face conferences. The collaboration, essentially unchanged since 2009, has been successful, but it is labor-intensive and depends on personal trust to keep it going. This is an untenable situation. The threat has expanded to attack the defense supply chain, an ecosystem of much smaller and less cyber-capable companies who are ill-suited to such a labor-intensive information-sharing programs.

Yesterday's policies and collaboration processes, however successful, do not reflect today's realities. Manual processes do not scale up to the dramatically larger number of suppliers. The buy-in costs for cybersecurity do not scale down to the investment profiles of small- or even medium-sized suppliers.

PROVINCIALISM

Regulation of the defense community is predicated on US-based companies operating on American soil. Yet the last decade's reduction in defense spending has led many defense companies to expand their sales and presence overseas. This creates a very different set of dynamics for cyber defense in the sector.

The requirements levied by the International Trafficking in Arms Regulations drives the defense industry into maintaining two distinct networks—one with access for US persons and the other for non-US employees. This makes a unified cyber defense both difficult and expensive.

ITAR also makes it difficult to deploy detection tools outside of the United States. Even a custom-developed tool by a defense company for internal use faces restrictions on deployment to foreign branch offices.

Conversely, overseas privacy laws further hinder unified monitoring environment. The collapse of the European Union Safe Harbor agreement is the most striking example of how complex global cyber defense has become.

Finally, most countries are now requiring coproduction or offset suppliers. In the past, these efforts have been at the lower end of the value chain where the cyber defense of an overseas supplier was not an issue. But as the demand for coproduction rises in the value chain, so does the need to defend the networks of the suppliers. These trends represent policy challenges to the defense industry in two areas. Current information-sharing policies generally preclude open sharing of information with foreign partners. There are provisions for subsidiaries but none for coproduction or offset suppliers, even when they are under the auspices of Foreign Military Sales oversight. This policy has the effect of precluding the kind of cyber-threat information-sharing that domestically has proven successful.

Second, the recently released Defense Federal Acquisition Regulation Supplement rules on safeguarding defense information make it mandatory to apply National Institute of Standards and Technology controls to overseas suppliers anytime covered information is involved. However, few foreign companies are likely to submit themselves to DoD-imposed standards. This leaves defense companies with the dilemma of continuing with a foreign supplier who is out of compliance with the DFARS rules or abandoning the supplier, thereby failing to meet contractual offset requirements.

RECOMMENDATIONS

Private companies in the defense sector operate in an environment where there is too much government focus on regulation and compliance, little support in addressing the problems faced in the defense supply chain, and small subcontractors and a decreasing pool of talent.

In light of these challenges, we propose several recommendations the federal government might consider to meet the cybersecurity needs of the defense sector.

INSTITUTE A TIERED MATURITY MODEL FOR GRADING CYBERSECURITY COMPETENCY

The fundamental problem with the cybersecurity regulatory compliance model in the defense sector is that it is a *compliance* model. It creates an incentive to check the block at the minimum level required to pass without improving defenses ways not easy to capture by auditors. In a compliance model, auditors, not cybersecurity specialists, run things.

Even worse, the compliance model is binary. You either do everything required, or you fail. There is no middle ground. There is a way to fix it: turn it into an incentive model. The key is to establish a way for companies to take credit for incremental improvements by structuring the system to have different levels, or tiers, of compliance. The tiers would be designed so that each successively higher level represents a concrete improvement in security. Lower tiers would be for companies achieving the basic foundations for security that require less investment. Higher tiers would reflect greater investment in high-end systems and operational processes.

Such a model would produce immediate benefits. It would help companies prioritize their efforts and tell them where to spend their next dollar. For example, adding a capability that would move them from tier two to tier three might be a better investment than buying a level-four capability that would, however, still leave them at a net tier-two level.

Such a model would also allow the government or prime contractors to tailor contract requirements to a level of security proportionate to the criticality of the information being protected. This would incentivize suppliers to move to the next level to be eligible for what would presumably be more important or lucrative contracts.

A tiered model should include a maturity component for each control to reflect a company's progress in taking advantage of each defensive control. Lower levels of maturity would indicate that a control was in place enough to satisfy an audit. A higher level would indicate that the control was being aggressively monitored with the results acted upon—that is, an indication of operational rigor rather than regulatory compliance. This would go a long way toward incorporating the operational aspects of security that differentiate a compliant organization from a secure organization.

Fundamentally, a tiered maturity model transforms the environment from one of compliance to one of competition. A compliance model is inherently adversarial, where regulators seek to explain any compromise as a consequence of noncompliance. It is a model where lawyers are more important than security professionals. A maturity model is inherently a measurement along a sliding scale. It introduces the concept of *better* rather than the binary of *perfect/failure*.

A tiered maturity model that recognizes defense contractors for their efforts would then be an incentive for companies to demonstrate their security posture. It would become a branding and competitive incentive, rather than a compliance mandate. The marketing possibilities for small and medium businesses in the defense supply chain would be significant, making it attractive for them to participate.

One of the greatest benefits of a maturity model, though, is that it allows small- and medium-sized defense contractors to realistically participate. In a binary compliance model, they are essentially excluded because most can never hope to ever become compliant under any type of realistic investment profile.

INFORMATION SHARING BEYOND THE ELITES

The other area where small and medium businesses have been institutionally excluded is information sharing. Here, too, we offer a way ahead. In the same way small- and medium-sized businesses are disproportionately impacted by compliance, they are disproportionately excluded from the benefits of a decade of information-sharing efforts.

The current close-hold information-sharing methods are designed for companies with the infrastructure and staff capable of manually receiving complex threat data, evaluating these data for their environment, and applying them to any number of defensive systems.

Small companies can do none of this. Instead, sharing with small companies requires a passive model where the company can accept threat data in an automated system and have these data applied to their network. They have neither the capability nor desire to analyze the data. They just want to have them take effect automatically. This type of unquestioning acceptance is very applicable to the practice of monitoring or blocking command and control channels. It looks very much like the antivirus model but on a different data set.

The Pentagon should work with industry to create a broader information-sharing environment that is both affordable and passive. It should be focused on attacker command and control channels to make it suitable for a perimeter or cloud activity. Such a system might well not include the most sensitive of the data currently shared, but the added benefit of sharing 90 percent more broadly far outweighs the value of protecting against that last 10 percent that are too sensitive to be shared outside controlled environments.

To understand the impact on small and medium businesses, consider an attacker that targets fifty companies. Not an uncommon occurrence at all. In every case of this kind, a couple of targets inevitably discover the attack. The other forty-eight never get the word. Cyber criminals and nation-state industrial espionage forces alike count on us being more concerned about secrecy than about sharing the information with the other forty-eight companies. We play right into the attackers' hands.

And therein lies the problem with cybersecurity today. We're split into the haves and have-nots. The unfortunate thing is that this is largely a self-inflicted wound. We all know we need to share, and we all say we want to share, but in the end, we either don't share or only share with a select few of our trusted partners. This is despite a decade-long drumbeat within government, industry, and the media on the need to share information on a wider scale.

Defense can address this by allowing the large system integrators to share DoD-provided unclassified threat indicators with defense contractors in their supply chain via automated monitoring systems. Many of the larger primes have such systems they use to monitor their own subsidiaries. Extending it to the supply chain will have a high payoff at low cost.

DOD SHOULD MOVE TO BETTER ACCOMMODATE A GLOBAL DEFENSE INDUSTRIAL BASE

Defense should work with industry to develop operating concepts for cyber defense in an increasingly global market. Overseas suppliers and coproduction agreements are structurally part of our industry for the foreseeable future and only likely to increase. Compliance regimes and information-sharing processes must both be modified to accommodate this new reality.

The department should immediately begin working with NIST to find an acceptable international standard that can serve as an overseas substitute for defense controlled-information cybersecurity controls.

DoD should also begin working with industry to develop a way to share cyber-defense information with foreign suppliers of critical items. It may well turn out that this will need to be in the form of a tamper-proof black box, but it may also turn out to be a recognition that cyber defense is a global problem and restricting information to US companies and their sub-sidiaries presents far more risk than does the possibility that a foreign sup-plier might leak threat information.

THE PENTAGON NEEDS TO INCREASE OUTREACH TO SMALL COMPANIES

Defense depends on small businesses to support its missions, spark in-novation, and develop technologies to support the warfighter. In 2014, FBI assistant director Randall Coleman testified that small businesses were in-creasingly targeted for theft of trade secrets and economic espionage by foreign entities—often with state sponsorship and backing.[9]

Defense maintains an Office of Small Business Programs to ensure small businesses receive a fair proportion of DoD contracts and subcontracts. This office, among other things, is responsible for providing small-business policy advice to the Office of the Secretary of Defense and for providing policy oversight to other DoD small-business offices. While OSBP is not required to educate small businesses on cybersecurity, OSBP officials ac-knowledge that cybersecurity is an important and timely issue for small businesses.

However, as of July 2015, a Government Accountability Office report found that OSBP had not identified and disseminated any cybersecurity re-sources in its outreach and education efforts to defense-sector small busi-nesses.[10] This lack of providing cybersecurity resources to small businesses DoD does business with comes despite the GAO noting the existence of more than a dozen existing programs within the federal government that could have been adapted by the DoD with little to no effort.

OSBP noted two primary reasons they were not able to provide these resources: lack of organization and communication between government agencies already using existing cybersecurity programs for small business and lack of coordination within DoD leadership on the subject due to high turnover rates.[11]

The next administration should ensure that cybersecurity is a compo-nent of OSBP outreach and take steps to stabilize the office's performance and leadership.

CONCLUSION

The consistent theme emerging within the defense sector is that the cyber-defense relationships and processes that have been so successful with the large US-based system integrators for the last decade are becoming ill-suited to an industry where much of what we need to protect increasingly lies with less capable or non-US suppliers. Those vendors find the emerging compliance culture untenable. Government and industry must revisit and revise the existing processes to find better ways to make the public-private partnership more inclusive. The year 2017 needs to be the *year of the supplier.*

---

1 Nathan Thornburgh, "The Invasion of the Chinese Cyberspies (And the Man Who Tried to Stop Them)," *Time Magazine*, Sept. 5, 2005, Web.

2 Fire Eye, *Maginot Revisited: More Real-World Results from Real-World Tests*, Special Report (Fire Eye, 2015), Web.

3 Sean Lyngaas, "DISA Chief: We're in 'an Economic Cyber Cold War,'" *FCW*, Nov. 18, 2015, n.p., Web.

4 US Department of Defense, Office of the Undersecretary of Defense for Acquisition, Technology and Logistics, *Task Force Report: Resilient Military Systems and the Advanced Cyber Threat* (Washington, DC: Department of Defense, Defense Science Board, 2013), p. 33, Web.

5 Frank Kendall and Daniel M. Tangherlini, *Improving Cybersecurity and Resilience through Acquisition* (Washington, DC: US Department of Defense and General Services Administration, Nov. 2013), p. 11, Web.

6 John Oates, "Dell Warns on Spyware Infected Server Motherboards," *The Register*, July 21, 2010, Web; Dennis Fisher, "HP Warns of Procurve Switches Shipped with Malware," *Threat Post*, Apr. 12, 2012, Web; John Leyden, "Olympus Apologises after Shipping Malware-laced Cameras in Japan," *The Register*, June 9, 2010, Web, Apr. 26 2016; Matthew Broersma, "Samsung Wave Smartphone Ships with Malware," *ZD Net*, June 4, 2010, Web.

7 David F. Melcher, Craig R. McKinley, Stan Soloway, and Dean Garfield, "Government Contracting Associations Letter to Mr. McDonough and Ms. Jarrett," *Letter to Denis R. McDonough and Valerie B. Jarrett* (National Defense Industrial Association, Government Contracting Associations, Aug. 3 2015), Web.

8 "Disclosure of Information," DFARS 252.204-7009, 2013; "Safeguarding Covered Defense Information and Cyber Incident Reporting," DFARS 252.204.7012, 2015.

9 *Economic Espionage and Trade Secret Theft: Are Our Laws Adequate for Today's Threats?*, 113th Cong. (2014) (testimony of Randall C. Coleman, assistant director, Counterintelligence Division, Federal Bureau of Investigation before the Committee on the Judiciary, Subcommittee on Crime and Terrorism, United States Senate), Web.

10 US Government Accountability Office, *Defense Cybersecurity: Opportunities Exist for DOD to Share Cybersecurity Resources with Small Businesses* (USGAO, Sept. 2015), Web, GAO-15-777.

11 Ibid.

Four

Cybersecurity in the Healthcare Industry

Dustin Wilcox, Vice President and Chief Information
Security Officer, Centene

INTRODUCTION

Anyone looking for a case study illustrating the speed of the evolving cyber threat need look no further than healthcare. Only a few years ago, aside from the commodity attacks that affected all verticals equally, the primary threat targeting healthcare was aimed squarely at intellectual property held by medical device manufacturers. While the industry, together with regulatory partners, understood the value of patient data and the need to protect these data, would-be cyberattackers had yet to divine how to monetize patient data. That is no longer the case, particularly for organized crime.

Nine in ten health-care organizations surveyed by the Ponemon Institute say they suffered a data breach involving the loss or theft of patient data during the past twenty-four months. Half of organizations say the root cause of their breach was criminal theft.[1] During any given year, healthcare data breaches now account from one-third to more than 40 percent of the recorded total.[2]

The rise in cyberattacks targeting healthcare over the last several years has been well chronicled in media headlines. Furthermore, we can logically assume that the sophistication of attacks against healthcare has evolved as it has across other industries.

WHAT MAKES THE HEALTHCARE SECTOR UNIQUE

PATIENT DATA ARE UNIQUELY VALUABLE TO CRIMINALS

By 2014, the cost of purchasing a stolen patient record on the cyber black market was approximately ten times the cost of purchasing that same individual's stolen credit-card data.[3]

An individual's healthcare record includes all the data elements necessary to impersonate the victim in order to receive credit on their behalf. The attacker's job is even easier if the victim's physician takes a photocopy of patients' driving licenses and includes those images in the electronic medical record.

What is worse, it is highly unlikely that anyone will detect financial fraud as stemming from a healthcare data breach. Even if it is detected, the essential data elements, such as name, date of birth, address, and Medicaid ID, are not likely to change. Healthcare data differ significantly from financial data. When your financial data are stolen, your bank simply issues you a new credit card and account number. But you can have just one date of birth. Put another way, financial data are additive to the individual's identity; healthcare data are indicative of that identity.

Hackers exploit health records in other ways besides credit-card fraud. They further monetize that data by billing fraudulent claims to Medicaid and Medicare. Both government programs still largely pay bills using the "pay-and-chase" model, meaning that fraudulent claims likely get paid and only afterward does someone attempt to recover the funds. Naturally, the attacker and the money are long gone by then. An ambitious attacker might fraudulently prescribe narcotics, sell the drugs on the black market, and bill the claim to Medicare. There are myriad ways to defraud the public healthcare system.[4] It is highly unlikely that we have seen them all. When all other methods are exhausted, the attacker may then file fraudulent tax returns.[5]

VALUE OF PATIENT DATA TO NATION-STATES

Perhaps the most interesting evolution in the cyber threat facing the healthcare sector in the last several years is the rise of the nation-state threat—governments of other countries directing their cyber warriors to hack into hospitals and health insurers to steal medical records.

It's likely that sophisticated nation-state actors, China and Russia in particular, are stealing patient data to build databases on American citizens for the purpose of nation-state espionage activities. The fact that two of the biggest healthcare breaches in 2015 included patient data on large populations of Boeing and Northrop Grumman employees supports this theory.[6]

If I were a nation-state hacker wanting to phish a defense-sector employee to install spyware, and I had access to that employee's medical history, his detailed financial records from the Morgan-Stanley breach, his purchase preferences from the Target breach, it is not hard to imagine that I could create a well-crafted attack and expect a high likelihood of success.

INSIDER THREATS

Employees who steal data from the inside are problematic everywhere. However, they are particularly insidious in the healthcare sector. In the healthcare environment, it is helpful to subdivide the insider threat into the intentional and unintentional categories.

The intentional insider threat is often an extension of organized crime and nation-state threats. A crime element or nation-state intent on stealing patient data from a well-defended healthcare enterprise may determine that the most efficient and effective method for doing so is to hire someone to take a well-placed job there. These harms typically manifest themselves in the form of stealing patient data, company funds, or intellectual property.

Although a relatively small fraction of healthcare data breaches are caused by insiders, their impacts are significant. The access to patient data available to intentional insiders means that the proportion of patient records captured by intentional insiders is much higher than the simple number of breaches. Healthcare data processors say malicious insiders account for just about 10 percent of data breaches but are the root cause of double the percentage of medical-identity thefts.[7]

Encryption is a common anti-hacking best practice, but it is largely ineffective when it comes to insiders. A database administrator in any healthcare company must have privileged access to protected health information. The best practice of least-privileged access—giving administrators the access to data they need, but no more—limits the opportunity of many to steal data. However, it will not eliminate it, since those same low-level administrators typically load plaintext patient data into the database. In other words, they have full access to sensitive data before these data reach an encrypted database. Further, a high-level administrator gone bad can be difficult or impossible to detect, since accessing large quantities of PHI is normal behavior for some job descriptions. Fraudulent use of that access is exceedingly difficult to detect with the tools available today.

The accidental insider threat is something else altogether. This threat is best described as well-intentioned, smart employees doing things as a part of their daily jobs that are not smart when viewed from a cybersecurity perspective. "Smart in other things" is the term we affectionately use in my practice. For example, the doctors who order nurses to rush ahead of them and log them onto their electronic health record accounts before they arrive in a patient's room. This practice might make patient care more efficient but can seriously compromise security. Other examples are laptops lost by well-intentioned providers wanting to take their work home or simply accidently transcribing numbers on a fax transmission.

In contrast to the intentional insider threat, the impact of the average breach caused by an accidental insider tends to be small, but the large number of these incidents makes the threat significant. The sheer volume of people in the healthcare industry that tend to engage in "smart in other things" activities makes this a very serious threat. In fact, accidental insiders cause more, albeit smaller, breaches than any other threat to the healthcare industry.

BUSINESS ASSOCIATES AND SECONDARY USE OF HEALTHCARE DATA
The final element of the cybersecurity problem facing healthcare is how many individuals need direct access to data. In the lifecycle of any

healthcare transaction, patient data must pass through a number of hands. Each hand represents another potential point of vulnerability or attack. Information security professionals describe this as an *attack surface* problem.

Imagine I go to my primary care doctor with a stomachache. A medical assistant holds a folder or a portable device loaded with electronic health record software containing my medical history. The assistant is about to add to it: Am I taking new medications? Where does it hurt? What have I eaten recently? My answers fall in with all my other information, including my name, date of birth, address, social security number, driver's license number, and insurance card.

After examining me, the physician orders lab work and an ultrasound. Orders sent on my behalf to the lab and the imaging center include a portion of my medical record, enough to identify me and bill my insurance. After reviewing the results, my physician prescribes an acid blocker and sends me home. However, my healthcare data still have far to go.

Each of the entities that rendered service to me—the doctor's office, the lab, and the imaging center—submits payment claims to my insurance carrier. That may include private insurance, Medicare, Medicaid, or some combination of the three. In today's world, there is still a high likelihood that at least one of those claims will be submitted on a paper form via fax or mail.

Let us say that two of the claims arrive at my insurer electronically and were processed automatically, even though many insurers process electronic claims with a high degree of manual review.

However, in my case, a third claim arrived via fax. That claim, including all of my healthcare information it contains, is picked-up by mailroom employee. Another employee scans it, converting it into an electronic image. Specialized software extrapolates data from the image. Because of the high error rate, another employee manually checks the scan. From there, the remainder of my faxed claim's journey through the process proceeds like those claims received electronically.

The journey for my healthcare information has not ended. There are administrative uses for my information. For example, an examiner might review my claims in detail looking for potential fraud.

Next, there may be what I would call medical management uses for that information. A case-review nurse might follow up to ensure that I am taking my medication.

Finally, there are population health use cases for my data. A health-care data scientist might combine claims data for people living in my state and run advanced analysis against it in an effort to discover what environmental factors contributing to a spike in doctor visits by people complaining of stomachaches. There may be countless additional analytic uses for my data, all serving to promote better health for the larger population, for months and years to come.

If you are counting, the important parts of my medical record—the parts that identify me—passed through no fewer than twelve people, or groups of people. In addition, all because of a routine doctor visit. If I have multiple insurance carriers, that number could easily expand to between twenty and twenty-five.

All of these touches to my healthcare data were necessary and proper. Regardless, it's this variety of uses for my healthcare data, combined with the quantity of data and their indicative nature, that make the data the biggest information security challenge facing healthcare.

CYBERSECURITY IS NOT, AND WON'T BECOME, THE PRIME FOCUS OF CONSUMER CHOICE

The doctor-patient relationship is a unique one insulated from the pressures that affect other sectors in the wake of a data breach. Patients are unlikely to abandon their medical provider over a data breach, whether because their choice in doctors or insurance providers is limited or in deference to the skilled care they receive from a medical practice. As things stand, there is little incentive, beyond regulatory consequences (that achieve poor outcomes), to spend more time and effort defending against that breach.

CHALLENGES FACING THE NEW ADMINISTRATION

THE INHERENT CONFLICT BETWEEN PATIENT CARE, TECHNOLOGY, COSTS, AND SECURITY

It is common knowledge that healthcare is vital (some would say a human right) and expensive. Both public concern and public policy have created massive incentives to expand excellent healthcare and control costs. Unfortunately, security has received neither equivalent concern nor adequate investment.

One of the earliest business uses for the iPad I can recall was my physician using it to consolidate his patient data record and other medical reference materials into a single, mobile, searchable device. Once in the physicians' hands, the number of mobile-enabled practice management systems grew rapidly. Like most every disruptive technology, the uses for it multiplied long before any serious thought was given to securing the technology. We are likely to see similar scenarios play out with other emerging technologies that are relevant to healthcare, such as cloud computing and wearable health monitors.

Medical providers "were woefully unprepared" to handle the cyber threats inherent in digitalization, former national coordinator for health IT David Brailer recently told *PoliticoPro*.[8] They still are. However, they are living with the unintended consequences of that headlong rush: an uptick in data breaches and a scary new rash of ransomware attacks.[9]

Other examples of these trends include the push for healthcare providers to use digital technologies, such as cloud computing and the Internet of Things, which can both improve critical patient care and drive down costs. PricewaterhouseCoopers's 2014 *Global State of Information Security Survey* found that use of cloud technologies is rising significantly in the healthcare world but only one-third of healthcare institutions are confident of the security of data placed in the cloud.[10]

Overall PWC has generally found that adoption of new technology in healthcare has not kept pace with security. Among the findings PWC has recently generated are that healthcare security strategies include cloud providers only 28 percent of the time, and only 46 percent of healthcare organizations have a strategy for mobile device security.

Comments filed by the College of Healthcare Management Executives and the Association for Executives in Healthcare Information Services before the Senate Judiciary Committee in June 2016 reported that "the digitization of personal health information and the sharing of data encouraged by the Medicare and Medicaid EHR Incentive Program, has led to an increase in the number and types of cyber threats facing healthcare providers." Meanwhile, providers with limited resources struggle to balance the huge demands for cybersecurity technology and information risk–management programs. Threats to healthcare organizations are growing more sophisticated every day, and too many health systems are not properly equipped to combat the myriad of attacks that could penetrate their networks. Even the largest healthcare delivery organizations, with the greatest investment in security programs, may still fall victim to bad actors as we have seen with some of the largest retail organizations, financial institutions, and even the federal government suffering large-scale breaches.

REGULATORY CHALLENGES

Already highly regulated, healthcare organizations are subject to divergent and duplicative guidance on data security and privacy by various federal entities, state regulators, and business agreements.

The two major laws governing healthcare cybersecurity practices, the Health Insurance Portability and Accountability Act of 1996 and the Health Information Technology for Economic and Clinical Health Act of 2009, were well intentioned but aren't functioning as intended when it comes to cybersecurity.

The massive 2013 "omnibus rule" updating HIPAA mandated by the HITECH Act has failed to have the desired effect of making the healthcare industry more secure.

More than a year after the rule took effect, the FBI issued a warning telling the healthcare industry that it "is not as resilient to cyber intrusions compared to the financial and retail sectors" and that the "possibility of increased cyber intrusions is likely."[11] The year after that proved a banner one for healthcare data breaches, with four of the five largest ever occurring in 2015.[12] The parade of damaged institutions include Excellus BlueCross BlueShield, Premera Blue Cross, and Anthem.[13]

Those companies do not suffer from a lack of regulatory compliance. Fortune 100, multinational insurance carriers have teams of lawyers and privacy professionals monitoring all aspects of the business to ensure that every HIPAA requirement is followed to the letter. They ensure every employee receives regular training and follows HIPAA requirements.

It is critical, however, to distinguish between security and compliance. Indeed, it is not unusual for healthcare institutions to do audit for regulatory compliance and not audit to security needs. This is indicative of the broader research cited in chapter 1, which highlights the general inefficiency of standards-based regulatory auditing as opposed to more sophisticated "risk-based" auditing generally indicative of the private sector.

Smaller and more rural primary healthcare practices, sometimes consisting of a physician, two midlevels, and an office manager, are especially vulnerable to the conflicting patient care/cost regulation/security tensions. Who on this team has the time or training to understand the omnibus regulation, let alone train others? I can tell you from experience that these clinics have two priorities: treating patients and billing claims. In that order. There are exponentially more players in the healthcare industry that resemble that small practice than a multinational conglomerate.

Moreover, not all the critical elements of the healthcare cybersecurity ecosystem are fully integrated into that system from a regulatory perspective. According the College of Healthcare Information Management Executives and the Association for Executives in Healthcare Information Security, "device manufacturers, for example, are not Health Insurance Portability and Accountability Act (HIPAA) covered entities, and CIOs and CISOs often describe scenarios in which medical devices are deployed with default passwords, some of which are unable to be changed by the providers, that can be easily penetrated by bad actors, potentially threatening the functionality and safety of the device. In other instances, inadequate technical controls exist to protect the medical devices that are already deployed. Additionally, some medical devices operate on private networks, not controlled by the providers, creating large holes in perimeters and firewalls."[14]

Moreover, current regulations take a retributive approach to cybersecurity, punishing organizations that get breached even if they have correctly done many things concerning information security. Companies can spend enormous amounts of capital on expensive technologies, such as encryption and data-loss prevention, and still experience a breach.

In healthcare, breaches spawn audits. Often those audits have punitive outcomes in the forms of substantial fines and other penalties. That substantial time and money put into preventing such breaches are often overlooked.

Two healthcare companies of a similar size might make substantially different commitments to cybersecurity. One can devote significant resources to implementing best practices, while a second spends less for a superficial implementation. However, thanks to a number of factors, perhaps including nothing more than the bad luck of a nation-state attack, the first company might be breached, while the second is not. The superficially secure company has realized a significant economic advantage over the organization that decided to take healthcare data security seriously. That advantage is further exacerbated when you consider the hefty fines the first, luckless firm will experience after the breach.

Even in the best-run and best-funded healthcare institutions, there is a limited supply of qualified personnel, but for healthcare and security. When the limited security personnel are pulled away to regulatory and audit compliance there is less time and energy to focus on critical and growing security issues. The limit on available security resources is an endemic problem that cannot be solved immediately and must be addressed quickly and with full understanding of the competing needs in this sector.

COST OF SECURITY

Another systemic barrier is the cost of security. Large healthcare enterprises have teams of dedicated information security staff focused on the achievement of regulatory compliance and the implementation of security best practices.

Surveys nonetheless indicate that most healthcare executives are confident in the effectiveness of their security practices. They believe their strategies are sound, and many consider themselves to be leaders in the field. While there is clearly a segment of the healthcare industry that is being proactive, that group is a distinct minority. PricewaterhouseCoopers found that only 42 percent have a cybersecurity strategy and proactive in executing it.[15] While 65 percent of healthcare leaders are confident that their cybersecurity practices are effective, that percentage is a 15 percent decline from 2009.

PWC also measured healthcare providers' self-appraisal against four key criteria of leadership:

- Have overall info security plan.
- The chief information security officer reports to "top of the house."
- Measure and review plan within the past year.
- Understand what types of events have occurred.

PWC found only 6 percent of heath care leadership were effective on the basis of these criteria.

These problems are magnified when one considers smaller practices with fewer resources. In such cases, the goal is not likely to go beyond regulatory compliance, which most in the industry agree is a poor substitute for true security.

The number of cyber incidents in the healthcare domain suggests a disconnect between industry leadership perceptions, current practice, and effective security. PWC confirmed this finding, reporting that 53 percent of healthcare IT professionals cited lack of funding a main reason for the vulnerabilities they faced. "Diminished budgets have resulted in degraded security. Incidents are on the rise and new technologies are being added faster than security safeguards. Healthcare practitioners need to understand they are playing a new game with different rules and they need to respond with new strategies," PWC wrote.[16]

Some might think of this problem as one of parity—all within the healthcare industry must abide by the same rules and regulations. However, not all within the industry have equivalent access to the financial resources and individual expertise necessary to comply. The high cost of compliance, and the higher cost of failure, further exacerbate the problem.

ESCALATING MALICE OF CYBERATTACKS

Ransomware is an epidemic raging in hospitals across the country. The prognosis is bad, especially with criminals focusing their attention on the healthcare industry.[17] Ransomware has become so commonplace that it was cited as a top new threat for 2016 by the Ponemon Institute in its annual study of healthcare data security and privacy.[18] To illustrate the ferocity of the bad actors, the chief information officer of a large East Coast, multibillion-dollar health system turned away more than one million ransomware-ridden e-mails during the month of March 2016 alone.

In a ransomware attack, hackers plant malware onto a computer or server, encrypting the hard drive in an uncrackable code. Attackers do not release the impossible-to-guess decryption key until they are paid off. The amount can be substantial, as ransomware attacks go. One Southern California recently paid out $17,000.[19] Of course, the real damage is not in ransoms paid, but in medical care deferred.

Ransomware attacks for now appear unconnected to data theft.[20] And attackers likely started targeting healthcare not because of the leverage that control over patient data afford them, but because of the obsolete state of their information technology infrastructure—replete with phased-out operating systems and web applications known to be pathways for malware.[21]

However, that is not going to stay the case. Having discovered the healthcare industry to be an easy and lucrative target, ransomware attackers are adopting the same sophisticated, lateral techniques involved in traditional network breaches.[22] Given the real value of patient data—in their theft for exploitation or resale—ransomware attacks will become the nasty second jab of what really are one-two punch attacks.

TERRORIST ATTACKS

Considerable attention is lavished on the possibility of a cyberattack against the electric grid.[23] Without minimizing the threats facing energy companies, anyone looking to sow terror via computer can do a lot better than turning off the lights.

In fact, there is a whole field of newly networked devices coming onto the market as we speak devices whose disruption could be quickly fatal. They are medical devices.

If hacking a pacemaker or the like seems a sensationalist television show contrivance (in fact, *Homeland*, season two), it is not so to security researchers. On the basis of researchers' findings, the Food and Drug Administration in August 2015 urged medical providers to cease using an infusion pump that "could allow an unauthorized user to control the device and change the dosage the pump delivers, which could lead to over- or underinfusion of critical patient therapies."[24]

Moreover, if the goal is terror, simply the threat of an attack, if credible to the public, could be sufficient to cause substantial damage. Much of the ransomware threat is enhanced by the potential to corrupt, not steal data. Substantial public concern could be generated if a terrorist accessed a health institution, or claimed they did, and altered as minimal a target as blood types, creating substantial fear and paralyzing patient care, as well as generating substantial costs until all the data validity were confirmed.

Not every medical device hack will be terrorism. Data thieves, too are making their mark here.[25] However, there is no denying that life-sustaining devices once isolated from public networks are now exposed to them. Terrorists unable to physically attack Americans may find reaching them through the Internet an appealing alternative. If terrorists' technical abilities today are wanting, their intentions are not.[26] Medical equipment is now part of the mix of databases and hard drives also once thought impervious to hackers. If the Internet teaches us anything, it has not to underestimate how easily the far-fetched or fantastical becomes normal reality.

COMPLACENCY

The final system obstacle in healthcare is best described as lack of urgency. Well into the computing age, few within the healthcare industry thought that our data had value, or feared that we would be the target of any serious cyber threat. We cured of the belief, but we are going to suffer the consequences of our failure to act earlier for years to come. Unfortunately, it took significant healthcare data breaches to convince many in our industry to get serious about committing people and capital. We are still struggling to catch up and will yet see attacks that damage our ability to provide care in a secure, private and efficient manner.

RECOMMENDATIONS

INCENTIVIZE HEALTHCARE TO IMPLEMENT BEST CYBERSECURITY PRACTICES

When discussing information security in the healthcare industry, a colleague of mine is fond of saying that "the bad guys are getting worse faster than the good guys are getting better." At an abstract level, the easy supposition is that we should force everyone within the healthcare industry to implement information security best practices. Unfortunately, that conclusion fails to account for the economic realities of the regulatory environment governing healthcare.

A course shift away from prescriptive regulation and to regulation that encourages security best practices is desperately needed. That encouragement would best be achieved through the strategic application of liability relief and other complementary incentives.

What I propose is regulation that would incentivize healthcare companies to aggressively implement security best practices by offering a sliding scale of liability protection on the basis of the company's progress toward implementing an objective set of practices. The National Institute of Standards and Technology Cybersecurity Framework, and the process used to develop it, could provide a good starting point.

Sector and government coordinating councils should develop a healthcare–specific framework on the basis of research that documents which best standards and practices are most cost effective for the sector and subsectors. Companies would be expected to voluntarily adopt standards and practices independently documented as cost effective as a matter of sound commercial security.

It is unreasonable to expect private healthcare organizations to fight off cyberattacks from entities who dwarf them in size and scope such as nation-states or larger crime syndicates (any of which as interrelated to nation-states). For a level of security necessary for national security but not reasonable for private institutions to provide on a sustainable basis, a new system of market incentives is needed.

This is another opportunity to level the playing field through the application of regulatory principles that incentivize desirable behavior. In this particular example, a system that would allow a company to accrue credits tied to its investments in security that it could use against future audits and fines in the event of a breach. This could be taken further by also offering modest tax incentives for certain high-value, but often-overlooked, security best practices, such as employee awareness training.

The system would also have to adapt to using sliding scales, since it is impractical to expect smaller or rural organizations to fund the same degree of security apparatus as large urban and multistate institutions. Differential cost-benefit calculations may be appropriate, and qualifications for liability, tax, or other incentives would also need to be adjusted taking into consideration these variables.

REDUCE REGULATORY COMPLEXITY

Congress should pursue legislation that harmonizes privacy, security, and information risk–management requirements to eliminate the complex patchwork of regulations. Healthcare organizations dedicate highly valuable resources on navigating these complexities to demonstrate compliance with regulators. If a streamlined regulatory framework were in place, these resources could focus more time on actively monitoring and protecting against the daily variable threats.

Streamlining HIPAA audit requirements put into place by the HITECH Act is another place good place security could be incentivized. Audits drain resources from security budgets because money and time must go toward compiling documentation in auditor-friendly ways. A passing audit combined with proof of ongoing investment into cybersecurity should elicit a less strenuous audit the next time around—a HIPAA-Lite version, as it were—or increased time interval between audits.

REPLACE SOCIAL SECURITY NUMBERS AS A PATIENT IDENTIFIER

At a more micro level, the College of Healthcare Information Management Executives and the Association for Executives in Healthcare Information Security have recommended two concrete measures: first, enabling the use of a healthcare–specific identification solution that reduces reliance on social security numbers and other identifiable patient identifier information; second, a sector-specific solution would immediately devalue health records on the black market.

Congress should remove language placed annually in federal spending bills that prohibits the Department of Health and Human Services from using any federal funds to promulgate or adopt any such standard.

Technology has provided for alternatives to a numeric or alphanumeric identifier as a solution, and the government does not need to be the arbiter of the identification solution. But HHS must be able to provide technical assistance to private-sector initiatives. The department has interpreted the annual funding ban to prohibit them from collaborating or assisting with private-sector efforts to improve patient identification on a national level.

USE SECURITY AS A FACTOR OF REIMBURSEMENT

Another very specific recommendations from CHiME and AEHiS is to include security as factor in reimbursement. The Centers for Medicare and Medicaid currently employs value-based reimbursement modifiers; Congress should allow CMS to consider a similar principle to be applied to healthcare enterprises investing in security. Similarly, improving an organization's cybersecurity readiness should be considered a recognized activity under the clinical practice improvement performance category under the Medicare Access and CHIP Reauthorization Act Merit-based Incentive Payment System reimbursement scheme.

CONCLUSION

An incentive-focused regulatory approach would encourage more companies in the healthcare industry to make the investments necessary to protect information assets. With the right incentives, we drive good information security behavior today and continual good behavior going forward.

The mounting threats facing our industry, combined with our inability to adequately defend against them, demonstrate that we need new ideas and a fresh approach. A new regulatory approach would be a good first step. Most importantly, we need to understand the tremendous potential that healthcare data have to serve the greater good, improve population health, and lower the overall cost of care. The challenge is in finding ways to protect these data that promote, not diminish, their utility.

---

1 Ponemon Institute, *Sixth Annual Benchmark Study on Privacy & Security of Healthcare Data* (Ponemon Institute, 2016), Web.

2 Identity Theft Resource Center, *Identify Theft Resource Center Breach Report Hits Near Record High in 2015* (Identity Theft Resource Center, 2016), Web.

3 Caroline Humer and Jim Finkle, "Your Medical Record Is Worth More to Hackers than Your Credit Card," Reuters, Sept. 24, 2014, Web.

4 "The $272 Billion Swindle: Why Thieves Love America's Health-care System," *Economist*, May 31, 2014, Web.

5 Department of Justice, US Attorney's Office Northern District of Florida, *Former Tallahassee Memorial Hospital Employees Sentenced in Tax Refund Scheme* (Department of Justice, June 13, 2013), Web, May 6, 2016.

6 Heather Timmons, "The US Department of Defense Avoided a Security Breach in the Anthem Hack," *Quartz*, Feb. 6, 2015, Web, May 2016.

7 Ponemon Institute, *Sixth Annual Benchmark Study on Privacy & Security of Healthcare Data* (Ponemon Institute, 2016), Web, June 13, 2016.

8 Arthur Allen, "Cyber Ransom Attacks Panic Hospitals, Alarm Congress," *Politico Pro*, May 25, 2016, Web.

9 US Cong. Senate, Committee on the Judiciary, Subcommittee on Crime and Terrorism, *Statement from the College of Healthcare Information Management Executives and the Association for Executives in Healthcare Information Security. Hearing, May 18, 2016*, 114th Cong. 2nd sess. (Washington, DC: GPO, 2016), Web. These comments reported that "the digitization of personal health information and the sharing of data encouraged by the Medicare and Medicaid EHR Incentive Program, has led to an increase in the number and types of cyber threats facing healthcare providers."

10 PricewaterhouseCoopers (PWC), *Defending Yesterday: Key Findings from the Global State of Information Security Survey 2014* (PWC, 2014), Web.

11 Jim Finkle, "Exclusive: FBI Warns Healthcare Sector Vulnerable to Cyberattacks," Reuters, Apr. 14, 2014, Web.

12 Alex Ruoff, "Outlook 2016: Cybersecurity to Become Main IT Concern for Hospitals," Health IT Law & Industry Report (Bloomberg BNA, Jan. 15, 2016), Web.

13 Jessica Davis, "7 Largest Data Breaches of 2015," *Healthcare IT News*, Dec. 11, 2015, Web.

14 US Cong. Senate, Committee on Energy and Commerce, *Testimony Before the United States House of Representatives Committee on Energy and Commerce Subcommittee on Health. Hearing, May 25, 2016*, 114th Cong. 2nd sess. (Washington, DC: GPO, 2016), statement of Marc Probst, Web.

15 PWC, *Putting Data Security at the Top Table: How Healthcare Organizations Can Manage Information More Safely* (PWC, June 2013), Web.

16 Ibid.

17 Nick Biasini, "SamSam: The Doctor Will See You, after He Pays the Ransom," *Cisco Talos Blog*, Mar. 23, 2016, Web.

18 Ponemon Institute, *Sixth Annual Benchmark Study on Privacy & Security of Healthcare Data* (Ponemon Institute, 2016), Web.

19 Richard Winton, "2 More Southland Hospitals Attacked by Hackers Using Ransomware," *Los Angeles Times*, Mar.22, 2016, Web.

20 Sean Gallagher, "Patients Diverted to Other Hospitals after Ransomware Locks Down Key Software," *Ars Technica*, Feb. 17, 2016, Web.

21 Sean Gallagher, "Two More Healthcare Networks Caught Up in Outbreak of Hospital Ransomware," *Ars Technica*, Mar. 29, 2016, Web.

22 Kim Zetter, "Why Hospitals Are the Perfect Targets for Ransomware," *Wired*, Mar. 30, 2016, Web.

23 Mike Masnick, "Ted Koppel Writes Entire Book about How Hackers Will Take Down Our Electric Grid...and Never Spoke to Any Experts," *Tech Dirt*, Nov. 19, 2015, Web.

24 US Department of Health and Human Services, US Food and Drug Administration, *Cybersecurity Vulnerabilities of Hospira Symbiq Infusion System: FDA Safety Communication* (US Food and Drug Administration, July 31, 2015), Web.

25 Akanksha Jayanthi, "MetroHealth Cardiac Cath Lab Attacked by Malware, 981 Patient Records Compromised," *Becker's Hospital Review*, May 18, 2015, Web.

26 Joseph Marks, "ISIL Aims to Launch Cyberattacks on U.S." *Politico Pro*, Dec. 29, 2015, Web.

Five

Cybersecurity in the Banking
and Financial Sector

Daniel Crisp, Chief Information Risk Officer and Head of Technology
Compliance, BNY Mellon
Larry Trittschuh, Threat and Vulnerability Leader, Synchrony Financial
Gary McAlum, Chief Security Officer and Senior Vice President, USAA

INTRODUCTION

N early a hundred years ago Willie Sutton supposedly answered the question "Why do you rob banks?" by saying "That's where the money is."
In a digital world where the number of targets ripe for hacking has grown exponentially, banks and other financial institutions remain a top target for cyberattacks, whether for financial gain, data theft, or retaliation. For nation-state adversaries or hacktivists, disrupting the financial services industry has the potential to grievously wound the global economy, given the interconnectedness and integrated nature of the society we live in today.

As cyberattacks continue to escalate in severity, financial service firms are investing in cybersecurity at industry leading rates. In its 2016 annual report, the Financial Stability Oversight Council notes that while cybersecurity continues to be a pressing concern, significant investments within the financial sector have reduced vulnerabilities.[1]

Financial institutions continue to be among the leading industry sectors in supporting above average cybersecurity programs. Nearly two-thirds of sector institutions have an overall security strategy.[2] Forward-leaning firms are greatly bolstering their cybersecurity programs through the use of innovative cybersecurity tools and emerging technologies. These organizations are setting high standards in security, availability, and privacy.

They have done all this in the face of heavy-handed and often-redundant regulatory scrutiny and oversight.

Yet, despite herculean efforts, the sector has been unable to fully immunize itself from sophisticated cyberattacks ranging from distributed denial-of-service attacks to high-profile breaches of personal and financial data. Theft of intellectual property such as proprietary business plans and business algorithms from financial institutions soared a stunning 183 percent in 2015.[3]

In its annual *Global State of Information Security Survey*, PricewaterhouseCoopers noted financial services companies saw a "striking year-over-year increase in incidents attributed to highly skilled adversaries in 2015." Not only is the involvement of nation-states (and their proxies) becoming more common but organized criminal attacks on the financial services sector also jumped 45 percent in 2015. Evidence is beginning to accumulate that nation-states and well-resourced, organized criminal syndicates are partnering to perpetrate cybercrime, sometimes engaging insiders for assistance.[4]

The impact of cyberattacks is not confined to losses suffered by the attacked institution. A 2015 study for the Centre for the Study of Financial Innovation highlighted the threats to the financial system itself, noting that "we may at some point see a cyberattack so powerful on an individual bank that it could bring down the institution necessitating a state bailout."[5] A cyberattack on key institutions could paralyze key activities such as interbank payments for several days, which could put the entire interconnected, global financial system into chaos.

WHAT MAKES THE FINANCIAL SERVICES SECTOR UNIQUE

Financial services was one of the first industries to adopt information and communication technology, automating back-office and branch operations and developing innovations like credit cards and ATMs.[6] Embracing such innovation has allowed for tremendous growth, but it has also changed the behavior of retail and commercial banking customers.

Today's consumers have higher expectations about service, given the proliferation of technologies available to them. Consumers are more likely to shop around for products and be more interested in direct and mobile channels than their predecessors. At the same time, competition for retail banking business is vibrant. New market entrants are attacking the value chain between banks and their customers. Established competitors are responding with new and compelling offerings. Through it all, new technologies, such as smartphones, biometric authentication, and cloud computing are shortening the innovation cycle and increasing the pace of change, particularly in the area of mobile payment applications and real-time money movements. In this environment, technology innovation is more important than ever for market differentiation and cyber protection.

However, while the use of innovations such as mobile devices and applications for consumer banking has exploded, the exploitation of these devices has increased significantly.

Commercial banking, too, has seen tremendous benefits from technology and is poised to reap even more as the new distributed ledger system, known as blockchain, enters the mainstream. Through the application of encryption and algorithms, blockchain has the potential to automate complex, multiparty transactions and improve the speed and accuracy of settlement systems.[7] In June 2016, a group of seven financial institutions used blockchain to move money across borders almost instantaneously via a real-time gross settlement system known as Ripple. They achieved in seconds what usually requires days.[8]

The world relies on US financial markets for economic security and stability. American stocks, shares and bonds are the bedrock for long-term growth.

Looking back in history, the United States gained an extraordinary advantage after World War II because its capital markets and economic infrastructure were undamaged, while Europe and Japan had to rebuild out of devastation.[9] This infrastructure continues to provide accessibility for broader participation and liquidity in the market while lowering volatility.

In the decades since, securities exchanges and record keepers have turned to enabling technologies to enhance the formulation, processing, execution, and settlement of highly complex investment trades that previously took hours, or even days and weeks. High-frequency trading is now widely used by institutional investors, pension funds, mutual funds, and other types of market participants to implement investment strategies in an effort to achieve higher returns for investors. The fabled trading floors at stock and commodity exchanges, with their jacketed traders and open-outcry trading, are essentially photo-op backdrops.[10]

Within the past ten years, there has been a massive shift in the adoption of algorithmic trading. "Algorithmic trading first accounted for at least 50 percent of orders in 2009, and accounted for over 40 percent of total trading volume in 2010."[11] With automation comes great responsibility to ensure that the tasks being run maintain high degrees of confidentiality, integrity, and availability of the information being processed, sustaining the trust and confidence in the financial markets on which the world relies.

Cybersecurity is "perhaps the single most important new risk to market integrity and financial stability," Commodity Futures Trading Commission chairman Tim Massad told attendees of a 2015 futures industry conference.[12]

Indeed, more than half of exchanges surveyed by the International Organization of Securities Commissions and the World Federation of Exchanges in 2013 reported experiencing a cyberattack during the previous twelve months.[13]

The insurance industry is not immune to the changes in how business is conducted in today's contemporary and interconnected society. "Insurers are prime targets to be victimized given the richness of data—credit-card information, medical information, and other underwriting information. It's not a matter of if but when it will happen," a risk-management director at a Canadian insurance company recently told researchers.[14] Insurance executive contacted for a biennial survey conducted in 2015 for the Centre for the Study of Financial Innovation listed cyberattacks against their firms as a key risk for the first time since the survey began in 2007.[15] Insurers are poised to collect continuous streams of real-time sensor data and transform those bits into highly detailed predictive models. In addition, the Internet of

Things with its connected sensors within homes and automobiles, coupled with the ability to automate decision-making (e.g., the water heater is leaking, so shut off the water supply), will create outstanding value propositions for consumers, but also amplify cybersecurity concerns. These revolutionary changes will drive technology innovation at an increasingly faster pace. This demands a greater, complimentary focus on cybersecurity and privacy innovation.

CHALLENGES FACING THE NEW ADMINISTRATION

OVERLAPPING, INEFFECTIVE AND CREEPING REGULATION

The current regulatory model for cybersecurity does not work. Cybersecurity is a uniquely twenty-first-century problem and traditional mechanisms such as consumer lawsuits and government regulation are proving ineffective in meeting the challenge. Because cyber technology and attack methods change constantly, the regulatory process, imbedded with time-consuming reviews, comments, and often litigation, has not kept pace. However, the tendency of the government agencies in the face of this daunting threat is to try more of what isn't working. For example, recently the Securities and Exchange Commission recognized the seriousness of cybersecurity challenges facing the financial system and "promised to step up regulation."[16]

Governmental oversight of the financial sector is notoriously fractured.[17] Duplicative and frequently uncoordinated state and federal governmental structures for regulating the sector are not just inefficient; they have downstream negative implications for the sector when financial institutions must divert resources from maintaining cybersecurity and direct them toward compliance with redundant inquiries from multiple regulators. It's no secret that federal regulation of financial services firms does not exist in a vacuum. Indeed, states place regulatory requirements on firms, resulting in a quilt of overlapping, duplicative, and sometimes conflicting regulations.

Regulations generally create a "floor," or a static set of required minimums. This static check-the-box approach does not work for the dynamic, complex, and ever-evolving nature of the cyber threat that more typically threatens the financial services industry. By its nature this approach is detrimental to cybersecurity. When scarce time and money are deployed toward look-back compliance exercises mandated by federal and state supervisors, there's less available to spend on proactive cyber-defense measures. Companies predict a 40 percent increase in compliance costs because of cybersecurity mandates on critical infrastructure protections in the coming years.[18]

Attempting to shoehorn cybersecurity into an outdated regulatory framework is not only ineffective but also counterproductive.

Despite the unsuitability of the regulatory model as a tool for enhancing cybersecurity, the financial services sector continues to see an increase in disparate and fragmented cybersecurity regulation.

One large financial institution communicated to the Internet Security Alliance that it had internal numbers showing a 121 percent year-over-year average growth over the last five years in regulatory cybersecurity inquiries. This drives the vicious circle of internal audit, compliance, and risk assessments, the cost of which tripled from 2014 to 2015 at the same institution.

It wasn't supposed to be this way. In February 2013, President Barack Obama issued Executive Order 13636, which led to development of the National Institute of Standards and Technology Cybersecurity Framework. Section 7(a) of the order specifically calls for the framework to be available to critical infrastructure owners and operators for *voluntary* adoption.[19] Instead, independent financial sector regulators are using what was supposed to be a voluntary framework in regulatory inquiries.

For many institutions, it began with the Federal Financial Institutions Examination Council—an amalgamation of five banking regulators—releasing in June 2015 a Cybersecurity Assessment Tool incorporating concepts from the NIST framework.

Although the FFIEC emphasized the "voluntary" nature of its tool, the Board of Governors of the Federal Reserve System, the Federal Deposit Insurance Corporation, and the Office of the Comptroller of the Currency all have made use of the tool during examinations of financial institutions.[20] The New York State Department of Financial Services has also expected banks within its jurisdiction to use the FFIEC tool.

As a result of this new de facto regulation, many large financial institutions expend an immense amount of time and resources in determining how to demonstrate compliance with the tool. In its current form, the Cybersecurity Assessment Tool perpetuates a checklist, compliance-oriented, approach to cybersecurity. It doesn't fully account for mitigating controls since the only options are to answer "yes" or "no" to the tool's prefabricated questions. In addition to the financial burdens, operating in this type of duplicative, expanding, check-the-box regulatory environment takes valuable resources that could be used for increasing cybersecurity.

In a perfect illustration of the disconnect that separates regulators from institutions, the FFIEC estimated in 2015 that it would take eighty hours to complete the assessment tool.[21] In fact, it takes considerably longer to provide answers to solicitations that are supportable during the regular examination process with documentation and the other typical evidence requested by regulators. For medium-sized institutions, the real amount of time is one thousand to two thousand hours. Larger institutions can require even more time.[22]

Complicating matters further are the duplicative cybersecurity inquiries emanating from different regulators, even coming from within different offices of the same regulator. These duplicative reporting requirements ask largely the same questions but require exhaustive tailoring for each regulator.

One large bank used to be able to easily coordinate between state regulators, federal regulators, and other independent regulatory bodies. However, the increase in overlapping and largely duplicative regulatory inquiries has resulted in substantial cost increases both in time and money. Institutions have indicated their compliance costs have jumped between with some claiming increases of 40 percent, while others offer higher estimates between 150 to 500 percent. While the cost estimates vary, they are all tend to be substantial. The counterproductive impact of these costs, coupled with the volatility of the data, underlines the need for processes such as the NIST framework and the subsequent instruments it has spawned to be evaluated for their cost effectiveness, as originally called for in the president's executive order.

There is no evidence that these new quasimandates result in tangible improvements in the cybersecurity practices of the US financial services security. As argued elsewhere, including this book's initial chapters, this regime needs an empirical study demonstrating the cost effectiveness of these new regulatory regimes, and public policy ought to be aligned with this cost-effectiveness research.

Potentially compounding the burden of this supposedly voluntary tool, the FFIEC announced in 2015 that it planned to update the assessment tool. While the prospect of rewriting the tool theoretically could realign it with the original vision in the president's executive order, most are skeptical that a realignment will happen. Unlike in the private sector, where market forces would demand that an expensive program that has not demonstrated its ability to meet its goals would be terminated, this costly and ineffective approach is likely being extended by the government, which of course operates immune to market forces.

Throughout this process, the FFIEC has essentially mandated compliance with supposedly voluntary guidance, which it plans on changing in the near future. Banks would then be expected to incur additional expenditures of time and effort to document their compliance with the modified assessment tool.

Financial sector businesses that don't fall under the FFIEC's auspices aren't necessarily excused from incipient regulation. The Securities and Exchange Commission is becoming ever more assertive in monitoring the cybersecurity of broker-dealers and registered investment advisers, even testing firms' implementation of cybersecurity controls.[23] In December 2015, the commission said it intends to impose cybersecurity requirements on transfer agents.[24]

SEC examinations pose a gamut of risks similar to those stemming from the FFIEC's assessment tool: an emphasis on documentation and policies that diverts resources away from genuine cybersecurity, especially given the SEC's power to levy fines. This activity and direction is ironic, given ongoing problems the SEC has with securing its own systems.[25] Indeed, these efforts are problematic and potentially counterproductive since SEC can't always guarantee that the sensitive data it collects about its regulated firms aren't at risk from hackers.

ONLINE RISKS

Technology innovations have eliminated borders for legitimate and criminal enterprises. Attackers can exploit vulnerabilities from anywhere and can impact entire networks in a matter of seconds. The exploitation of such vulnerabilities poses a risk of cascading failure across the entire sector.[26] A cyber incident at a smaller institution such as a community bank can result in a domino effect across the industry, impacting larger, systemically important financial institutions, and possibly other industries and economies.

While such an attack is firmly within the bounds of plausibility and may yet shock us from complacency, attacks against our sector have, for now, resulted just in theft and service disruption. These disruptions have been very serious, including schemes resulting in hundreds of millions of dollars in losses and a year-long campaign aimed at crippling dozens of banks' online portals that was directed by the Iranian government.[27]

A main pathway for cyber theft is an old-fashioned method that attackers have seen no reason to abandon—it's simply too effective to give up: phishing. That is, e-mails designed to trick users into providing sensitive information or to download malware.

According to a survey from cybersecurity firm Cloudmark, "91 percent of companies encountered phishing attacks in 2015, with the lion's share—84 percent—of companies claiming attacks successfully snuck past their security defenses."[28] More pernicious is spear-phishing, which are e-mails tailored to look like they come from a trusted source sending a legitimate message. The pattern of sending a message to the accounting department purportedly from the company CEO has become quite popular, with 63 percent of companies having encountered the tactic.[29]

The use of phishing is widespread, unrelenting, and a low-cost, high-payoff technique for attackers. Phishing is a low-percentage game. One of the Internet Security Alliance's financial sector members works with an outside vendor to shut down thirty to thirty-five phishing sites per day. Any one of those sites can generate tens of thousands of e-mails with the goal of getting just one attachment opened or link clicked by a consumer or employee. Phishing continues its upward trend as being a primary method through which attackers infiltrate corporate networks. Nearly 30 percent of recipients continue to open phishing e-mail messages, and another 12 percent click on attachments, according to the 2016 Verizon Data Breach Investigations Report.[30]

MOBILE DEVICE RISKS

Mobile banking is a boon for consumers but opens up a new front for attackers to exploit. Cyber thieves target banking data by crafting malicious apps known as Trojans, since their benign appearance masks malicious intent.

One particularly vicious Trojan variant distributed through the Google Play store as a Flash Player or as a pornography app overlays nearly every other downloaded mobile app with a fake screen designed to capture log-on information, including for PayPal, Skype, Facebook, and Twitter.[31]

E-mail phishers are also doing their part to stay current with the mobile revolution. Security firm TrendMicro exposed in 2014 a Russian-speaking criminal crew hitting German and Swiss victims with e-mails purporting to come from popular European retailers.[32] The antivirus resistant malware attached to the e-mail substituted requests to online banking web pages with a fake one that prompted users to download a mobile app in order to receive an account log-on verification PIN sent via SMS. Through that malicious app, attackers intercepted actual SMS PINs.

RECOMMENDATIONS

GOVERNMENT SHOULD RETHINK ITS APPROACH TO CYBERSECURITY

The federal government's credibility in educating, let alone regulating and mandating, cybersecurity practices in the private sector is severely undermined by its track record of inefficiency.

At the top level, government needs to fundamentally rethink its approach. Punitive checklist compliance is a waste of resources. However, examinations can produce data that, when aggregated and analyzed, would at least suggest sector-wide areas for improvement and ways to streamline examinations into the most useful areas of inquiry. The problem is that regulators treat each examination as a one-off event.[33] Agencies need to adjust their perspective to the interconnected nature of cybersecurity. The security of any one individual institution is important, but not as important as the collective security of the entire sector.

Another illustration of this outdated mentality comes in how regulatory agencies cope with the shortage of cybersecurity talent in their pool of regulatory examiners. The shortage is problematic enough, since personnel charged with assessing the strength of sector defenses should reasonably be expected to have cybersecurity expertise. But the numbers of examiners with specialized information technology training at regulatory agencies are low—just one hundred examiners at the Office of Comptroller of Currency and sixty examiners at the Federal Deposit Insurance Corporation, according to a 2015 Government Accountability Office report.[34]

Even worse, examiners with expertise tend to get tasked to large banks, where the level of cybersecurity expertise is high. Small and medium institutions get generalists. The rationale is that large banks pose a greater risk to financial stability. But when it comes to cybersecurity, it's not size but expertise and interconnectedness that matters. Small and medium banks lack the former and are a pathway for hackers to penetrate larger institutions.

In addition, information sharing by the federal government continues to be problematic. Many of the data coming from the government are out of date and so stripped of context as to be useless. One sector executive told GAO investigators that government data were "similar to telling the institution that it might be attacked by a criminal in a red hat."[35]

In short, although government recognizes that cybersecurity is pressing and serious, regulatory agencies are approaching the problem as if it were a static problem addressable through existing formulations. Our fundamental recommendation is for federal recognition that new challenges presented by cyber threats call for new approaches to the regulatory supervision of how industry meets those challenges.

HARMONIZE, STREAMLINE, AND IMPROVE REGULATIONS
Regulatory and legislative mandates and compliance frameworks that address information security for the financial sector, such as Sarbanes-Oxley,

Gramm-Leach-Bliley, the Fair and Accurate Credit Transactions Act, as well as state compliance regimes, must be consolidated and streamlined.

A harmonized compliance model would eliminate any wasteful overlaps and eradicate inconsistencies in cybersecurity guidance and requirements. While there may be some justification for occasional variation and tweaks, the extent of uncoordinated, and therefore costly, inefficient, and counter-productive requirements is unjustified by any serious rationale, other than turf wars.

Just as the private sector has learned to integrate multiple and far-flung consumer needs into practical, cost-justified services, so too must government learn to adapt to the digital world. If compliance with one set of meaningful regulations were to be considered compliance with all, the material reduction in compliance costs would free up additional resources to be reinvested in cybersecurity initiatives, rather than in compliance ef-forts. The obligation ought to be on government to justify the need to vary from core requirements, not for industry to prove a negative in that they are unnecessary.

The rationale for consolidation isn't hard to find. "Not only do com-mon standards make it easier for product development and sales, compa-nies can more easily maintain and enhance network defense and resilience, which are vital in today's world of diverse cyber threats," said White House cybersecurity coordinator Michael Daniel in late 2015 when announcing a strategy for engaging the international community on harmonizing cyberse-curity standards.[36] What applies internationally is equally true domestically.

Regulations should encourage banks to take a risk-based approach, which is customized to the threats they face and takes into account the bank's business model and resources available. Utilizing a standard mecha-nism such as the NIST Cybersecurity Framework to align the proliferation of different legal and regulatory cybersecurity requirements enables harmo-nization and adopts unified fundamental guidance for developing cyberse-curity policies and practices within the industry.

Specifically relating to the FFIEC Assessment tool, we recommend the FFIEC abandon its binary approach to Cybersecurity Assessment Tool ratings. Yes-or-no answers incentivize the wrong kind of behavior.

And zero credit for partial improvements obscures areas of real improvement, as well as spheres that may have incomplete or overinvestment. In addition, the tool should better allow for different levels of maturity within the industry—and different needs—by defining a set of cybersecurity tiers, each one representing a greater level of organizational support, investment, and successful adoption of security measures. This way, too, the assessment tool can be tailored not according to a preset assumption of cybersecurity but according to what's relevant to a particular organization.

Populating those tiers with relevant information shouldn't be a job assigned exclusively again to the FFIEC, nor to the National Institute of Standards and Technology. Industry, through the Financial Services Coordinating Council, should receive funding to perform a function that Executive Order 13636 has long called for: determining what controls of the NIST Cybersecurity Framework are most cost effective, and where gaps lie between the limits of cost-effective cybersecurity investment and the most robust defense possible. Assessment tool ratings, in turn, will pinpoint where investment shortfalls occur and will suggest a path for incentivizing their closure.

OPERATIONAL IMPROVEMENTS

Toss the Password into the Dustbin of History

The realities of today's cyber-threat environment have resulted in the widespread leakage of Americans' sensitive information, thanks to a data-breach epidemic. For consumers, the fallout has been an upswelling of identity theft and account takeovers. And as a result, the security model of identity authentication by user ID and password, including the use of "security questions," is no longer acceptable. Increasingly, financial institutions and other online entities require more effective methods of achieving online authentication without an undue level of inconvenience.

"Killing the password" has been a long-standing Obama administration priority, one that it reiterated in the National Cyber Action Plan unveiled in February 2016.[37]

We enthusiastically support moving consumer authentication from traditional passwords to one of "multifactor authentication"—as also recommended by the FFIEC in its 2005 guidance on authentication in Internet banking environments.[38] But we're concerned that enthusiasm for supplanting passwords with alternatives such as facial or fingerprint recognition isn't translating into results, despite high-level support from the administration. Although it launched in 2011 a program called the National Strategy for Trusted Identities in Cyberspace charged with creating market conditions favorable to a wholesale replacement of passwords, it's clear today the effort has stalled.

Partial fault lies with NSTIC and its private-sector stakeholders, which bogged down the effort in inward-facing debates over governance. Blame goes to Congress too, which has cut NSTIC funding and treated it as a political football for scoring points during the appropriations process. We'd like the program to accelerate its output and do so with the full support of Congress. In addition, the rollout of multifactor authentication for government websites, such as tax-related sites operated by the Internal Revenue Service, is far overdue.

We also urge NIST to continue its engagement with the Fast Identity Online Alliance, an industry consortium for developing standards for identity authentication. The alliance, known as FIDO, is making it possible for the private sector to build innovative new ways for consumers to validate their identities by publishing widely adhered-to technical standards. NIST's decision to join the alliance in June 2015 is laudable and the next administration should ensure the agency remains actively engaged.

Incentivize ISPs to Become More Active in Cybersecurity

Internet service providers are a critical player for improving cybersecurity across the Internet. However, the majority of ISPs do not have incentive to implement well-established security protocols that would make launching cyberattacks harder for hackers. The system used to lookup web addresses, the domain name system, can be tricked into diverting users to legitimate sites. The domain name system security extensions protocol would mitigate that problem. Similarly, the protocol used to route Internet traffic between large network chunks, the border gateway protocol, is highly vulnerable to false routing. BGPSec is the protocol for preventing that hijacking of traffic through dodgy routers, but it, too, is underutilized.

We believe the government should help coordinate the wider adoption of ISP cybersecurity standards for the benefit of all. In our view, ISPs are like airports across the global aviation system. Airports have to meet certain level of security, or major airlines won't use them. We are not advocating for heavy-handed regulation but a common set of strong security standards that ISPs can be evaluated against in the market place, much like the "5-star safety rating" system developed years ago by the National Highway Traffic Safety Administration. With a common set of standards to use, the marketplace will help drive the level of ISP cybersecurity.

Adopt Antiphishing Technology

We previously discussed the scourge of phishing. There is no silver bullet to eliminate this problem, but there are things that can be done by private and public-sector organizations. Specifically, the existing Internet technology standard known as DMARC should be implemented by the federal government, and even further in private sector. DMARC, which stands for domain-based message authentication, reporting, and conformance, is an e-mail authentication standard. It builds on widely deployed existing e-mail policy standards, adding a reporting function that allows senders and receivers to reject fraudulent e-mails. An Internet Security Alliance member that recently implemented DMARC achieved tremendous results but discovered many e-mail domains—.gov and .mil especially—had still not implemented this standard or didn't implement it strictly enough. While there is some momentum and recognition of the effectiveness of DMARC, more widespread implementation is necessary to gain greater benefits. Widespread implementation by federal, state, and local governments along with private-sector entities would significantly reduce the phishing problem.

ENCOURAGE DEVELOPMENT OF MORE CYBERSECURITY EXPERTS

The need for talent specialized in cybersecurity is growing exponentially, while the supply of qualified experts is limited. The need is pervasive across the public and private sectors. There is a small number of specialized technology examiners employed by the federal banking regulators. Government, industry, and ultimately the nation will reap rewards from prioritizing the development of individuals trained in cyber defense. The new administration should consider leveraging the federal science, technology, engineering, and mathematics program to promote wider interest among students in technology jobs. The current national goal of graduating an additional one million students with STEM majors should be reassessed with an eye toward increasing both that number as well as the number of technology graduates represented within it.[39]

---

1 US Department of Treasury, Financial Stability Oversight Council, *FSOC 2016 Annual Report* (Financial Stability Oversight Council, 2016), Web.

2 PricewaterhouseCoopers (PWC), *Turnaround and Transformation in Cybersecurity: Financial Services Key Findings from the Global State of Information Security Survey 2016* (PWC, 2016), Web.

3 Ibid.

4 Ibid.

5 Centre for the Study of Financial Innovation, *Banking Banana Skins 2015: The CSFI Survey of Bank Risk* (PWC and Centre for the Study of Financial Innovation, Dec. 2015), Web.

6 Irving Wladawsky-Berger, "Measuring Technology's Impact on the Evolution of Financial Services," *The Wall Street Journal* (blog), June 26, 2015, Web.

7 US Department of Treasury, Financial Stability Oversight Council, *FSOC 2016 Annual Report* (Financial Stability Oversight Council, 2016), p. 127, Web.

8 Ben McLannahan, "Banks Claim Blockchain Breakthrough in Money Transfer," *Financial Times*, June 22, 2016, Web.

9 Mark J. Roe, "Legal Origins and Modern Stock Markets (December 2006)," *Harvard Law Review* 120 (2006): 460–527; Harvard Law and Economics Discussion Paper No. 563.

10 Jeremy Olshan, "This Is the Last Photo We'll Ever Run of the NYSE Trading Floor," *Market Watch*, Oct. 1, 2014, Web.

11 US National Archives and Records Administration, Commodity Futures Trading Commission, "CFTC Concept Release on Risk Controls and System Safeguards for

Automated Trading Environments," *Federal Register*, vol. 78, no. 177, pp. 56542, 56545, Sept. 12, 2013, Web.

12 Gregory Meyer, "NYSE Owner Warns of Cyber Risk to High-frequency Trading," *Financial Times*, Mar. 13, 2015, Web.

13 Rohini Tendulkar and Gregoire Naacke, "Cyber-crime, Securities Markets and Systemic Risk" (working paper no. SWP2/2013, IOSCO Research Department and World Federation of Exchanges, July 16, 2013), Web.

14 Centre for the Study of Financial Innovation, *Insurance Banana Skins 2015: The CFSI Survey of the Risks Facing Insurers* (PWC and Centre for the Study of Financial Innovation, July 2015), Web, June 6, 2016.

15 Ibid.

16 Maria Korolov, "Regulators: Cybersecurity Poses Biggest Risk to Global Financial System," *CSO*, May 25, 2016, Web, June 27, 2016.

17 US Government Accountability Office, *Financial Regulation: Complex and Fragmented Structure Could Be Streamlined to Improve Effectiveness* (Feb. 2016), Web, GAO-16-175.

18 Ponemon Institute, *2015 Global Megatrends in Cybersecurity* (Ponemon Institute and Raytheon, Feb. 2015), Web.

19 Exec. Order No. 13636, 3 C.F.R. Section 7(a) (2013).

20 Tracy Kitten, "Will FFIEC Revamp Cyber Assessment Tool?" *Bank Info Security* (Information Security Media Group, Jan. 13, 2016), Web.

21 Stuart E. Feldstein, "Agency Information Collection Activities: Information Collection Renewal; Comment Request; FFIEC Cybersecurity Assessment Tool," Notice and Request for Comment 2015-17907, Office of the Comptroller of the Currency, Department of the Treasury, July 22, 2015, Web, June 7, 2016.

22 Russell Fitzgibbons, "FFIEC Cybersecurity Assessment Tool," letter to Ms. Shaquita Merritt, OCC Clearance Officer Legislative and Regulatory Activities Division Office of the Comptroller of the Currency (Financial Services Information Sharing and Analysis Center [FSISAC], Financial Services Sector Coordinating Council [FSSCC], Sept. 21, 2015), Web.

23 Office of Compliance Inspections and Examinations (OCIE), *OCIE's 2015 Cybersecurity Examination Initiative*, Risk Alert Announcement (US Securities and Exchange Commission, Sept. 15, 2015), Web.

24 US Securities and Exchange Commission (SEC), *SEC Seeks Public Comment on Transfer Agent Rules* (SEC, Dec. 22, 2015), Web.

25 US Government Accountability Office, *Information Security: Opportunities Exist for SEC to Improve Its Controls over Financial Systems and Data* (Apr. 2016), Web, GAO-16-493.

26 US Departments of Treasury and Homeland Security, *Financial Services Sector-Specific Plan 2015* (Financial Services Sector Coordinating Council and Financial and Banking Information Infrastructure Committee, Department of Homeland Security, 2015), Web.

27 Office of Public Affairs, Department of Justice, *Seven Iranians Working for Islamic Revolutionary Guard Corps-Affiliated Entities Charged for Conducting Coordinated Campaign of Cyberattacks Against U.S. Financial Sector* (Department of Justice, Mar. 24, 2016), Web.

28 Robert Lemos, "Phishing Attacks Continue to Sneak Past Defenses," *EWeek.com*, Feb. 11, 2016, Web.

29 *Cloudmark 2015 Annual Security Threat Report: Measuring the Impact of Spear Phishing* (Cloudmark, 2015), Web.

30 Akamai Technologies, Anti-Phishing Working Group (APWG), et al., *2016 Data Breach Investigations Report* (Verizon, 2016), p. 18, Web.

31 "Acecard Trojan: Android Users of over 30 Banking and Payment Apps at Risk," *Kaspersky Lab*, Feb. 22, 2016, Web.

32 David Sancho, Feike Hacquebord, and Rainer Link, "Finding Holes: Operation Emmental," research paper (Trend Micro, July 22, 2014), Web.

33 US Government Accountability Office, *Cybersecurity: Bank and Other Depository Regulators Need Better Data Analytics and Depository Institutions Want More Usable Threat Information* (July 2015), Web, GAO-15-509.

34 Ibid.

35 Ibid.

36 J. Michael Daniel, "Engaging the International Community on Cybersecurity Standards," *The White House* (blog), Dec. 23, 2015.

37 Office of the Press Secretary, the White House, Fact Sheet: *Cybersecurity National Action Plan* (White House, Feb. 9, 2016), Web.

38 Federal Financial Institutions Examination Council, *Authentication in an Internet Banking Environment* (Federal Financial Institutions Examination Council, 2005), Web.

39 "Science, Technology, Engineering and Math: Education for Global Leadership," US Department of Education, n.d., Web.

Six

Cybersecurity in the Power
Utility Sector

Scott DePasquale, Chairman and CEO, Utilidata

INTRODUCTION

In 2015, the Ukraine fell victim to a highly coordinated cyberattack on its electric grid, leaving more than 230,000 residents in the dark and stranding backup power supplies in multiple locations. More than two months after the attack, affected control centers were still not fully operational. The attack was the first of its kind, foreshadowing how unprepared the utility sector may be as a primary target for disruption.[1]

Most experts agree that the United States is exposed to a similar, if not worse type of cyberattack.[2] According to a recent study by Lloyd's, a highly orchestrated cyberattack on the US power grid could "trigger a rise in mortality rates as health and safety systems fail, a decline in trade as ports shut down, disruption to water supplies as electric pumps fail, and chaos to transportation networks as infrastructure collapses." Such an attack could have a $1 trillion impact on our economy.[3]

The system of power generation, high voltage transmission, regional control, and local distribution that we call our power grid is one of the most complex, integrated, and now obsolete machines ever engineered. With the obvious vulnerabilities related to such a complex, and now highly connected machine, we find a utility sector struggling to keep up. In 2015, BitSight Technologies published a report that analyzed the security performance of six key sectors including finance, federal government, retail, energy and utilities, healthcare, and education. Of particular concern was the finding that energy and utilities were performing worse than the retail sector and in line with the poorly performing healthcare sector.[4]

So where do the vulnerabilities exist? Over the past decade, the bulk power system (which includes power generation and high voltage transmission) has seen improvements and increased investment in both resiliency and cybersecurity. However, local power-distribution systems are still a significantly underprotected part of our nation's critical infrastructure.

Local power-distribution assets are not only more vulnerable to cyberattack but also more critical to national electricity delivery than previously contemplated. Since cyberattacks can result in physical damage to power-grid equipment in the field, long replacement and recovery times could cause significant disruption.[5] A 2013 federal study concluded that as few as nine of the fifty-five thousand distribution substations in the United States could be taken offline to cause coast-to-coast blackouts.[6] A similar scenario studied by the Centre for Risk Studies at the University of Cambridge suggests that six weeks of power loss to roughly ten million electricity customers in the United Kingdom would result in £29 billion of direct economic losses and £129 billion of lost gross domestic product over the subsequent five years postdisruption.[7]

WHAT MAKES THE POWER UTILITY SECTOR UNIQUE

MARKETPLACE INNOVATION IS LAGGING

While products to protect information technology infrastructure are readily available and mature (e.g., firewalls, intrusion-detection system, and incidence and event management systems), there are far fewer products in the marketplace that provide security for the highly connected operational technologies that control physical assets on the power grid. Product innovation and new product development within this segment of the utility sector have been hampered by multiple rate-limiting factors for innovation and commercialization. Vendors in the cybersecurity space have long-standing relationships with utility IT professionals and understand the more conventional network security requirements well. However, relationships between vendors and utility engineers on the operational technology side of the business are only recent, and security weaknesses are still poorly understood—even within many of the larger utilities themselves.

To add complexity, many power utility executives struggle with the uncertainties associated with recovery of security-related costs and overhead on the basis of the traditional state rate making procedures they are subject to. State utility commissions, not Congress, approve utility spending—which in many cases has fostered inadequate investment in utility-wide cybersecurity. A 2014 report from the Bipartisan Policy Center attributed that to many reasons, including the limited proficiency state commissions have with cybersecurity. "Few public utility commissioners have experience with the management of information and control systems," the center noted. "In fact, many commissioners come from outside the utility industry and face a more basic learning curve in understanding electric utility operations generally."[8]

Even if there were adequate funding by utilities to address their normal (i.e., "commercial") cybersecurity risk, there will inevitably be a gap between vulnerabilities that can be cost-effectively mitigated and the residual risk posed by sophisticated nation-state powers seeking to disrupt the grid. Even utilities, duty-bound by public-good considerations, are still private-sector businesses unlikely to invest far beyond the thresholds of normal commercial risk. Defending against foreign attacks requires both financial and operational assistance from the federal government.

Lastly, even if the outsized product and regulatory risk can be accommodated, the vendor community is still faced with the multiyear purchasing cycles exacerbated by rigorous reliability testing requirements. These factors make it difficult for vendors to justify investing resources to develop operational technology–centric cybersecurity products, putting significant pressure on government sponsored grants to catalyze innovation.

Not only is vendor-driven innovation lacking but utilities themselves also fall short on research and development spending. The National Science Foundation notes that the sector typically spends 0.1 percent of their sales on R&D, competing only with the transportation and logistics industry for the lowest spending on R&D compared to all other major industries. The industry-wide national average is more than 3 percent.

LIMITED INFORMATION TO INFORM CYBERSECURITY DECISIONS

Power utilities also face unique challenges that make planning and response to cyberattacks more difficult. Utility executives have fewer data points to work with when evaluating defense and response strategies related to widespread power-grid vulnerabilities. Unlike commercial IT networks where attacks are frequently reported and analyzed across a range of entities, attacks on operational grid assets are less frequent and less frequently talked about. In addition, grid infrastructure is typically targeted by nation-states, making the attacks more sophisticated, bespoke, and harder to detect.[9] In many cases, operational system compromises may go undetected for years. These challenges point to the important role of the federal government both as a clearinghouse of information as well as a partner in defense against nation-state threats.

Exacerbating the situation is how utility asset vendors sell closed-source devices and software solutions, which typically come bundled with significant contractual prohibitions against tampering or reverse engineering. This results in a difficult situation, preventing utilities from processes that might allow them to verify the integrity of hardware and software they purchase (i.e., ensuring malware was not unintentionally preinstalled). In addition, it creates an impractical hurdle for utilities preparing response plans for cyberattacks such as by running war games premised on maliciously tampered-with devices or software, a reality that occurred in Ukraine and is likely in future attacks. Ultimately, power utility security professionals may not be able to predict what a compromised grid asset would do, how it would impact their systems, or how best to recover from it.

CHALLENGES FACING THE NEW ADMINISTRATION

A GRID THAT IS BECOMING INCREASINGLY DIFFICULT AND COSTLY TO DEFEND

Local distribution systems are undergoing a significant transformation. For the past fifteen years, the electric power industry, with significant support from government, has invested heavily in making the distribution system smarter, more efficient, and more connected. The Department of Energy has granted millions of dollars to install smart meters. Hundreds of companies are working to build a more advanced electrical infrastructure capable of handling the renewable and decentralized energies of the future. While these efficiencies and transformative innovations are critical to our energy economy, they undoubtedly are making the grid more susceptible to cyberattacks. Previously air-gapped devices at substations and on local circuits are becoming increasingly digitized and Internet protocol addressable, thereby linking them to the Internet directly.

Smart grid technologies have been incentivized and implemented with little regard for the increased exposure and cyber risk associated with their deployment. Equally concerning is that utilities are sourcing advanced technologies and products from multiple vendors with little or no ability to properly assess the supply-chain risks associated with them. Furthermore, the core legacy systems that utilities are building from were not developed with modern information and communications technology in mind.

CREEPING POSSIBILITY OF A TERRORIST ATTACK

In contrast to other sectors, the complexity and limited financial gain of attacking a utility suggest that most attacks will either be state-sponsored efforts or acts of terrorism. The level of sophistication required to effect widespread damage to the grid has typically suggested that only nation-states will be effective. However, a growing community of postnational actors are being contracted by states as an extension of their offensive capabilities, which is creating an international marketplace for sophisticated disruption capabilities. This means that it may not be long from now until more complex tools and capabilities are available for purchase by less sophisticated groups such as the Islamic State of Iraq and the Levant—which will surely be less constrained in how they exercise them.

Today, conventional thinking suggests that China and possibly two other countries have the capacity to effect wide-scale damage to our power grid, although it remains unlikely in peacetime that they would exercise this capability, as it would likely constitute an act of war.[10] Also deterring major states from using cyber means to attack the grid is the fact that major economies are closely integrated so that economic fallout from a grid attack in the United States would quickly rebound to harm the attacking nation's quite possibly weaker economy. ISIS would have no such fear.

RECOMMENDATIONS

Compromises of the power sector by nation-states and terrorist organizations are fundamental national security concerns. It is critical that the private sector not bear all of the cost to combat these quickly evolving and asymmetric threats. Most agree on the importance of our national and local regulatory processes. However, it is not possible to regulate our way to safety. As threats and risks evolve, utilities must be incentivized to innovate and invest to protect their assets—and customers—from cyberattacks. There are several important considerations that can help strengthen utility cybersecurity and incentivize market-led innovation.

Energy resource resiliency is a core national security issue, as are the persistent state-sponsored attacks on the US power grid. Power utility companies must do their part, but they can't solve this problem alone. The most effective solutions will align incentives across the various stakeholders and most certainly will require the government to work in closer partnership with private industry.

Key policy recommendations from this chapter cover the need for (1) improvements to how information is shared between the government and utility sector, (2) prioritization of clearances for executives within the sector, (3) policy support for an evolving private-sector cybersecurity-related insurance market, (4) continued support from the Department of Energy as the core liaison between utility companies and the broader homeland security and intelligence communities, (5) investments in grant programs that foster cybersecurity innovation specifically focused on the power grid, (6) greater cybersecurity focus by state-level regulators and legislatures, and (7) public sector–private sector collaboration toward improving vendor investments in security and supply-chain risk management.

ENHANCE INFORMATION SHARING BETWEEN UTILITIES AND THE FEDERAL GOVERNMENT

Utilities, as highly regulated entities, have a long history of collaborating with government. But there are obvious caveats. They require a better understanding of how the government and the national security apparatus use the information they supply, and what protections will be put in place to keep sensitive data confidential. These issues will need to be addressed in order to foster sound public-private partnerships and a fundamental relationship of trust and collaboration between the private-sector stakeholders responsible for delivering our nation's electricity and the government.

Greater transparency will not only increase the volume of communication but also improve the quality of information exchanged to assist in government-led investigations. In the past, utilities have been reluctant to share certain data with the government due to privacy concerns. Many utilities have noted that they will only be comfortable sharing more detailed information on cyber intrusions if they know, understand, and trust the processes the government uses to protect it.

Separately, it is in the business interest of industry to appropriately share information on cyber incidents with their customers. In the face of an attack, many utilities note that it is better to be upfront than attempt to hide system or data compromises. Being less than frank is redolent of conspiracy and once facts inevitably become public, changes the focus from how the utility was victimized to how it hid the truth. However, certain disclosures may be seen by the law-enforcement community as compromising ongoing investigations. In this regard, the law-enforcement community has work to do finding a suitable middle ground toward the goal of better alignment with the power utility sector's business imperatives.

The next president should instruct the existing utility industry sector coordinating council and the corresponding government coordinating council established under the National Infrastructure Protection Plan to engage on these information-sharing issues and report back to the administration within three months on their plan to create greater clarity and transparency regarding information sharing within the sector, including any legislative adjustments that may be needed.

REFORMING THE CLEARANCE-ATTAINMENT PROCESS FOR PRIVATE-SECTOR EXECUTIVES

Long processing times and an insufficient number of security clearances being made available are significantly hindering the utility industry's ability to support the US cybersecurity mission. In order for utilities to prepare themselves effectively for cyberattacks, executives need to be able to speak transparently and productively with the intelligence community about how to best prepare. This process encompasses information that is, due to its gravity, highly classified.

In addition, collaboration in public-private partnerships often requires working within government or defense contractor facilities that have rigid clearance requirements. Simply stated, gaining facility access is a requirement for effective collaboration.

Currently, utility executives face long delays in obtaining the clearances necessary to work with government counterparts to discuss and resolve cyber concerns. This applies not only to individuals who have never obtained a clearance but also to individuals who simply need to renew their clearance because they moved from one utility company to another. "Requiring an act of Congress" is a phrase used to describe the difficulty of the current clearance-attainment process for utility executives. The safety of the domestic power grid is fundamentally core to national security, making resolution of this issue a high priority.

Executives who have clearance and change companies require flexibility to renew their clearances quickly if the industry is to keep up with the quickly evolving threats. Affording executives who are obtaining clearance for the first time secret clearances within six months would allow a significant uptick in industry participation and effective information sharing. It is unlikely that any government initiatives to further enhance public-private collaboration will be effective without developing more streamlined processes for getting power utility sector executives cleared.

The next president should instruct DHS to coordinate among security clearance granting agencies and develop an expedited "TSA pre-check" style system to enable already cleared individuals to maintain their clearances more easily and generally modernize the clearance process to include the use of transferable clearances from department to department.

ENSURING DOE REMAINS THE PRIMARY LIAISON BETWEEN UTILITIES AND THE FEDERAL GOVERNMENT

Under the Cybersecurity Act of 2015, companies only receive liability protection for sharing data with the federal government when they do so through the Department of Homeland Security.[11] Under current procedures, DHS then forwards these data to the Department of Energy but still issues most security advisories to utilities directly. While Homeland Security has a critical role to play as utilities face cybersecurity challenges, the Department of Energy remains best suited to be the main point of contact. Energy has decades of experience working with utilities and is best positioned to provide meaningful, contextual, and actionable analysis.

The next president and Congress should consider amending the act to expand the benefits currently granted for sharing information with DHS to other appropriate agencies such as Energy.

CATALYZE AND ACCELERATE THE DEVELOPMENT OF THE PRIVATE CYBERSECURITY INSURANCE MARKET

The use of private cybersecurity insurance is an undervalued tool and a critical part of the future of safeguarding utilities. Just as insurance companies were a driving force in the development of automobile standards, such market-driven strategies can have a similar impact on enhancing information and operational security and resiliency for the power utility sector.

To date, the cybersecurity insurance marketplace has been focused on data-breach fallout, which while necessary and beneficial, is not enough given the uncertainties and risks that utilities face today. The cybersecurity threat has escalated beyond the realm of traditional information technology venues and now affects physical devices and operating systems in the field. Real-world assets can now be compromised such that equipment is physically damaged, causing blackouts, risk of life, and millions of dollars of damage.

Even where existing cyber-related insurance policies do exist, it is often unclear exactly what types of damage are covered. For example, the cost of mitigating damages where personal data are stolen may be covered. However, property damage costs related to cyberattacks often are not. In a situation where prolonged power outages cause damage to personal property, the reach and protection of the existing coverage models will likely be insufficient, putting the solvency of companies responsible for power delivery deeply at risk. Additionally, there is confusion and a lack of clarity around pricing this risk for power utility assets given the lack of any government backstop.

Furthermore, a cybersecurity attack of potentially catastrophic magnitude on a major utility by a terrorist organization or a nation-state would constitute a serious national security issue, not merely a commercial security issue. This justifies the government's role in taking an active interest in the matter.

In the aftermath of the September 11, 2001, terror attacks, there was a gap in the insurance market for policies covering damage from terrorist attacks. The federal government addressed this gap by passing the Terrorism Risk Insurance Act, creating a reinsurance backstop that enabled the development of appropriate and economical terrorism-related insurance policies by private-sector underwriters. The administration and Congress should follow the same path by updating or replicating TRIA to create a similar reinsurance backstop for cyberattack-caused real-world damage to utilities and their customers. The importance to national security, and the ability to push utilities to invest in cybersecurity in a market-driven fashion, motivates the federal government's involvement.

PROMOTE INNOVATION THROUGH GOVERNMENT GRANTS

The government should fund grants and cooperative agreements in support of commercial product development. Initiatives such as Rapid Attack Detection, Isolation and Characterization Systems at the Defense Advanced Research Projects Agency and Cybersecurity for Energy Delivery Systems at Energy encourage investment in commercial products by appropriately reducing risk for potential vendors and helping bring together all relevant stakeholders. These programs should be continued and expanded.

INCREASE CYBERSECURITY FOCUS OF STATE-LEVEL REGULATORS AND LEGISLATURES

Electricity distribution utilities need state-level regulators who are educated participants in the cybersecurity dialogue. In their absence, it is difficult for utilities to motivate appropriate cybersecurity investments.

Federal efforts to foster cybersecurity awareness at the state level have consisted largely of education and knowledge-sharing initiatives. The federal government can go one step further by asking states to demonstrate that they have considered whether or not to include cybersecurity standards in their ratemaking proceedings. This "states-must-consider" approach was used in the Energy Policy Act of 2005 and the Energy Independence and Security Act of 2007 to effectively drive awareness and uptake among state regulators of beneficial new electricity standards including advanced metering infrastructure, demand response, and smart-grid technologies. For example, the "states-must-consider" approach pushed state regulators to perform cost-benefit analysis of advanced metering infrastructure and therefore drove education, common understanding of the technology across states, and eventual uptake without mandating new state regulations.

The federal government should pass a cybersecurity "states-must-consider" law so that states must demonstrate they have considered appropriate cost-effective cybersecurity standards for their electric utility ratemaking proceedings. Doing so will effectively increase the focus on distribution cybersecurity at the state level without imposing new regulations on distribution utilities.

ENCOURAGE PUBLIC-PRIVATE COLLABORATION TO MANAGE VENDOR RISKS

The grid is composed of assets from vendors, both hardware and software. As such, vendors must play their part in the security of the grid. A new balance needs to be struck between the commercial needs of vendors, who would prefer not to reveal the workings of their products, and the needs of electric utilities to both ensure assets are not prepackaged with malware and understand better how assets would behave if they were to be controlled maliciously. Utilities need more transparency into the assets they install onto their grids, and they need to be able to modify those same assets to test the possible impact of malicious tampering in real-world settings.

Current efforts are uncoordinated and duplicative. The Electricity Subsector Cybersecurity Capability Maturity Model framework (developed by the departments of Energy and Homeland Security to guide utility cybersecurity efforts) creates duplicated effort whereby each utility conducts its own independent risk assessments of each vendor and equipment, with attendant variation in quality on the basis of utility capability.

Solving this requires a dialogue between utilities, vendors, and the government to evaluate possible solutions that cost-effectively increase confidence in US grid assets and help utilities prepare for cyberattacks. The Obama administration's proposal for a National Center for Cybersecurity Resilience, where companies could test the security of systems under controlled conditions, is a good start in this direction. So is the Federal Energy Regulatory Commission's proposed rule regarding supply-chain risk management.[12] The government and utilities themselves could play a valuable role in incentivizing vendors to adopt the Underwriter's Laboratories model—this would ensure that all vendor products are rigorously and transparently inspected to ensure they meet baseline cybersecurity standards.

---

1 Kim Zetter, "Inside the Cunning, Unprecedented Hack of Ukraine's Power Grid," *Wired*, Mar. 3, 2016, Web.

2 Kim Zetter, "Everything We Know about Ukraine's Power Plant Hack," *Wired*, Jan. 20, 2016, Web.

3 Trevor Maynard and Nick Beecroft, *Business Blackout: The Insurance Implications of a Cyberattack on the US Power Grid*, Emerging Risk Report (Lloyd's and the University of Cambridge Centre for Risk Studies, 2015), Web.

4 BitSight Technologies, *Third Annual BitSight Insights Industry Benchmark Reports* (BitSight Technologies, Sept. 2015), Web, June 1, 2016.

5 Wikipedia contributors, "Aurora Generator Test," *Wikipedia, The Free Encyclopedia*, Mar. 31, 2016, Web.

6 Rebecca Smith, "U.S. Risks National Blackout from Small-Scale Attack," *The Wall Street Journal*, Mar. 12, 2014, Web, June 5, 2016.

7 S. Kelly et al., *Integrated Infrastructure: Cyber Resiliency in Society, Mapping the Consequences of an Interconnected Digital Economy*, Cambridge Risk Framework Series (Centre for Risk Studies, University of Cambridge, 2016), Web.

8 Michael Hayden, Curt Hébert, and Susan Tierney, *Cybersecurity and the North American Electric Grid: New Policy Approaches to Address an Evolving Threat; A Report from the Co-chairs of the Bipartisan Policy Center's Electric Grid Cybersecurity Initiative* (Bipartisan Policy Center, Feb. 2014), Web.

9 US Department of Homeland Security, Office of Intelligence and Analysis, *Intelligence Assessment IA-0060-16: (U///FOUO) Damaging Cyberattacks Possible but Not Likely against the US Energy Sector* (ASIS International, Inc., Jan. 27, 2016), Web.

10 Jamie Crawford, "The U.S. Government Thinks China Could Take Down the Power Grid," *CNN Politics*, Nov. 21, 2014, Web.

11 Cybersecurity Act of 2015, Pub. L. 114-113 (2015).

12 US Federal Energy Regulatory Commission, 18 C.F.R. Part 40, Docket No. RM15-14-000, *152 FERC ¶ 61,054: Revised Critical Infrastructure Protection Reliability Standards* (Federal Energy Regulatory Commission, July 16, 2015), Web.

Seven

Cybersecurity and the Information Technology Industry

Art Coviello Jr., Executive Chairman (Retired), RSA

INTRODUCTION

The next president starts at an unprecedented crossroads in human history. The digital world being created by the IT sector permeates every facet of our lives and has enormous potential not only for the good of humanity but also for its destruction.

The physics of the digital world are different from anything we have ever experienced. They ignore national borders. They smash together cultures, ages, continents, kids, adults, criminals, and spies into one big global stew, where laws, morals, and politics fuse in ways we never could have imagined.

It is something we did not plan, and we are unprepared for it.

We are unready because the digital world is not just about technologies. It is a new dimension where individuals, organizations, and governments must be able to interact in ways that are productive, safe, and socially acceptable. However, the laws, policies, and social norms we developed over centuries for our physical world are not capable of providing the structure we need to prosperously inhabit this new dimension.

We see the results daily: crimes unpunished, loss of trust in governments and corporations, and nation-state–directed attacks. We may be Americans, but our digital society is global and increasingly homogenous.

Without some set of norms of behavior and standards for privacy and security here at home and across the world, we will not know how to tell these technologies to behave appropriately any more than we know how to tell our children or ourselves. This is particularly alarming in a world where actions in one dimension have real implications in the other, with less knowledge of who is doing what to whom.

Mastering this world will require bold, enlightened leadership. The next president must acquire the skill and knowledge to provide that leadership, taking advantage of the vast reservoir of talent available across our country and particularly in the IT sector.

WHAT MAKES THE IT SECTOR UNIQUE

Technology developed by US companies fuels the operating engine of the global economy and enables and facilitates social interaction and communication worldwide.

Uniquely, the IT sector has radically altered the operations and the very nature of all of the other industry sectors. No industry has escaped transformation by the remarkable innovations in IT that have occurred since President Barack Obama came to office. The economic impact and the effects on globalization have been astounding. Just consider these figures, taken from the McKinsey Global Institute: Approximately 12 percent of global trade is conducted via international e-commerce. Nine hundred million people have international connections on social media and 360 million take part in cross-border e-commerce. In 2014 (the last year statistics are available) data flows accounted for an additional $2.8 trillion in world gross domestic product.[1]

The changes are not only economic; they are societal as well. We now communicate with new services such as Skype and FaceTime. We shop online at eBay, Craigslist, and Amazon. Even our political process has fundamentally been changed, the effects ranging from social media's role in Arab spring, and jihadi recruitment, through this year's presidential campaign.

As impressive as all of this IT innovation has been, the pace is accelerating, and it is important to understand why—and why a side effect of that speed has been an increase in cyber vulnerabilities.

It starts with Moore's law, the prediction by Intel cofounder Gordon Moore that computing power doubles every two years at roughly the same cost, a forecast that only recently has shown signs of slowing down.[2] It has enabled us to build smaller and smarter devices and is enabling us to embed intelligence into almost every conceivable machine. Connected through the Internet, these devices and machines can communicate, give or receive instructions, and pass data, building what is dubbed the Internet of Things.

Coupled with continued advances in bandwidth and storage capacity, we are amassing and analyzing huge amounts of data. Over the next few years and beyond, big data applications will enable organizations to understand everything about us and the world around us. Rapid development techniques and cloud computing–based services and capabilities will allow for incredible advances in research. Combined with advances in other technologies such as battery life, satellite tracking, and video technologies, the opportunities for innovation are almost endless. However, so are the opportunities for security breaches and the misuse of private information. The increase in our attack surface is becoming unfathomable and the risks immense. Over the past eight years, we have already witnessed an escalation in attack methodologies form intrusive, to disruptive, to destructive. The consequences are being felt everywhere.

Nevertheless, there is hope. The same innovations that create increased risk also create opportunities for advances in cybersecurity technologies. While we can no longer rely on any discernible network perimeter for protection, we can build an array of smart capabilities to give ourselves the ability to stop attackers at multiple places and times through defense in depth.

Development of products with artificial intelligence and the use of machine learning and big data applications are giving us the ability to prevent attacks from developing, see attacks coming, prevent intrusions, detect breaches, and respond to them as never before. We now, or will soon have, the ability to more easily find security vulnerabilities in products, the information and knowledge to identify attackers and their methodologies as they appear, artificial intelligence to block malware, user behavior analytics to spot fraudulent or abnormal behavior, and infrastructure analytics to spot anomalies in the flow and use of information and transactions.

However, we should not mistake improved technical abilities for a true solution to today's bad state of computer security. The challenges are equally embedded in policy and management.

A final distinctive characteristic of the IT sector, particularly in comparison to other sectors such as electric and telecommunications, is that IT has grown and flourished in a generally unregulated environment. The culture of the IT industry embraces innovation, risk, new ideas, and the desire to create disruptive products and services that are antithetical to the centrally managed structures governing sectors that are more traditional. The overwhelming consensus of the industry's major players is that this unregulated environment has been an essential feature, and primary driver, of the historic growth and productivity that the sector has achieved and brought to the rest of the economy and culture that now rely on it.

CHALLENGES FACING THE NEW ADMINISTRATION

THE INTERNET OF THINGS
Upward of one hundred billion intelligent and networked devices with embedded applications are poised to control our power grids, our hearts, our automobiles, our thermostats, and our kids' new playthings over the next five to ten years. Overlooked in the excitement over smart homes or smart cities is how much personal data generated by everyday users will become part of the mix. In the Internet of Things, humans will be the ultimate things.

Do we know better than to create this new world without first seeing to securing the data, especially given the sensitivity of what's collected—personal data including medical indicators, lifestyle choices and religious beliefs? Evidently we do not, because we are doing all of these things anyhow. A recent survey of IoT apps found a litany of concerns. Seven out of ten did not encrypt network connections and 60 percent of user interfaces contained well-known cybersecurity vulnerabilities.[3]

CYBER WAR AND TERRORISM

Cyber intrusions that cause significant economic or physical damage create the possibility of escalation into traditional armed conflict. Even absent direct escalation into a shooting war, cyberattacks will cross the plane from bits to atoms and become kinetic in the damage they cause. That is particularly the case as we use IoT devices and connect them to other machines and devices that control physical processes. In consequence, it is becoming more and more probable that cyberattacks by nation-states or terrorists will kill people at some point in time in the next decade. Stopping those incidents altogether or keeping them isolated, and containing their escalation, is essential. Clearly, the proliferation of cyber weapons and the ease with which they can proliferate and be used will become the single biggest existential threat to humanity.

COMMERCIAL CYBER ESPIONAGE

Nation-states and foreign agents have been hacking into the systems of US companies and stealing corporate secrets for years. Intellectual property theft is a particularly insidious form of attack because many of these acts have gone undetected, and we still do not understand how to measure the downstream economic effects and competitive disadvantages.[4]

It is no exaggeration to say that these thefts are an act of economic war, harming a critical driver of global economic growth. The main culprit, it should come as no surprise, is China.[5]

Theft of IP is a critical issue for the IT sector, whose wealth stems in no small measure from proprietary software licensing, proprietary hardware sales, and services. Victims have included many American tech companies, including Cisco, Google, and others.[6]

Once competitors steal that IP, they become an "instant international competitors without becoming innovators themselves," noted the Commission on the Theft of American Intellectual Property.[7] The damages are multiple: Companies lose profit from lost sales and unrecovered research and development costs. Workers lose jobs as company's cutback payroll because of the unfair competition. In addition, providers of capital are cheated out of the value of their investment.

Reliant as it is on venture capital, the IT sector is especially exposed to this last consequence of IP theft, particularly when the beneficiaries are state-sponsored companies unencumbered by strict return-on-investment requirements.

With all of this as a backdrop, perhaps the greatest disconnect of all is what steps has the government taken to protect us?

After years of token protests and a mostly-for-show indictment of five junior-grade Chinese military hackers in 2014, the United States coaxed Chinese president Xi Jinping in 2015 into agreeing that neither country "will conduct or knowingly support cyber-enabled theft of intellectual property...with the intent of providing competitive advantages to companies or commercial sectors."[8]

It is a start, but the agreement's strength is proving dubious. "Don't expect China to rein in its legions of hackers just yet," wrote Council on Foreign Relations senior fellow Adam Segal in January 2016.[9] "The jury is still out," concluded the director of national intelligence, James Clapper, a few weeks later.[10]

PROPOSALS FOR BACKDOORS

Not only is the IT sector one of our most successful industries but it also enjoys one of our largest favorable trade balances. We have earned this position through continuous innovation and trust in the quality of our products. Sustaining it depends on keeping its reputation.

Even so, for years the IT industry has been accused of not doing enough to make its products secure. Ironically, there is now serious discussion in policy circles of deliberately weakening those same products through encryption backdoors meant to make it easier for the intelligence community and law enforcement to do their jobs.

Given heightened tensions around terrorism, the possibility of cyber war and ongoing theft of IP, such policies appear well intentioned. But a special security vulnerability built for good intentions is still a vulnerability and will benefit our adversaries, who will find it and exploit it.

Adoption of such proposals would also provoke legitimate privacy concerns among our own citizens and cause a further deterioration of trust between the United States and the world community. Without trust in American IT, other countries will shy away from buying our products and pull back from the premise of global interconnectivity that the Internet promises. Revelations of pervasive Internet surveillance conducted by the National Security Agency have already damaged foreign sales. If we are not careful, we could be saying good-bye to that favorable balance of trade and America's preeminent position in IT.

Knowing that the US government could peep at will into their communications, our best trading partners and even close allies would place restrictions on the use of US-based products and services and force the adoption of competing technologies. Individuals would not wait for their governments to act, damaging consumer-level product sales. American companies have already suffered from the appearance of too-close ties to the federal government. Loss estimates in forgone cloud computing sales tied to fallout from Edward Snowden's disclosures range from $25 billion over three years to $180 billion over the same period.[11]

What is worse, accommodating backdoor proposals would not even accomplish the stated national security objectives. Adversarial nations, criminals, hacktivists, and terrorists would simply obtain encryption applications from abroad. Open source versions of encryption tool kits (the algorithms in software necessary to build or embed encryption applications) have been available for decades. They have been used to create applications that encrypt voice or data communications and stored data. Many such applications are sophisticated enough to cause data or voice communication to self-destruct within a predetermined time limit.[12]

By recent estimates, more than eight hundred secure messaging apps exist worldwide, and roughly two-thirds of them have been developed outside the United States. One of the more popular of these applications is Telegram, developed by a dissident trying to protect himself from the prying eyes and ears of the Russian security apparatus.[13]

It is for these reasons that a former secretary of homeland security and two former heads of the NSA have argued against backdoors.[14] They also note the example the United States would set for nations that do not respect the individual rights and freedoms of their citizens in the same way we do. If one of the most open governments on earth sanctions backdoors expressly for state surveillance, then other, less free nations, will demand the same type of access in exchange for doing business in their countries.

GOVERNMENT CYBERSECURITY

Government systems have repeatedly failed at security. Piecemeal attempts to improve them have fallen dangerously short—to the point where it is probable that a Chinese intelligence agency stole from the Office of Personnel Management the background security investigation data of twenty-two million Americans.[15]

Government officials have acknowledged that years of neglect and a slow progress on continuous monitoring is not meeting agencies' needs.

Let us not overlook the role of funding, either. Cybersecurity funding at the Department of Homeland Security and elsewhere in government has gone up at a steady clip. Yet, according to the Ponemon Institute, total private-sector spending on cybersecurity has doubled in the past few years and now exceeds $100 billion annually.[16]

Federal spending on cybersecurity is about $13 billion and nearly half of that goes to the military for offensive oriented cyber programs, which, while vital, are not security in the sense discussed here.[17] For an example of how big the gap between private- and public-sector spending on cybersecurity is, consider that two major banks have a combined cybersecurity budget of close to a billion dollars.[18] The DHS cyber budget, which includes government-wide cybersecurity as well as efforts to improve critical infrastructure, is about $1.3 billion. Barely two percent of DHS's total $61 billion budget goes to cybersecurity activities.

Nor is cybersecurity spending the only place where the federal government has fallen behind. In many agencies, the information technology infrastructure underpinning federal operations is obsolete. Modern new systems pile on top of a rotting core, resulting in a rickety system difficult to administer and to secure. Rather than funding upgrades, federal agencies spend most their dollars keeping the old systems going.[19] Years of costly IT modernization failures have left Congress and administration officials rightly skeptical of new upgrade projects. However, a reckoning with obsolesce can only be postponed, not avoided. The longer we wait, the harder it becomes.

INFORMATION SHARING

For all of the rhetoric, we have not seen the kind of consistent and sustained action needed on information sharing. We cannot seem to navigate the legitimate concerns of privacy groups around the information that can be shared and the legitimate concerns of the business community around legal liability. The new information-sharing law does not go nearly far enough to do any tangible good. Well into the implementation of the Cybersecurity Act of 2015, administration officials are acknowledging that it is a tough sell to get industry to participate as looming trust issues remain with regard to government's use of information shared with entities such as NSA and state governments.[20] Moreover, liability protections are available only for sharing through DHS and no other preferred entities such as the FBI. It is ironic that ecosystems of criminal groups and hacktivists, who now even work with rogue nations and possibly terrorists, do a better job sharing information about attack methodologies, malware for sale, and credentials for sale.

PUBLIC-PRIVATE PARTNERSHIP

The IT sector can help itself and others by playing a pivotal role in a structured and close public-private partnership. The sector has been ready to engage with government on numerous occasions. In addition, it has, through efforts like the Enduring Security Framework, a mostly moribund outreach effort convened by the departments of Defense and Homeland Security to work with companies on technology issues larger than any one firm. Also during development of the NIST Cybersecurity Framework industry is played a major part.

Rather than engage in a productive relationship dedicated to rooting out cybersecurity problems, trust and cooperation between the IT industry and government is at an all-time low. So long as government continues to threaten industry, this situation will persist.

DATA BREACH NOTIFICATION

Today forty-seven states plus the District of Columbia maintains separate laws for data breach notification, creating an undue burden on industry. Business costs for notifying consumers about a data breach are inching upward—increasing from an average per incident expense of $1.41 million in 2013 to $1.64 million in 2015, according to survey data from the Ponemon Institute.[21] The cause is not hard to trace. State laws are a welter of differing definitions for what constitutes a reportable breach, deadlines for consumer notification, and company obligations.

A national data breach law preempting state laws would establish a badly needed common set of definitions and obligations and help contain costs.

RECOMMENDATIONS

CREATE A CABINET-LIKE POSITION TO UPGRADE CIVILIAN IT AND SECURITY INFRASTRUCTURE

It is time to bring the IT infrastructure of the federal government into the twenty-first century. The government can and should be reaping more of the productivity and operational benefits of the digital age.

Whether it's tax collection, healthcare.gov, or background investigation data, there is far too much at stake to not do a better job protecting government infrastructures. Cybersecurity is an issue that cuts across individual departments and all sectors of the economy, an issue that is everywhere but is treated as if it is nowhere, since it lacks a bureaucratic power base. Attempts to build one through the position of cybersecurity coordinator were well intentioned, but a White House policy czar lacks the authority needed to effect real change.

Creating a "Department of Cybersecurity" is not the recommendation here. Setting up a new department would be costly, time consuming, and sap the urgency from the challenges we have identified. One federal agency, the Department of Homeland Security, should be tasked with the operational duty of extending help and assistance to all civilian agencies. The authority for cyber should flow to DHS so the department can become a managed security service provider, the federal equivalent of commercial consultants who set up security infrastructures, provide and train personnel, and assist with incident response.

We also need to better leverage the extensive capabilities of the defense and intelligence agencies on the civilian side. Appreciating the legal separation required, the new president should find ways to take advantage of this expertise so our best cyber people can assist in civilian defense and law enforcement and generally better coordinate all of their respective efforts.

In addition, much needs to be done organizationally, operationally, and technologically on the civilian side. Currently, the responsibility for the adoption and implementation of IT and security technologies is held by agency chief information officers whose average tenure is approximately two years. By comparison, the average tenure in the private sector is four to five years. As a result, on average, CIO's in the federal government, inherit a budget in their first year, propose a plan and budget for a follow-on year, staying a year to implement it while proposing a third year budget that their successor will inherit. Confused? You should be. They are assisted by career and appointed staff, including the chief information security officer. Unsurprisingly turnover across the board is high due to poor morale caused by continuous uncertainty.

The following also play a prominent role in policy, procurement, and oversight of IT and security technology and operations in the government: the chief technology officer and CIO of the federal government, Office of Management and Budget, the General Services Administration, the Under Secretary of Science and Technology of the Department of Homeland Security, and the Under Secretary of National Protection and Programs Directorate, also of DHS. In all of this, one needs to distinguish between the civilian agencies being referred to and the defense and intelligence communities, which function reasonably well.

Nevertheless, there's an old adage in IT and security, "you can't secure what you can't manage, and you can't manage what you can't secure." In the civilian agencies, the lack of organizational tenure; the lack of sufficient resources, human and financial; the decentralized nature of overall operational and governance responsibility; and an IT environment that requires agility and scalable operating discipline that just doesn't exist make the task of securing government systems virtually insurmountable.

Given the importance of IT in the running of our government, the need to manage and secure critical infrastructure, and the ongoing productivity benefits of continued innovation, shouldn't a project on this scale be one of the highest priorities for the next administration? Shouldn't the responsibility for digital and IT infrastructure warrant a cabinet level–like position, with full authority and funding?

While it has been noted that there is skepticism in Congress about "IT Projects," there really is no alternative to getting this done. Historically, Americans have shown time and time again an ability to achieve anything we set our minds to.

And, with respect to IT-specific projects, there is a model we can learn from. The State of India decided to pursue a massive IT project, the Unique Identification Authority of India, to issue physical and logical identity cards to all of their citizens through a combination of a number and biometric data. Although an identity project, itself, would be a nonstarter in the United States for cultural reasons, the management model for such a project could be appropriate for a massive upgrade to US government IT infrastructures. Although India is hardly known for bureaucratic efficiency and has had continuous issues with corruption over the years, their project has been a resounding success. While they are still wrestling with the utility of the program, the infrastructure was built out in three years at a cost of approximately $425 million. Through the first quarter of 2016, seven years into the project, approximately one billion identities have been collected at a cost of just over $1 billion for implementation and ongoing support, including three layers of security.

Nandan Nilekani, the founder and CEO of the IT services company, Infosys, managed the project and was given ministerial authority to get the job done. With centralized authority, sufficient financial resources, and the ability to hand pick his executive team, he was able to achieve the results outlined above. Instrumental in the success of the project was adherence to the following tenets: an open policy in selecting hardware and software, multiple private vendors, and technology neutrality to ensure maximum flexibility and agility.

While any project of this magnitude would have to follow existing procurement regulations, these concepts, at a high level, are an example of what can be done with the right mind-set.

WORKFORCE DEVELOPMENT

Government should work with colleges and universities across the country to obtain a steady flow of recruits for cybersecurity positions. Current research shows that the government is simply not competitive in attracting top cyber students. Elsewhere in this volume, creative ideas for starting recruitment for cybersecurity professionals well before college are detailed. With respect to colleges and universities, Congress should pass legislation to fund programs for education and research to lubricate the education system to create the best source of cybersecurity talent in the world.

One model might be to provide government scholarships (not loans) to individuals who will commit to a specified number of years in government cybersecurity positions (perhaps one-year service for every year tuition paid). Government investment would be offset by accessing top-level talent otherwise unavailable to the government at well below market rates. The government experience would also help facilitate future industry-government collaboration, which we have shown is critical to overall cybersecurity.

Because such talent is in high demand, government must plan for regular employee turnover, as many of these recruits will ultimately move to the private sector. Although this would be especially true and somewhat problematic for DHS, this would not be a bad outcome, as cybersecurity trained experts leaving the government for the private sector would create a steady supply of talent that is sorely needed.

INCREASE AND IMPROVE INTERNATIONAL LAW ENFORCEMENT AND COOPERATION TO PREVENT CYBER WAR AND TERRORISM

Internationally, much can be done to improve cooperation among nations on the tracking, apprehension, and prosecution of cyber criminals and terrorists. Currently, best estimates are that we are losing up to a half trillion dollars a year to cyber criminals and successfully prosecuting less than 2 percent of the culprits.

Not only is it vital for the United States to lead here but it is also in our own interest. Because Americans adopt technology early and at scale, we are living in the biggest digital glass house in the world. The United States has the most at risk. However, if we are to continue to have an interdependent global economy, increasingly dependent on digital technology, all nations ultimately share that risk. Without a global partnership that acknowledges sovereignty rights of nations, individual rights of privacy, and rule of law, no progress can be made. Given its preeminent position in technology, intelligence, and law enforcement, US leadership is fundamental to making any progress.

Obviously, this would be a major undertaking requiring multiple sequential steps. The new president can initiate this effort by making fighting cybercrime a priority reflective of its economic impact. This should start with the president instituting a full review of national law-enforcement spending to assure that fighting digital crime is far better resourced. This may well need to include an examination of the degree of legacy law-enforcement investments currently being made. Operationally, it is likely that US law enforcement will, at least in the immediate term, need to aggressively upgrade international cooperation including allowing other nations to leverage US resources.

Reviewing federal grants to states and localities and stressing the need for greater coordination between agencies (backed by funding ties to this coordination imperative) would be part of this review. At a different, but related level, reprioritizing Cold War–era US collaborative investments abroad (e.g., large land-force military bases in Europe and Japan) ought to be considered.

Simultaneously, the new president should prioritize and initiate a concerted process to modernize international law and procedures with respect to clarifying criminal laws internationally. As suggested in several chapters in this volume, this would include a clarification of the roles and responsibilities nation-states have in protecting private organizations from international cyberattack including those launched or supported by nation-states.

Selecting the correct forum to start this effort is a critical step. Utilizing more cohesive coalition, such as NATO members, might be more efficient and effective process than more unwieldy institutions such as the United Nations or the International Telecommunication Union. Recognizing the need to develop a sensible international criminal code as soon as possible, it may be wise to decouple the criminally focused efforts (e.g., theft and destruction of property) from the more sensitive, though important, issues like privacy.

Work should also commence to minimize the possibility of cyber war and the proliferation of cyber weapons. Although we know chemical weapons exist and can be created, we have international treaties to limit their creation and outlaw their use. We need a similar effort in international cooperation to insure we have the same abhorrence to cyber war that we have for chemical war.

INCREASE GOVERNMENT RESEARCH AND DEVELOPMENT FUNDING FOR RISKY TECHNOLOGY RESEARCH

The federal government has a significant role to play in incentivizing the development of new and innovating technologies. Investors tend to shy away from fundamental research and development, unless they see an apparent potential for commercial application. Investments geared to promote the general welfare are understood to generally fall within the province of government. In the interconnected digital world, and notwithstanding the fact that private entities may profit from use of the commons, the general security of the commons is the province of government.

Other countries see the need for greater investment in IT too. China, for example, through institutions such as the Ministry of Industry and *Information Technology*, places such an emphasis on the IT sector.

In the United States, IT innovation is funded through a variety of institutions, and totals have decreased since 2010.[22] That is absurd, since federally funded research and development rewards the general welfare through economic growth. Besides the Internet, government funding played a heavy role in the development of optical storage, supercomputing and silicon chips.

Rather than routinely cut research and development funding, the United States should emulate what our competitors are doing in other countries by providing increased government support for basic IT research and general-purpose digital programs. We do not necessarily need to duplicate their precise models, but we should study and adapt theirs for our purposes.

PUBLIC-PRIVATE PARTNERSHIP

Much can be done in cooperation with the government, if there exists a true dialogue based on trust. The first issue is a macro one, protecting the cyber side of critical infrastructure: telecommunications, transportation, financial systems, and the power grid.

Specifically, there ought to be a collaborative effort between the public and private sectors using the existing partnership model as laid out in the National Infrastructure Protection Plan to test the effectiveness of the NIST Cybersecurity Framework. A great deal of effort went into development of the framework, and the document now deserves the same sort of systematic testing that any private-sector entity would undertake prior to a releasing a new product or service. At a minimum, we need to define what using the framework entails in a practical sense, which, in turn, would be suitable for eligibility of access to a menu of federal incentives. By testing the framework in real-world conditions with volunteer critical infrastructure companies, we could also discover what aspects of the framework need more specificity as well as which aspects are cost effective, important knowledge to have if our goal is to sustain cybersecurity over the long haul.

An atmosphere of cooperation would also allow the Enduring Security Framework to be reenergized and perhaps expanded to include our allies. The timely sharing by the government of information about vulnerabilities in IT products before they are exploited against us, and threat intelligence would not only go a long way to reestablishing trust but would also significantly enhance our ability to defend ourselves.

LAW ENFORCEMENT SHOULD STOP PUSHING THE "GOING DARK" NARRATIVE

In 2011, Peter Swire, a professor at the Georgia Institute of Technology and former counselor to Presidents Obama and Bill Clinton, coined the phrase "golden age of surveillance" to describe the reality of today's environment for law-enforcement and intelligence agencies.[23]

Numerous technology-related ways exist to gather evidence were either unavailable or only modestly available ten years ago, including location information from mobile devices, information about contacts and confederates, and an array of databases that create "digital dossiers" about individuals. Technology, far from causing law enforcement to "go dark" as they claim (largely because of encryption) is instead digitally capturing activities that until recently went unrecorded.

Much of this information is data about data—metadata—and has significantly fewer legal protections than so-called content data, such as the substance of electronic messages. However, oftentimes it is hardly necessary to know what people say in an e-mail or voice call to know their gist. Increasingly, metadata generated by mobile devices is stored in the cloud and accessible by lawful court order. New enabling capabilities for the Internet of Things and advances in computer power and storage capacity for big data applications using metadata can be used by law-enforcement and the defense and intelligence communities in lawful ways to assist them in their missions. Although there's a debate to be had about where to draw the line in metadata privacy and law-enforcement access, law enforcement should spend more energy in adjusting their investigative techniques to this new world than fighting the inevitable continued use of encryption.

CONCLUSION

In many ways our situation at the dawn of the digital age—fraught with possibility and danger—is not unlike what we faced at the dawn of the nuclear age. At the height of the Cold War, six months after the Cuban Missile Crisis, President John F. Kennedy delivered a commencement speech at American University. This is what he said:

Our problems are man-made; therefore they can be solved by man. And man can be as big as he wants. No problem of human destiny is beyond human beings. Man's reason and understanding have often solved the unsolvable and we believe they can do it again.[24]

In that same speech acknowledging the real differences between the United States and the Soviet Union, he went on to say this:

So let us not be blind to our differences—but let us also direct attention to our common interests and to means by which those differences can be resolved. Moreover, if we cannot end now our differences, at least we can help make the world safe for diversity. For, in the final analysis, our most basic common link is that we all inhabit this small planet. We all breathe the same air. We all cherish our children's future. And we are all mortal.

A few months later, after eight years of negotiations, President Kennedy and Premier Nikita Khrushchev signed the nuclear test–ban treaty.

Confronting forces previously unimagined in human history, we were, and have been, able to manage the nuclear age. The next president has the responsibility to provide that leadership for the digital age.

---

1 James Manyika, Susan Lund, Jacques Bughin, Jonathan Woetzel, Kalin Stamenov, and Dhruv Dhingra, *Digital Globalization: The New Era of Global Flows* (McKinsey Global Institute, Mar. 2016), Web.

2 Tom Simonite, "Intel Puts the Brakes on Moore's Law," *MIT Technology Review*, Mar. 23, 2016, Web.

3 Hewlett Packard Enterprise Security Research, *Internet of Things Research Study* (Hewlett Packard Enterprise, 2015) Web.

4 The Commission on the Theft of American Intellectual Property, *The IP Commission Report: The Report of the Commission on the Theft of American Intellectual Property* (The National Bureau of Asian Research, May 2013), p. 11, Web.

5 Ibid., p. 2.

6 Chandler Mark, "Huawei and Cisco's Source Code: Correcting the Record," *Cisco Blogs*, Oct. 11, 2012, Web, May 14, 2016; Kim Zetter, "Google Hackers Targeted Source Code of More than 30 Companies," *Wired*, n.p., Jan. 13, 2010, Web.

7 The Commission on the Theft of American Intellectual Property, *The IP Commission Report: The Report of the Commission on the Theft of American Intellectual Property* (The National Bureau of Asian Research, May 2013), p. 10, Web.

8 Office of the Press Secretary, the White House, Fact Sheet: *President Xi Jinping's State Visit to the United States* (White House, Sept. 25, 2015), Web.

9 Adam Segal, "Why China Hacks the World," *The Christian Science Monitor*, Jan. 31, 2016, Web.

10 Cory Bennett, "Spy Head: 'Jury's Out' on Whether China Quit Hacking after Deal," *The Hill*, Feb. 25, 2016, Web.

11 Daniel Castro, *How Much Will PRISM Cost the U.S. Cloud Computing Industry?*, white paper (Information Technology and Innovation Foundation, Aug. 2013), Web; James Staten, "The Cost of PRISM Will Be Larger Than ITIF Projects," *Forrester* (blog), Aug. 14, 2013, Web.

12 Sarah Perez, "Forget Self-Destructing Messages, Buzz's New App Offers Self-Destructing Connections," *Tech Crunch*, Oct. 30, 2015, Web.

13 Danny Hakim, "Once Celebrated in Russia, the Programmer Pavel Durov Chooses Exile," *New York Times*, Dec. 2, 2014, Web.

14 Mike Masnick, "Former NSA Directors Coming Out Strongly *Against* Backdooring Encryption," *Tech Dirt*, Oct. 7, 2015, Web.

15 Damian Paletta, "U.S. Intelligence Chief James Clapper Suggests China Behind OPM Breach," *The Wall Street Journal*, June 25, 2015, Web.

16 Ponemon Institute, *2015 Cost of Data Breach Study: United States* (Ponemon Institute and IBM, May 2015), Web.

17 Office of Management and Budget, Executive Office of the President of the United States, the White House, *Annual Report to Congress: Federal Information Security Modernization Act* (White House, Mar. 18, 2016), Web.

18 Emily Glazer, "J.P. Morgan to Accelerate Timeline for Cybersecurity Spending Boost," *The Wall Street Journal*, Aug. 3, 2015, Web; Dakin Campbell, "Moynihan Says Bank of America Cybersecurity Unit Has Blank Check," *Bloomberg*, Jan. 21, 2015, Web.

19 David Powner, *Information Technology: Federal Agencies Need to Address Aging Legacy Systems*, GAO-16-468 (US Government Accountability Office, May 2016), Web.

20 Tim Starks, "Politico Pro Q&A: Andy Ozment of DHS," *Politico Pro*, Mar. 15, 2016, Web.

21 Ponemon Institute, *2015 Cost of Data Breach Study: United States* (Ponemon Institute and IBM, May 2015), Web.

22 Walter D. Valdivia and Benjamin Y. Clark, *The Politics of Federal R&D: A Punctuated Equilibrium Analysis*, white paper (Center for Technology Innovation, Brookings Institute, June 2015), Web.

23 Peter Swire and Kenesa Ahmad, "Encryption and Globalization (November 16, 2011)," *Columbia Science and Technology Law Review*, vol. 23 (2012); Ohio State Public Law Working Paper No. 157.

24 John F. Kennedy, "1963 Commencement," American University's 1963 Spring Commencement, American University, Washington, DC, June 10, 1963, Web.

Eight

Cybersecurity in Telecommunications

Richard Spearman, Group Corporate Security Director, Vodafone

WHAT MAKES THE TELECOMMUNICATIONS SECTOR UNIQUE

Telecommunications in all forms is increasingly central to our working and personal lives. Dependence on the rapid availability of data and instant communications continues to rise. Even for those that did not grow up with the Internet, it has become almost impossible to imagine life without connectivity.[1]

The global telecommunications sector is a mix of government, former government, and commercial operators. The networks are a critical part of the business infrastructure and increasingly seen as part of the critical national infrastructure. They deliver services for customers, but also wider benefits for society. It is in everyone's interest for the telecommunications industry to be competitive, to prosper, to invest in the latest technologies, to be well defended against hostile actors and to behave in ways that balance the needs of customers with requirements of government. This is not easy to achieve and requires transparency, engagement from all stakeholders, leadership from government, and the ability to reach agreement on balancing the requirements of the business, the government and the customer.[2]

The telecommunications industry stores, manages, and transports a vast amount of valuable data for individuals and society, digital commerce, and critical national infrastructure. Telecommunications can also be a tremendous force for social good. The means to communicate, share, innovate, and prosper is inextricably linked to the way in which the telecommunications industry can mobilize technology and innovation on a global scale.[3] Bringing new technologies, services, and interoperability to new and existing markets in a responsible way is more challenging when there is uncertainty, disagreement, and conflict in cyberspace.

The telecommunications industry faces a massive increase in demand for data. Customers want a rapidly expanding range of services, which depend on faster data speeds and ever-greater reliability. There is a demand for greater personalization of services and for more control of privacy and better security. To meet this challenge by 2025, networks need to support up to a thousand times more capacity, reduce latency to milliseconds, and reinvent telecommunications for the cloud.[4]

Enabled by powerful new devices, the app ecosystem fuels demand for data by continuously inventing new categories of applications that test the limits of the network.[5] By 2025, people might demand mobile networks that allow them to broadcast live video feeds to thousands of other users in real time. To meet such demands, the industry is turning to software defined network architectures that combine greater efficiency with flexibility. Greater interworking between networks and services across a range of technologies of varying maturity levels will introduce new complexity. These changes could create new vulnerabilities or magnify existing weaknesses, making them more exploitable.

The threat from cyber actors is increasing in sophistication, persistence and variety—and the risks posed are not easily mitigated.[6] Cybersecurity needs to be multidimensional, transcending the risk management and response capabilities of any single enterprise, industry, or government. The damage inflicted by successful cyberattacks is not just financial and commercial but can also lead to long-term reputational damage and regulatory action. Consumer confidence once lost is hard to regain. Strong security basics that are well implemented can make a significant difference but are not a sufficient response in an environment in which consumers and businesses are seeking to exploit modern connectivity in increasingly ambitious ways. The telecommunications sector needs to be at the forefront of efforts to develop and maintain better defense and recovery capabilities for itself and for customers both in the public and private sectors.

The stakes are high. For the digital economy to flourish business needs to be able to take full advantage of the opportunities offered by new technology and the Internet of Things. It is vital that companies secure the services they run and the data they hold. There is also a need to recognize the risks of serious harms that could be enabled if the Internet becomes an impenetrably secure network for criminal activity. The dangers are real, and as we get more connected, the risks could multiply. Finding ways to manage these risks well is very important if we are to avoid a cycle of crises followed by government reactions, which if not managed carefully, could have unintended consequences and restrict the ability to fully exploit the opportunities offered by the Internet and exciting new technologies.

Customer confidence is crucial. Customers need to know that their data are safe and to understand how companies will use these and the basis on which the government can secure access to these data. Customers need to trust service providers to behave responsibly in this regard. Telecommunications is a regulated business. Service providers are required to give government's access to customer traffic and data in accordance with licensing regulations and the laws of the jurisdictions in which they operate. Our policy is clear: telecommunications companies should not hand over customer data unless they are lawfully required to do so.

CHALLENGES FACING THE NEW ADMINISTRATION

MAINTAINING TRUST BETWEEN BUSINESS, GOVERNMENT, AND SOCIETY

Without trust we risk failing to fulfill the potential presented by the digital economy, making the most of new technology and a hobbling of the IoT. We need a balanced and engaged debate, not a shouting match at distance. We need to align the interests of customers with those of business and government. The experience of Apple versus the FBI might suggest that the interests of industry, government, and society are divergent. We would argue absolutely not. It is about reaching an agreed compromise, a question of balance not absolute choices. Crucially it is about trust and transparency.

Encryption is a valuable tool that increases security but it is also valuable to criminals. Abuse of encryption is a shared problem for society. It is not for government, academics or technology companies alone to make judgments about the use of data in general or encryption in particular.[7] Our role is to say what can and cannot be done in the telecommunications industry under various legal and operational frameworks, and what impact proposed changes will have on the risks posed to the public, trust in the telecommunications sector, and sustainability of telecommunications business models.

REGULATION LAGS BEHIND GLOBALIZATION AND THE PACE OF CHANGE

There is a real tension between technologies that transcend borders and rules based on national jurisdictions. There are opportunities for companies to provide services once and deliver them to many, but government requirements based on local service provision could interfere with this. Data localization requirements and conflicting national laws imposed on cross-border technologies could affect the technology and architecture choices made by telecommunications companies.

In a globalized information economy, telecommunications companies will often deliver products and services using centralized platforms and infrastructure located across multiple jurisdictions. Regulations that unduly restrict the cross-border transfer of personal and machine-generated data are likely to impede service delivery and distort investment decisions. The extent to which it is possible to develop a common approach to these issues has an impact on the choices companies will be able to make in deploying new technologies, the delivery of potential benefits to customers and potential for improved profitability from economies of scale.

The speed of technology change challenges existing regulation. Services come and go rapidly and the development cycle is shortening. There is a real challenge for those charged with making the rules in keeping up with the pace of change and in leading the debate toward sensible legislation and international cooperation. Not all law is well drafted and in some situations there are gaps, even conflicting laws. We welcome clarity in both legislation and oversight arrangements and as much transparency as possible. Legislation should clearly outline the purpose and offer clarity about the types of government agency who can require access to customer data, along with the process by which that data can be secured. The process should be auditable, and it should be possible, through that audit, to verify that the lawful system is being used. Transparency about the outcome of the audit process and verification of the integrity of the system should also be possible.

The differences between licensed service providers and so-called over-the-top players are blurring and disappearing. Current regulation and legal requirements are not applied consistently, leading to an uneven playing field. It cannot be in the interests of strong cybersecurity to have rules that apply to one set of communications services and not to others. There needs to be a level playing field across all sectors, encouraging sustainable competitive advantage on the basis of good cybersecurity practice.

THE NEED TO KEEP UP WITH THOSE WHO THREATEN OUR NETWORKS

The volume, sophistication, and persistence of attacks are increasing, taking advantage of systematic vulnerabilities in software. The scale and changing nature of the challenge are disrupting industry attempts to build internationally compatible safeguards and making it more difficult to have a mature debate with customers about privacy and security. The digital economy generates between $2 trillion and $3 trillion annually and is expected to grow rapidly. If the estimates on cybercrime are right, then crime currently extracts between 15 and 20 percent of the value created by online activity.[8] There is a need for more attention to be paid to creating proper disincentives for crime by targeting the market mechanisms that allow criminals to profit from their activities. Existing measures to combat organized crime and the proceeds of crime involving complex warrants and international cooperation are too slow. We need government to invest more in bringing offenders to account. The message from government should be clear and straightforward: if you attack the telecommunications sector, there is no time limit or safe haven to retreat to.

RECOMMENDATIONS

INCIDENT REPORTING AND INFORMATION SHARING

Governments can do more to set the framework and do more to incentivize and reward good behavior. Following an incident, everyone needs to be clear and precise about what has happened, but government decisions about incident notification and public disclosure of major incidents (or audits) should not be allowed to disrupt or undermine industry attempts to mount an appropriate and proportionate response. Furthermore, incident notification should account for disruptive effects in adjacent sectors and obligations on other parties to share relevant information in a timely manner. Cooperation and information sharing should be voluntary and protected and the law should favor incentives above regulation.

For the industry to make meaningful headway on standards and standardization, we need to see more intergovernment coordination on standards work to deliver globally accepted outcomes that strike at the heart of the issues. A consensus-based international standards development process needs clarity from governments about the role of organizations such as the International Telecommunications Union relative to the Internet Engineering Task Force, the National Institutes of Standards and Technology, 3rd Generation Partnership Project, and other global standards bodies.

The telecommunications industry also requires a legal and regulatory framework to promote and uphold technology neutrality and provide a legal framework to encourage investment in future-capable networks that will carry exponentially growing data in virtualized cloud-based environments. The law should also be a catalyst for standardization in the industry and channel stakeholder priorities to achieve this. The way in which data are collected, shared, and used is increasingly complex and global in nature. Nations should disincentivize data localization and support the free flow of data.[9]

TAKE A LIGHT HAND WITH REGULATION

It is for industry to take appropriate and proportionate technical and orga-nizational measures to manage risks posed to the security of network and information systems. Flexibility is important as solutions may differ depend-ing on the nature of organizations, services, and markets. Government, wherever possible, should avoid prescribing risk frameworks, risk tolerance, appropriate controls, and oversight mechanisms.

Government needs to lead and support national and international con-versations required to find the appropriate balance between the need to protect the privacy of the individual and the need to ensure the collec-tive security of society. Without a broader national consensus and more effective international standards and agreements, there is a real risk that the development of the digital economy could be hampered or distorted. Jurisdictional clashes and national data laws are already having an impact. A smart debate about the use and potential abuse of encryption will be key.

Where there must be regulation, make it smart. Policy and regulation must be developed with the specific needs of the enterprise sector in mind, rather than as a by-product of regulation designed for consumer needs.[10] Regulations that unduly restrict the cross-border transfer of personal and ma-chine-generated data are likely to increase the costs of providing global tele-communications solutions. This can reduce the range of services available, increase costs and complexity for businesses working to provide the services, and in the extreme, threaten the commercial viability of some services. It is also vital to ensure that regulation, intentionally or otherwise, does not un-duly restrict the transfer of industrial data and services across borders.[11]

BROADEN THE VISION OF THE PUBLIC-PRIVATE PARTNERSHIP BETWEEN TELECOMMUNICATIONS AND GOVERNMENT

In the digital age, private companies are on the frontline of defense when it comes to cyber threats. Many attacks are not launched at telecommuni-cations companies but through them, in some cases against government or national-security targets. Third parties may struggle to manage the im-pact of high-level attacks if their prevailing business models don't allow for further investment in cybersecurity. In these situations it might be cost effective for government to use telecommunications companies to provide enhanced security in situations where further investment is needed to reduce the impact of high-level threats and provide a broader common level of defense that it beyond the reach of some organizations but ultimately in the national interest.

CONCLUSION

The digital economy and communications technology has changed the world and the pace of change will increase. Industry, particularly the telecommunications industry, is making enormous investments to update and improve the functionality and security of its systems. However, the pace of change raises new issues relating to what will, and ought to be, the roles of industry and government. Policy makers need to approach these issues with open minds and with an understanding that there are no simple fixes and that balance between the interests of all the elements on the positive side of the equation (citizens, industry, and government) need to be balanced in order to unite against the criminals and rogue nation-state operators on the other side of the equation.

---

1 Today we communicate, collaborate, buy, sell, and trade about everything in our lives using digital technologies that are already so ubiquitous that we don't even notice them, but that are destined to become exponentially more intimate parts of how we live.
Art Coviello, et al., "Advancing the Dialogue on Privacy and Security in the Connected World," paper, the Digital Equilibrium Project, Mar. 2016, Web.

2 With privatization came an increased discretion on the part of those managing telecommunications infrastructure in the choice of systems and technology. Private sector owners of telecommunications infrastructure accept responsibility for securing their systems to the point that it is profitable—that is, as far as the cost of dealing with an outage promises to cost more than preventing it. However, there is a distinction between protecting against low-level threats and protecting against an attack on the state. This disjuncture is arguably at the heart of the tension in the public-private partnership between government and the telecommunications sector.

Madeline Carr, *Public–private Partnerships in National Cyber-Security Strategies*, Paper, the Royal Institute of International Affairs, 2016, Web.

3 Ibid. Only the private sector has the skills and abilities to manage the complex process of developing new technologies and bringing them to market.

4 Telecommunications organizations are recasting themselves as technology companies that offer a broad array of digital communications, connectivity, and content services.

Thomas Tandetzki, *Communications Review* (PWC), Web, July 7, 2016.

5 In 2014, Apple announced that seventy-five billion apps had been downloaded from its App Store (two years earlier, the number was thirty billion), while Google reported fifty billion in 2013 (more than double the number in 2012).

"Cumulative Number of Apps Downloaded from the Google Play as of May 2016 (in Billions)," *Statista*, the Statistics Portal, 2016, Web.

6 The result is a society worried, frustrated, and unsure how to respond.

Art Coviello, et al., *Advancing the Dialogue on Privacy and Security in the Connected World*, Paper, the Digital Equilibrium Project, Mar. 2016, Web.

7 "Director Robert Hannigan Dispels Myths about Encryption in MIT Speech," *GCHQ*, Mar. 7, 2016, Web.

8 Center for Strategic and International Studies, *Net Losses: Estimating the Global Cost of Cybercrime. Economic Impact of Cybercrime II* (McAfee, June 2014), Web.

9 Examples where industry-agreed standards and self-regulatory initiatives have been introduced to address concerns around privacy and security provide evidence of proactive measures taken by industry players to provide alternative measures to data localization laws and regulations in order to address legitimate public-policy concerns.

KPMG LLP, *Securing the Benefits of Industry Digitisation: A Report for Vodafone* (KPMG International and Hogan Lovells, Nov. 2015), Web.

10 Ibid.

11 In a globalized information economy, providers of ICT will often deliver their products and services using centralized platforms and architecture, located across multiple jurisdictions. Therefore, any requirement for data localization can impede effective service delivery as well as increasing costs and altering investment incentives. The economic consequences of this can be significant.

Nine

Winning the Cyber-Talent War: Strategies to Enhance Cybersecurity Workforce Development

Dr. David Brumley, Professor of Electrical and Computer Engineering and
Director of Carnegie Mellon's CyLab Security and Privacy Institute

RISING DEMAND AND UNFILLED POSITIONS: AN OVERVIEW OF THE CYBERSECURITY WORKFORCE CHALLENGE

Meeting the nation's cybersecurity challenge will require a multipronged effort. Sustained investment in research and innovation, successful implementation of new models for public-private collaboration, and the continued advancement of incentives that spark continued private-sector investment in cybersecurity capabilities are all vital components of an effective strategy.

Key to success in each of these areas will be the ability of the United States to launch a national initiative to nurture and develop a national cybersecurity workforce. Vacancies are in the hundreds of thousands and are expected to grow. Stanford University analyzed numbers from the Census Bureau and estimated that more than two hundred thousand cybersecurity jobs go unfilled.[1] Cisco places the global gap at nearly one million.[2] Symantec CEO Michael Brown projects the total demand for cybersecurity professionals to reach six million—and that over one million positions could be unfilled by 2019.[3] This current and projected gap exists despite the fact that these jobs routinely pay $100,000 or more.

The increasing demand will be driven by the collision of bits and atoms disrupting a host of industrial sectors. The rapid convergence of wireless technologies, sensors, microelectronic systems, and the web—the rise of the Internet of Things—is dramatically increasing the need for cybersecurity skills. Connected devices bring new threats, vulnerabilities, and the imperative for new approaches to security, because securing IoT devices demands strategies fundamentally different than locking down personal computers or mobile devices.

For example, the resurgence of American manufacturing is increasingly tied to advanced digital capabilities. These include the increased use of flexible robotics and autonomous systems, the integration of design and production through 3-D printing technologies, and creation of new products ranging from appliances to clothing with embedded microelectronics. The number of sectors for which cybersecurity will be central to their operations will continue to grow.

In addition, the development of wearable digital tools to augment human intelligence (Google Glass was an early taste) will further extend the impact of digitally mediated services and applications in our lives. The deployment of artificial intelligence tools applying machine learning to augment our interaction with machines will also intensify the demand for cybersecurity experts.

The emergence of these innovations will impact the private sector and the delivery of public services. Simultaneously meeting the workforce demands of industry and government will require a comprehensive strategy that focuses on fostering a wide range of skills and building a cybersecurity talent pipeline.

There will be no quick fixes or silver bullets. Analysis undertaken by Carnegie Mellon University has found little recognition of cybersecurity as a career path by high-school guidance counselors.[4] The next administration must be prepared to pursue a national scale initiative that addresses the overall talent pipeline.

A SYNOPSIS OF THE CYBERSECURITY WORKFORCE

The National Institute of Standards and Technology Cybersecurity Workforce Framework unveiled in December 2015 provides a starting point for sketching the broad building blocks of capabilities needed for the future.[5] The framework was crafted with input from public, private, and academic sector cyber leaders to sketch out the essential workforce skill and position building blocks.

NIST identified the following seven core areas as the central components of a cybersecurity workforce.

Positions and Skills Needed to Secure Provision—specialties responsible for conceptualizing, designing, and building secure information systems. Positions in this area include those engaged in software security engineering and systems security architecture, information assurance compliance, research, prototype development, and testing.

Positions and Skills Needed to Operate and Maintain—specialties responsible for providing support, administration, and maintenance necessary to ensure effective and efficient information technology system performance and security. NIST highlighted positions related to network services, data administration, systems security analysis, and customer IT support as part of the component of the workforce.

Positions and Skills Needed to Protect and Defend—specialties responsible for the identification, analysis, and mitigation of threats to internal information technology systems or networks. Incident response, network defense analysis, and vulnerability capabilities are critical to positions in the protect and defend component area.

Positions and Skills Needed to Investigate—specializations for the investigation of cyber events and crimes of information technology systems, networks, and digital evidence. Digital forensics capabilities needed to analyze computer-related evidence as well as trained professionals having the full range of investigative capabilities are central to this area.

Positions and Skills Needed to Collect and Operate—specialty areas engaged in specialized denial and deception operations and the collection of cybersecurity information that may be used to develop intelligence.

Positions and Skills Needed to Analyze—specialty areas responsible for review and evaluation of incoming cybersecurity information to determine its usefulness for intelligence. These professionals must engage in threat analysis and exploitation analysis.

Positions and Skills Needed for Oversight and Development—leadership, management, direction, development, and advocacy to enable the effectiveness of overall cybersecurity operations. Personnel in this area will have positions such as the chief information security officer or will come from legal and education and training support divisions.

The NIST workforce framework further delineates specific position titles that align with these skill areas. It provides a tool for organizations to identify and map specific components of their cybersecurity workforce needs. Perhaps more critically, the framework illuminates the imperative for shaping a strategy that meets the evolving multidisciplinary demands of cybersecurity—technical skills across a range of areas including business, policy, law, psychology, and social science.

EXAMINING PROGRESS TO DATE IN EFFORTS TO STRENGTHEN THE CYBERSECURITY WORKFORCE

The NIST workforce framework is one of several examples of progress made over the last several years by all levels of government and public-private cooperation to strengthen the cybersecurity workforce. Four initiatives provide a launchpad for envisioning an even broader and more comprehensive national strategy.

A PARTNERSHIP FOR BUILDING THE FUTURE PUBLIC-SECTOR WORKFORCE—THE SCHOLARSHIP FOR SERVICE PROGRAM

Funded by the National Science Foundation and operated in partnership with the Department of Homeland Security, the Cyber Corps of the Scholarship for Service program has demonstrated significant impact in encouraging students to pursue cybersecurity careers and creating a pipeline of talent for the public sector.[6] The program has increased in funding to $50 million in fiscal year 2016. Support is provided to four-year institutions with certified cybersecurity degree programs. More than sixty institutions ranging from public and private research universities to historically minority serving institutions participate in the program. The funding is utilized to support student tuition and educational services. After graduation, students must serve in an information assurance position in federal, state, local, or tribal government organization for a period of time equal to the length of the scholarship.

NATIONAL CENTERS OF ACADEMIC EXCELLENCE IN CYBER DEFENSE

The National Security Agency and the Department of Homeland Security jointly sponsor the National Centers of Academic Excellence in Cyber Defense (CAE-CD) program. This program sets criteria and mapping curricula to assist institutions in building effective cybersecurity education and research programs—helping to establish a national framework for cybersecurity education. All four-year baccalaureate, graduate education, and two-year institutions are eligible. Currently more than 160 institutions are designated as meeting the program criteria.

PRESIDENTIAL INNOVATION FELLOWS

While not focused exclusively or even predominantly on cybersecurity, the Presidential Innovation Fellows program provides a window on a future where an improved flow of critical cybersecurity talent could be a vital resource for meeting major short-term challenges and raising the overall level of skills in the cyber workforce.

The fellows program is designed to engage early career IT professionals and engage them in short stints in government.[7] The fellows bring fresh thinking and leading edge skills and approaches to major IT challenges facing federal agencies.

NATIONAL GUARD AND MILITARY RESERVE CYBER OPERATIONS

The military provides another model for developing this cross-sector collaboration. The regional centers being developed by the National Guard and Reserve are creating a nexus of talent within states and cities that draws on professionals engaged in industry and academia who can be mobilized to support government needs in the case of major incidents. Programs such as Cyber Guard, operated by the Software Engineering Institute at Carnegie Mellon, utilize online capabilities to deliver effective exercise training to support these efforts across the country. This training model is now also being utilized by the civilian workforce as well.

ENGAGING VETERANS IN CYBERSECURITY CAREERS

A number of promising initiatives have also been launched in the last few years to focus cybersecurity education on veterans. These efforts include specific outreach and degree programs—including those launched by the state of Virginia and boot camp programs launched by companies such as PricewaterhouseCoopers, among others.[8]

INITIAL STEPS TO NURTURE CYBERSECURITY CAREER PATHS FOR YOUNG AMERICANS

Progress has also been made to begin to create a foundation for a long-term cybersecurity talent pipeline. As part of the National Initiative for Cybersecurity Education (more often known as NICE), federal agencies collaborate to strengthen K–12 student and teacher engagement. One of the leading examples of this effort is the GenCyber initiative supported by NSF and the NSA. GenCyber supports collaborations with academic institutions to conduct cybersecurity summer camps for students and teachers. In 2016, 133 camps will be undertaken across the country.[9]

The growing focus on hacking contests is also an important step toward nurturing the talent pipeline by providing an exciting engagement for middle- and high-school students on the essence of cybersecurity. Hacking contests conducted by Carnegie Mellon's CyLab have engaged over eighteen thousand students.[10]

The Obama administration's Cybersecurity National Action Plan calls for initiatives that would strengthen a number of these core elements. The administration proposed funding the Scholarship for Service program to expand the number of participating institutions, developing a core cyber curriculum and a loan forgiveness program for individuals willing to join the federal workforce.[11]

As with progress made in advancing information sharing, these proposals can be regarded as important starting points for consideration by the next administration as a step toward the creation of a comprehensive cyber workforce strategy. But meeting the critical talent challenge will require nothing less than a national commitment to creating a broader workforce strategy.

SHAPING AN AGENDA FOR THE NEW ADMINISTRATION: PRINCIPLE BUILDING BLOCKS OF AN EFFECTIVE NATIONAL CYBER WORKFORCE STRATEGY

The progress over the last several years to strengthen federal investment in cybersecurity education and engagement with federal employment opportunities provides a starting point for crafting a broader workforce initiative. The following three principles will be key to a truly comprehensive strategy.

FOCUS A NATIONAL INITIATIVE ON BUILDING THE TALENT PIPELINE

Attracting students into the federal government must be augmented by an aggressive strategy to build the pipeline of interest in earlier grade levels. This will require a broad range of engagement with K–12 education that includes classroom initiatives, expanded teacher education, and after-school competitions to spark interest.

Carnegie Mellon's experience in building effective cybersecurity programs leads us to conclude that it is possible, as we've seen through programs like picoCTF, a hacking contest that has reached tens of thousands of high-school student participants. The contest lets young students hone existing skills while also generating excitement in students with no prior experience. A major lesson is that it is essential to structure academic programs around holistic, interdisciplinary curricula and experiences that prepare individuals for the evolving nature of cybersecurity challenges. Efforts to strengthen the core curriculum for cybersecurity should focus on hands-on experiences in building operating systems so that students are prepared for and confident enough to ask the "what if" questions essential to thinking several steps ahead of potential attackers. The curricula should blend deep technical training with courses in the humanities, business, and policy to prepare cybersecurity professionals for challenges in areas of privacy and human computer interaction that will increasingly define the field and the demands of industry and government.

In addition to energizing the entry levels of the pipeline, it is important to note the crucial impact of research initiatives that attract and nurture graduate students, a key component of a vital talent pipeline. Over the long term, graduate students engaged in research-based education will be the cadre that provides the energy to advance the field and shape overall workforce education. The federal government has been very effective at fostering networks among agencies and higher-education institutions engaged in cybersecurity degree programs. Fostering stronger networks and collaboration among research institutions in cybersecurity would be a valuable complement to general workforce strategies.

In keeping with the strength of the higher-education system, a close synergy among security and privacy research and education is an essential ingredient to create a better-prepared workforce and to generate real impact on transforming the overall environment for the future of cyberspace. Finally, it will be critical for programs to blend offensive and defensive training and education—particularly to train a workforce that will be expected to lead major cybersecurity operations. This blending of offensive and defensive training necessitates that the education experience involve regular exposure to operational exercises. Achieving more holistic cybersecurity education programs across the broad landscape of higher education will necessitate much stronger collaboration and partnership among institutions.

EMBRACE THE POSITIVE ELEMENTS OF THE HACKER DYNAMIC

Hackers are ultra-curious, highly imaginative professionals who are able to spot even the most hidden vulnerabilities in systems. Indeed, hackers have entered the workforce pipeline and protect both industry and governmental systems from attackers. The actions of a handful of rogue hackers have led to the demonization of hacking, but these rogue hackers are a small subset and are not representative of the field as a whole. Meeting the nation's cybersecurity talent needs will require nurturing the natural curiosity and imaginative creativity that defines the hacker experience and that can create professionals capable of discovering the most difficult vulnerabilities to uncover. We need to stop stigmatizing hackers and start emphasizing that hacking skills can be applied to highly in-demand careers in cybersecurity.

CREATE NEW VEHICLES FOR INDUSTRY, GOVERNMENT, AND EDUCATION COLLABORATION

While policies to date have focused on the needs of the federal government, the national cybersecurity workforce is a challenge for the private sector as well. Opportunities must be explored to foster closer coordination among government, industry, and the higher-education community as the nature of the cybersecurity challenge evolves.

POLICY RECOMMENDATIONS FOR NEW NATIONAL FEDERAL CYBERSECURITY WORKFORCE

The following policy recommendations would provide the core elements for a broader national strategy to build the cybersecurity workforce of the future.

INTENSIFY INITIATIVES TO CREATE A CYBER-AWARE GENERATION

While expanding and deepening the training of cybersecurity professionals is vital, it is important to recognize that the first line of defense is the cyber decision making that individuals do every day as they consider downloading apps, posting pictures, or connecting devices to their cars. Just as STEM education is required in most K–12 curricula, cyber needs to be included in classrooms. Incorporating basic cybersecurity education into curricula at all education levels and work experiences would enhance this first line of defense.

Along with this effort, we need to invest in research and applied development of innovations that continue to make security and privacy easier for consumers. Security and privacy actions must be less of an obstruction and more frictionless. Action in this area provides a vital opportunity for public-private collaboration and the use of incentive-based policies.

LAUNCH A COMPREHENSIVE INITIATIVE TO BUILD THE TALENT PIPELINE

The nation's cybersecurity workforce needs will never be met without greater attention to nurturing interest in cybersecurity in middle schools and high school. We need an initiative that matches the scale of the challenge. The following elements could be central components of this effort.

Develop a Core Cybersecurity Curriculum That Can Be Adapted and Applied at All Education Levels and Start Building Cybersecurity into STEM Programs

While curricula and programs must always be adapted to the unique dynamics of students and the particular focus of programs, efforts to engage industry, government, and primary, secondary, and higher education in crafting a core curriculum would provide a valuable accelerant to expanding programs. Similarly, recognizing the importance of cybersecurity as a fundamental element of STEM education will also enhance the growth of programs and stronger student interest.

Engage Industry and the Higher-Education Community in Commitment to Train One Hundred Thousand High-School and Middle-School Teachers in Basic Cybersecurity Education in the Next Five Years

This component can tap the development of new online and gamification tools that have the potential to significantly impact the ability to bring cost-effective education resources to schools throughout the nation. Carnegie Mellon experienced the success with picoCTF, and nationwide adoption of this model, specifically aimed at educators who can run their own versions of the contest, could have an exponential impact.

Using the FIRST Robotics League as a Model, Advance a National Strategy for Middle-School and High-School Hacking Contests to Excite the Next Generation of Cybersecurity Professionals

Now in its twenty-fifth year, FIRST reaches seventy-five thousand students around the world each year and provides a broader portal to STEM careers.[12] A national hacking contest initiative can have a similar impact.

Expand the Scholarship for Service Program and Foster Even Deeper Cross-Institutional Collaboration

The proposal to increase the number of institutions in the program is a valuable component of a talent initiative. This effort would be further enhanced by supporting and incentivizing collaboration among institutions on course delivery, professional development, and best practices. One model for such an effort is the *Cyber Stakes* program, which has fostered collaborative education and exercises between Carnegie Mellon and service academies.

Explore Creation of a Cybersecurity ROTC Program

A cyber-specific ROTC-like initiative would underscore the sense of national mission that is vital to addressing the environment for strengthening the cybersecurity talent pipeline. A key to this effort would be to create a strong network among institutions operating this program to ensure that the development of these students included both deep technical and operational experiences.

Additionally, consideration should be given to development a "2+2" model for this effort, where a student who has a potential interest in cybersecurity can receive a modest financial-aid supplement in their first and second year. At the end of the second year, these students (and any other students in the program) can choose to apply for acceptance into a program fully funding their tuition during the third and fourth year, if they commit to a cybersecurity minor in addition to their computer science or electrical and computer engineering major. In return, the student would be required to sign up for three years of service in a government cybersecurity position.

Create New Mechanisms for Industry, Government, Higher Education Collaboration

One strategic approach to fostering these new mechanisms would be to support the development of regional test beds for collaboration on the emerging Internet of Things. These test beds could focus both on innovation in cyber applications and advancing opportunities for formal education programs as well as ongoing training initiatives.

CONCLUSION

Recent administrations of both parties have sought to advance recognition of the vital challenge that faces the nation in securing cyberspace. Those efforts have resulted in historic bipartisan cooperation to enact cybersecurity legislation.

Now, greater attention must be focused on the talent and workforce challenges at the heart of an effective cybersecurity strategy. Among the most important steps the next president can take will be to elevate recognition among government and industry leaders, teachers, parents, and most critically, young Americans of cybersecurity as a uniquely skilled profession. Each day individuals across industry and government engage to protect commerce and the functioning of government. Recognition of these individuals and the profession at the highest level of government would be as powerful as the key programmatic and policy tools outlined above.

1 "VA Launches New No-Cost Training Programs," *VAntage Point: Official Blog of the U.S. Department of Veterans Affairs*, Aug. 5, 2015, Web; Ariha Setalvad, "Demand to Fill Cybersecurity Jobs Booming," *Peninsula Press*, Stanford Journalism, Mar. 31, 2015, Web.

2 Steve Morgan, "Cybersecurity Job Market to Suffer Severe Workforce Shortage," *CSO*, July 28, 2015, Web.

3 Ibid.

4 Peter Chapman, *PicoCTF: Teaching 10,000 High School Students to Hack* (Carnegie Mellon University, Jan. 15, 2014).

5 "National Cybersecurity Workforce Framework," The National Initiative for Cybersecurity Education (NICE), Web.

6 "CyberCorps: Scholarship for Service," CyberCorps: Scholarship for Service, US Office of Personnel Management, Web, July 8, 2016.

7 "Presidential Innovation Fellows," *The White House*, 2015, Web.

8 Colin Wood, "U.S. Cyber Commands Launches 13 New Cyber Protection Teams," *Government Technology*, Dec. 16, 2015, Web; Anne Fisher, "PwC Is Turning to Vets and Grads to Fill High-Paying Tech Jobs," *Fortune*, Jan. 13, 2016, Web.

9 National Security Agency, NSA Public and Media Affairs. *NSA GenCyber Camps Triple in Offerings* (National Security Agency, Central Security Service, May 18, 2016), Web.

10 CyLab, Web.

11 Office of the Press Secretary, the White House, Fᴀᴄᴛ Sʜᴇᴇᴛ: *Cybersecurity National Action Plan* (White House, Feb. 9, 2016), Web.

12 FIRST: For Inspiration & Recognition of Science & Technology, FIRST Robotics Competition, FIRST Inspires, 2016, Web.

Ten

Cybersecurity in the Manufacturing Sector

Brian Raymond, Director of Innovation Policy,
National Association of Manufacturers

WHAT MAKES THE MANUFACTURING SECTOR UNIQUE

Connected devices are everywhere. They make homes comfortable and vehicles safer. They make offices more efficient and drive down energy costs. They increase crop yields and monitor pipelines. They track inventory and manage logistics. What was unimaginable just a decade ago is now a reality. This ubiquity of connected devices is known as the Internet of Things. And there is one industry behind all of this innovation: our nation's manufacturers.

Manufacturers are the creators, users, servicers, and installers of the Internet of Things. Billions of connected devices are pervasive throughout manufactured products and on the shop floors where they are made. This technology is creating enormous opportunity and driving transformative change. It has made all manufacturers into technology companies.

The days of interacting with the customer only during a single transaction are over. Connected technology enables manufacturers to provide real-time performance monitoring and usage patterns for their customers throughout the entire lifespan of a product. This will create a positive feedback loop resulting in better and more efficient products that will be sold and bought for their promise of measurable results. A tire manufacturer won't just sell tires, but a package to reduce costs through sensors that collect data on fuel consumption and tire pressure.

The IoT will make services like predictive maintenance a standard offering, as well as enable efficiencies and flexibility across the entire manufacturing process and down the supply chain that feeds it. Productivity could go up by as much as 30 percent. McKinsey & Company estimates the economic impact of the Industrial IoT could reach $3.7 trillion by 2025.[1] Manufacturing will build the IoT and be transformed by it, simultaneously.

While connected technology drives innovation in the manufacturing sector, it also creates new challenges. Manufacturers are now the first line of defense in securing our nation's most critical online assets. They place cybersecurity at the highest priority level.

One of the primary targets for cyberattack inside the manufacturing ecosystem is industrial control systems. This is the class of computers that help manage the shop floor. ICS are configured in growing numbers to be reachable through the Internet, including systems retrofitted with modern networking capabilities.

Even when companies take measures to secure their Internet-addressable ICS, they often link their factory production and enterprise information technology networks. That connection results in benefits such as increased productivity, but a new class of malware is exploiting those links to target ICS, likely for espionage.[2] A recent survey of ICS cybersecurity specialists found that three-quarters of them believe their operation has undocumented external network links, a condition the IoT will exacerbate.[3]

In short, what's keeping the number of physically damaging ICS attacks so low isn't good security but probably a lack of motivation on the part of for-profit hackers and nation-states. The former hasn't yet learned how to monetize ICS attacks and probably sees no reason to start, given the bountiful opportunities present elsewhere. Nation-states are apparently content to limit themselves to surveillance. Neither condition is permanent.

CHALLENGES FACING THE NEW ADMINISTRATION

THE IOT IS GOING FASTER THAN SECURITY CAN KEEP UP

Although in its infancy, the Internet of Things is already a target of cyberattacks.[4] Symantec identified in 2013 a worm apparently engineered to attack devices such as television set-top boxes.[5] Although the report was later debunked, one cybersecurity firm made waves when it claimed to have uncovered a smart refrigerator used by attackers to send out spam.[6] The mere fact that a household appliance may be a target has elevated the level at which manufacturers must consider securing the IoT.

Many IoT devices will possess minimal processing power. That is the nature of the thing—ubiquitous and cheap devices everywhere whose power comes through networking. As a result, many devices may not have capability for basic cybersecurity best practices, such as encryption and operating system updates. Even where capacity exists, manufacturers might not find it economical to patch devices made on a slim margin in a market relentlessly focused on the next generation of products.[7]

Devices are only one part of the IoT universe. Databases holding telemetry generated by the devices are another substantial component, one that likely to become another target for hacking. Cybersecurity firm iPower Technologies already spotted in 2015 malware targeting newly purchased police body cameras, likely in order to access law-enforcement data.[8]

CYBER ESPIONAGE

Only the government tops the manufacturing sector as a victim of cyber espionage.[9] Primarily perpetuated by nation-states or their proxies, cyber espionage doesn't seek to disrupt computing infrastructure but exploit it for the information locked away inside. That includes intellectual property as well as business intelligence. Nation-states have targeted information such as pricing, production numbers, and business strategies in addition to vacuuming out high-tech design information.[10]

The IoT will increase the attack surface for manufacturers. The more that shop floors become imbued with intelligent machines, the more those machines will contain data worth stealing. They will contain intellectual property worthy of theft by itself, but also metrics on production that bad actors have already shown a gargantuan appetite for illicitly acquiring.

Espionage isn't just a matter of lost revenue. It's a threat to economic security with implications for national security. "Our economy depends on the ability to innovate. And if there's a dedicated nation-state who's using its intelligence apparatus to steal day in and day out what we're trying to develop, that poses a serious threat to our country," recently explained John Carlin, assistant attorney general for national security.[11]

A secondary threat to national security stems from the manufacturing sector's global supply chain. Larger companies have the resources and sophistication to be sensitive to cyber vulnerabilities and take steps to contain them, but smaller enterprises may not. This leaves the entire supply chain vulnerable—creating threats in every sector, including the defense industrial base.

INDUSTRIAL CONTROL SYSTEM SECURITY IS UNDERRATED

Attackers seeking to disrupt industrial processes don't need to exploit an underlying software vulnerability, the way that sophisticated hackers do when attacking enterprise IT systems. They simply need to gain access to the ICS (perhaps through the corporate IT network) and use the exposed digital controls to manipulate the system into failure. No further hacking required.

Operational technology is a different beast and much of the hard-won knowledge about mainstream technology cyber defense isn't transferable. Although ICS more and more incorporate commercial-off-the-shelf parts and operating systems, the objectives and priorities of an automated shop floor are different than a data center. "The number-one goal of IT security is rooted in the concern about privacy—'Protect the Data'—whereas the number-one goal of ICS security is based on the concern for safety— 'Protect the Process,'" notes a blog post from an ICS security provider.[12] As a result, company cybersecurity and operational personnel who are hands-on with the automated systems are working hard to coordinate their efforts and cybersecurity strategies.

The Department of Homeland Security stood up in 2009 the Industrial Control Systems Cyber Emergency Response Team in recognition of this challenge, but the years since have proved disappointing. As Dale Peterson notes, ICS-CERT should be "developing secure ICS protocols and standards, accurately informing government and industry, analyzing ICS attack code," but its main output is further transmitting alerts already widely available to industry.[13]

RECOMMENDATIONS

INCENTIVES FOR IMPROVING CYBERSECURITY

Small- and medium-sized manufacturers in particular face bad economics when it comes to achieving a level of cybersecurity robust enough to stand up to nation-states, manufacturing's main cyber threat. Market forces stymie private-sector businesses from standing up cybersecurity capacity beyond the threshold of normal commercial risk, forces particularly strong below the threshold of large businesses.

"It's not a fair fight. A private company can't compete against the resources of the second largest economy in the world," said John Carlin, assistant attorney general for national security, discussing attacks from China.[14]

This gap between commercially sustainable levels of cybersecurity and what's necessary to counteract foreign adversaries isn't just a market failure. It's the space that federal government was designed to fill by dint of its constitutional charge to provide for the common defense. If the notion of national security depending on strengthening the network defense of a tractor plant in the Midwest seems strange, that's only because cybersecurity has altered what used to be geographic borders into digital frontiers. On the Internet, the domestic and the foreign rub shoulders without having to cross oceans.

But filling the gap with better cybersecurity isn't something the government can do on its own; it doesn't own the Internet, nor the tractor plant's computers. What's necessary is a public-private partnership that uses economic tools to encourage investment beyond ordinary levels of commercial cybersecurity spending.

Specifically, the government should complete the task begun with creation of the National Institute of Standards and Technology Cybersecurity Framework in determining what the most cost-effective elements of cyber defense are. The executive order that resulted in the framework's creation never saw it as an end in of itself. The order charged the network with setting out a "prioritized, flexible, repeatable, performance-based, and *cost-effective approach*" to cybersecurity (emphasis added).[15]

For NIST to determine how to use the framework cost-effectively is, admittedly, no easy task. But the structure for setting up studies with private-sector cooperation already exists with the sixteen critical infrastructure sector coordinating councils and their sibling government coordinating councils. In a nutshell, the councils for each critical infrastructure sector should seek out representative companies and solicit their voluntary participation in studies to test practical application of the framework in their information technology infrastructure. The studies would measure costs and benefits and identify where the chasm between commercially sustainable cybersecurity protections and nation-state-level protections opens up.

FUND IOT SECURITY RESEARCH

No amount of incentives can overcome a key characteristic of the Internet of Things: ubiquity of cheap computers with minimal computing power. The ability to seed the environment with cheap computers is what makes the IoT possible. Durable goods will likely possess sufficient capacity for cybersecurity measures such as firewalls. But they will be the exception. What makes the IoT possible is also what makes it vulnerable.

This is an irreducible problem that requires a different approach to cybersecurity, one premised on building secure systems from insecure components. This isn't a new notion, but it's one that's needs urgent revitalization, forearmed as we are with the certain knowledge of a planet's worth of devices coming online in the near future. The National Science Foundation, the Defense Advanced Research Projects Agency and the research arm of the Department of Homeland Security should make funding research into this a priority.

ICS-CERT SHOULD BE STRENGTHENED

The Industrial Controls Systems Cyber Emergency Response Team performance needs to enhance its focus on development of best practices and on research. The organization's outreach to the manufacturing sector should also be improved.

"We tend to count things—how many alerts, how many advisories, how many incidents do you respond to," said ICS-CERT director Marty Edwards in May 2016.[16] "I think we have to get to the point of measuring what impact did we make inside of a company, or how is a sector improving or degrading over time in the cybersecurity area," he added. The manufacturing sector concurs.

---

1 James Manyika, Michael Chui, Peter Bisson, Jonathan Woetzel, Richard Dobbs, Jacques Bughin, and Dan Aharon, *Unlocking the Potential of the Internet of Things* (McKinsey Global Institute, June 2015), Web.

2 Robert M. Lee, "Fourth Sample of ICS Tailored Malware Uncovered and the Potential Impact," *SANS Industrial Control Systems Security Blog*, Apr. 25, 2016, Web.

3 Derek Harp and Bengt Gregory-Brown, *The State of Security in Control Systems Today* (InfoSec Reading Room, SANS Institute, SurfWatch Labs, and Tenable Network Security, June 2015), p. 18, Web.

4 Hewlett Packard Enterprise Security Research, *Internet of Things Research Study* (Hewlett Packard Enterprise Development LP, 2015), Web; *HP Study Reveals 70 Percent of Internet of Things Devices Vulnerable to Attack* (Hewlett Packard Development Company, LP, July 29, 2014), Web.

5 Kaoru Hayashi, "Linux Worm Targeting Hidden Devices," *Symantec Official Blog*, Nov. 27, 2013, Web.

6 Paul Thomas, "Despite the News, Your Refrigerator Is Not Yet Sending Spam," *Symantec Official Blog*, Jan. 23, 2014, Web.

7 Bruce Schneier, "Security Risks of Embedded Systems," *Schneier on Security* (blog), *Wired*, Jan. 9, 2014, Web.

8 Patrick Sweeney, "Insecurity of Things: The IoT Devices You Deploy May Be Trojan Horses," *Venture Beat*, Apr. 17, 2016, Web.

9 Akamai Technologies, Anti-Phishing Working Group (APWG), et al., *2016 Data Breach Investigations Report* (Verizon, 2016), p. 53, Web.

10 David Talbot, "Cyber-Espionage Nightmare," *MIT Technology Review*, June 10, 2015, Web.

11 "The Great Brain Robbery," interview by Lesley Stahl, *60 Minutes—Business*, CBS Interactive Inc., Jan. 17, 2016, television and transcript.

12 Heather Mackenzie, "SCADA Security Basics: Why Industrial Networks Are Different than IT Networks," *Tofino Security*, Oct. 31, 2012, Web.

13 Dale Peterson, "Lies, Damned Lies and Statistics—Part 2," *Digital Bond*, Apr. 3, 2015, Web.

14 "The Great Brain Robbery," interview by Lesley Stahl.

15 Exec. Order No. 13636, 3 C.F.R. (2013).

16 "S4x16 Video: Interview with Marty Edwards, Director of ICS-CERT," interview by Dale Peterson, *Digital Bond*, May 24, 2016, Web.

Eleven

Cybersecurity in the Food and Agriculture Sector

Dr. Robert Zandoli, Global Chief Information
Security Officer, Bunge Limited

WHAT MAKES THE FOOD AND AGRICULTURE SECTOR UNIQUE

A t a distance, grain silos and feedlots look the same as they ever did. Up close, the food and agriculture sector has seen huge changes wrought by digital connectivity. A combine isn't just a grain-harvesting machine; it's a data-gathering platform.

Be it wired-up off-road equipment and agricultural machinery, high-tech food and grain processing, radio frequency ID-tagged livestock, or global-positioning-system tracking, the sector has become dependent on information systems to sustain and improve operations, competiveness, and profitability.

Wringing out even more efficient yields is a global and domestic necessity. Demand for agricultural products will increase significantly in the future, owing to population growth and rising living standards in emerging markets. Breadbasket countries like the United States must find sustained growth in yields to meet such exploding demands. Not just as a matter for growth but also to prevent domestic food costs from spiraling upward. Domestically, that means finding yet more efficient ways to farm.[1] And without making use of remote sensing and computer science, significant increases in agricultural yields will be impossible.[2] To meet the demand the agriculture industry will increase its dependency on information systems and other technologies.

That embrace of technology comes with risks. The agriculture sector finds itself being targeted as never before, thanks to an explosion of food and agriculture intellectual property coveted by foreign competitors. "I don't think it's a question of if a company is going to get hacked. It's when," warned an American Farm Bureau Federation executive in 2015. "Farmers have to know that."[3]

Hacktivists, too, have left their mark. Agriculture biotech firm Monsanto and its customers face ongoing harassment and attacks launched by the Anonymous hacking collective.[4]

The sector has been a slow starter but now realizes that cyberattacks are a major risk. Until recently most companies in this sector did not invest in cybersecurity defense and were lax in fortifying their infrastructure and developing sound cybersecurity practices. That is beginning to change.

Certainly the big four of agriculture, the "ABCD of agriculture"—Archer Daniels Midland, Bunge, Cargill, and Dreyfus—aren't staying passive in the face of these new threats.

For example, Bunge hired their first global chief information security officer in 2015, a title not typically seen in agriculture companies, not even in firms that have reached the Fortune 150. Bunge has raised cybersecurity as a board-level concern, and the directors are supporting and investing in the security program.

This delay in grasping the threat wasn't limited to the private sector. In 2010, the two federal oversight agencies, the Department of Agriculture and the Food and Drug Administration, classified cybersecurity as a low tier risk:

Because cyber-attacks on food and agriculture [critical infrastructure and key resource] offer little financial gain and likely pose only minimal economic disruption, the sector does not perceive itself as a target of such an attack. DHS has not identified the Food and

Agriculture Sector as a target of cyber-crime; therefore, sector partners agree that addressing cybersecurity issues is not a top priority.[5]

In retrospect, the thought that this sector is not threatened or that a cyberattack against it wouldn't cause economic disruption was myopic. This
sector needs additional focus and should be treated as an equal to other
sectors. To their credit, the agencies reversed course in 2015.[6]

On the one hand, the oversight may be forgivable. If we missed a chance
to get ahead the problem, in the past there also seemed to be little interest
among hackers in the agriculture sector. This was probably due to the lack
of "name brand recognition."

On the other hand, we made a terrible mistake, especially when considering what makes the food and agriculture sector especially unique:
our product. All sectors of critical infrastructure are interlaced with dependencies, but the biological requirement for food is arguably at the
root of them all. An extreme coordinated cyberattack on agriculture
companies would have human and financial crisis. As stated in the book
Starving in the Shadow of Plenty, Loretta Schwartz-Nobel stated that
"a three-week disruption of fuel supply could cause a year's supply of
food to be lost."[7] Now, we could replace "disruption of fuel supply" with
"cyberattack."

CHALLENGES FACING THE NEW ADMINISTRATION

SUPPLY CHAIN

Between the seed seller and the supermarket shopper lies a huge, complex, and volatile supply chain. Affected by everything from weather to the
monetary policies of foreign nations, not to mention fickle consumer trends,
it's among the most complex in the world.

Its components are vastly different in size and sophistication. They
range from multinational seed, fertilizer and machinery companies to small
crop farms—the number of which are going up in the United States.[8] They
include slaughterers, millers, fruit and vegetable shippers, and then whole-
salers, distributors, and retailers.

One thing that unites these disparate components is fierce competition in an economy that optimizes for the lowest possible cost.[9] Slim margins haunt many subsectors, especially in agricultural production.

This level of diversity and size combined with small budgets for overhead isn't the best recipe for robust cybersecurity, since it results in huge disparities among individual components. And as a result, the food and agriculture sector as a whole will be confronted with the same weakest-link problem familiar to sectors such as defense and retail.

DIGITIZED OPERATIONS

Agricultural and food production and operations already depend on a host of software and hardware applications vulnerable to cyberattacks. That'll only increase. Farmers are poised to reap the rewards of a development known as precision agriculture. Its promise is the tailored application of inputs for each precise location in a field, resulting in better yields and cost savings. Through satellite and drone imaging, location tracking, and data analytics, algorithms will assist farmers in spraying at each step just the right amount of fertilizer or pesticide.

Looking ahead, it's not unreasonable to expect smart farm machinery to handle many of the labor-intensive and repetitive jobs that still require manual work, even delicate tasks such as fruit harvesting.[10] Similarly, smarter and more robust automation will expand into food processing to a greater degree as machines become abler to cope with irregular sizes, shapes, and quality-control problems.

But this expanding array of operational data collected and made by high-tech equipment is increasing concerns that the sector will become a bigger target of hackers.

And the tendency to adopt technology without adequately considering security is common in the sector, too. A recent Farm Bureau survey of 3,380 farmers found more than half plan to invest in new data technologies that support precision agriculture. More than 87 percent were unaware or unsure of what to do if a company holding their farm data suffers a data breach. And only 4.7 percent of farmers said their data holder communicated a security breach plan.[11]

This new level of connectivity creates vulnerabilities besides data theft that the sector hasn't fully contended with, especially not in the operational environment. These vulnerabilities include distributed denial of service attacks, ransomware, and botnet infections. Some of these attacks may reach our sector randomly by dint of automatic probing for network weaknesses. However, intentional attacks virtually identical to those found in other sectors are occurring and can be expected to continue and grow. A DDoS attack could result in a significant disruption of delivery of food products.

INTELLECTUAL PROPERTY THEFT

Seed and chemical companies have long guarded their technology with patents and security measures. This concern has shown to be well placed. In 2011, the Office of the National Counterintelligence Executive warned that foreign spies were stealing agricultural technology, particularly data on genetic engineering, improved seeds, and fertilizer.[12] Law-enforcement officials recently said information related to organic insecticide, irrigation equipment, and rice were also targets.[13]

"Here in America's heartland, you are producing a valuable product that adversaries want. It is why they are, and will continue, targeting you," said John Carlin, who heads the Justice Department's National Security Division, during an April 2016 trip to Iowa.[14]

China figures prominently in the list of foreign nations trying to illegally get ahold of American food and agriculture know-how.

America's status as China's largest exporter of agricultural products is a fact fraught with discomfort for Beijing, which wants to boost domestic production despite limitations in arable land and water.[15] Yet its dependence on exporters like the United States is only poised to grow. A growing taste for protein will drive corn consumption in China up 41 percent by 2024, vastly outpacing domestic production, according to the Agriculture Department.[16]

The inevitable result has been Chinese espionage. Famously, a Chinese national with suspected government ties was caught leading a trade secrets theft conspiracy that included digging up genetically modified corn seeds from furrow rows.[17] The man, Mo Hailong, pled guilty in January 2016.[18]

Mo wasn't the first to be accused. Two Midwest-based agricultural scientists originally from China were charged in 2013 with trade secrets theft after they allegedly facilitated the pilfering of designer rice samples by a Chinese delegation.[19] Their trial is set for November 2016.

Both cases were espionage done the old-fashioned way. But it would be naive to assume that cyber espionage will not, as in other critical sectors, become a major element of commercial espionage. Major agricultural firms are already seeing indications of serious cyberattacks and the degree of activity may be underestimated due to the low levels of security and detection investment that has characterized the sector. Moreover, given the Chinese government's determination to improve domestic agriculture through technology, the outlook for cyber espionage in the sector is high and rising.

TERRORISM

"For the life of me, I cannot understand why the terrorists have not attacked our food supply because it is so easy to do," marveled then secretary of Health and Human Services Tommy Thompson, in 2004.[20]

We needn't exaggerate the prospect of agroterrorism or food-supply attacks to be concerned about them. Terrorists have traditionally favored large cities as starting points for sending out shockwaves into society. But terrorists are unpredictable, and attacks on less heavily defended targets have grown more common. The underdeveloped status of information security in the food and agricultural sector, especially when compared with other critical sectors, combined with the potential impact of an attack to undermine confidence in the food supply, suggests far greater unwanted attention will be devoted to this critical infrastructure sector.

Osama bin Laden argued for attacking the US economy as a way of destroying the nation's ability to project military power abroad.[21] The food and agriculture sector is a significant contributor to the economy, constituting more than 9 percent of total employment and $835 billion of gross domestic product.[22] A sophisticated terrorist attack could wreck America's status as a trusted food exporter and undermine domestic confidence in the food supply chain.

The sector's growing digitalization brings with it new opportunities for terrorists to attack places that previously have been too remote or too difficult to strike. Cyber terrorism is a relatively low-cost venture with a high payoff potential. Today's would-be cyber terrorists probably lack the technical savvy and organization to launch a significant cyberattack. However, sophisticated attack methods are becoming increasingly common as the attack community grows larger and shares information better. Attack methods termed "advanced persistent threats" that only a few years ago were exclusively the tools of nation-states and military contractors are now relatively common throughout the economy including less prominent sectors like retail and manufacturing.

It would be a mistake to assume that modern groups such as the Islamic State or their followers won't gain knowledge and act accordingly. Jihadi sympathizers make no secret of their desire to hack with lethal consequences.[23] Knowledge that terrorists have penetrated the food supply could by itself terrorize Americans into losing trust in the packaged products in the supermarket. It an open question whether there be enough raw materials available for substitution. Consider the damage to confidence in the food supply caused by recent outbreaks of salmonella. A deliberate contamination of even middling scale could have far worse consequences.

The risks of agroterrorism are too plausible and too large to ignore.

RECOMMENDATIONS

INCREASE AWARENESS

Neither branch of government gives food and agriculture cybersecurity the attention it demands. We're certainly not calling for Congress or the executive branch to enact new regulations. But executive branch agencies charged with interacting with the sector should recognize cybersecurity for the priority issue it is. At the very least, the FDA and USDA should start educational programs promoting good cybersecurity practices among sector industries.

While there are literally scores of congressional subcommittees that discuss cybersecurity, there is no subcommittee charged with food and agriculture cybersecurity oversight, or over communication technology's new dominant role in sector growth. We propose committees within the full Senate and the House agriculture committees be assigned this task.

DEFINE WHAT CONSTITUTES A NATION-STATE ATTACK AGAINST THE FOOD AND AGRICULTURE SECTOR

Physical attacks on the United States are an act of war. At what point does a cyberattack in the heartland similarly constitute an act of war—and what type of defense will the government offer our sector against such attacks? These aren't theoretical questions that can be indefinitely postponed. Answers are needed urgently, and they should advise the extent to which the government should subsidize cybersecurity in our sector.

Cyberspace has changed old definitions of what constitutes a national frontier; in cyberspace, a Kansas grain miller is just as exposed to foreign attack as any costal city. Providing for the common defense is the very first responsibility given to the federal government under the Constitution. Yet now, nearly two decades after the dawn of the Internet, we have still not properly defined what this role is in the cyber age despite widespread attacks on our companies and citizens by foreign powers, nor have we undated and adjusted our defense spending in light of this modern threat.

While a certain amount of ambiguity over exact lines may be necessary in international diplomacy, today's confusion encourages adversaries to be aggressive in their probing of the permissible. The next president should be aggressive in outlining the types of activities are unallowable in cyberspace and the strategy it will pursue for deterring and punishing those involved in perpetuating them.

INCENTIVES

As is the case with all sectors, increasing cybersecurity will cost money. In some sectors it may be comparatively easy to address the economics of cybersecurity, such as by building cost recovery into the rate base of a regulated industry. Finding the needed funding for cybersecurity in the agriculture and food industries may not be as simple.

This sector is governed by tight margins and faces a highly competitive world market. Americans spend record low amounts of their paycheck on food.[24] They don't allow for additional overhead spending. But federal involvement in correcting food and agriculture market failures goes back to the New Deal. There are myriad ways that the federal government can incentivize better cybersecurity. One of the roles for the congressional subcommittees suggested earlier should be to investigate and update this involvement and incentivize the security of the infrastructure the modern digitalized agriculture and food industry relies on.

Other actions should include loan forgiveness or grants tied to cyber-security practices measured against an objective benchmark such as the National Institute of Standards and Technology Cybersecurity Framework, or other frameworks. Benchmark testing of these frameworks within the sector could yield information about which standards practices and tech-nologies are cost effective, information that will drive private investment. For standards, practices, or technologies that are not cost effective, but may be deemed necessary for national security reasons, current incentive programs could be modified, or new ones implemented.

Obviously, the framework would need to be developed further as origi-nally envisioned by Executive Order 13636. Determining the framework's cost effectiveness was a fundamental part of that order and remains essen-tial to sustaining cybersecurity. The Internet Security Alliance has long pro-posed that usage of the framework be tested by private-sector volunteers in a program designed to produce objective results. The need for such a program is doubly urgent in our sector, where haphazard or blind spending on cybersecurity even with government incentives is unaffordable.

IMPROVE THE FOOD AND AGRICULTURE GOVERNMENT COORDINATING COUNCIL

The two government agencies designated as the sector-specific agencies lack the bandwidth and capability to be effective overseers of food and agriculture cybersecurity. Individually, the USDA and FDA are plagued by lack of cyber talent, poor morale and turnover when it comes to promoting private-sector cybersecurity. Collectively, the two agencies have failed to get into a cohesive unit, turning the combination of their efforts into less than the sum of its parts.

This state of affairs is partially a consequence of a notoriously frag-mented system of federal food safety oversight. But improving food and agriculture cybersecurity is too urgent a task to wait on a consolidation proposal that clears Congress. The sector has an opportunity to embrace cybersecurity before insecurity becomes entrenched and improving it becomes the tedious work of retrofitting a long tail of infrastructure.

Improving the two agencies will require greater willingness to fund cybersecurity efforts by the agencies themselves and the congressional appropriators who approve their budgets. Money can't cure poor morale, but can alleviate it and reveal the nonmonetary sources of ineffectiveness.

The next administration and Congress alike should ensure cybersecurity is a higher priority at the USDA and FDA and take measures to ensure they cultivate a staff of cybersecurity experts with knowledge of the sector.

ENHANCE INFORMATION SHARING

Cybersecurity information sharing within the sector lacks a center. There are plenty of data exchanges dedicated to various threats, such as food-borne illnesses or crop diseases. Cyber threats get lost.

Past attempts to stand up a federally recognized Information Sharing and Analysis Center to be that center, collapsed, partially because DHS favors the "all hazards" approach to information sharing among ISACs.[25] That is, the department is prone to seeing cybersecurity as just one element of threat data. Combined with the often poor quality of data emanating from DHS, that turned the ISAC into yet another redundant online portal.

What we propose here isn't a retread of the past but a dedicated cyberthreat information-sharing mechanism designed for chief information security officers at large corporations, industry associations, and agricultural cooperatives. For smaller, individual enterprises, this mechanism should provide the option of automated updates to threat-protection software. Automated threat updating is a well-established Homeland Security goal that has made some strides, but not enough.

---

1 "Although its population has more than doubled in the last six decades, the United States now uses about 25 percent less farmland than it did in 1950," Sun Ling Wang, Paul Heisey, David Schimmelpfennig, and Eldon Ball. Agricultural Productivity Growth in the United States: Measurement, Trends, and Drivers, ERR-189, US Department of Agriculture, Economic Research Service, July 2015.

2 Intelligence Community Assessment—Global Food Security, ICA 2015-04, Sept. 22, 2015, p. 13.

3 Tom Vilsack, "Remarks as Delivered by Secretary Vilsack and Panelists at 2015 Agricultural Outlook Forum Plenary Panel on Innovation, Biotechnology and Big Data," 2015 Agricultural Outlook Forum Plenary Panel on Innovation, Biotechnology and Big Data, Webcast, Washington, DC, Feb. 19, 2015, United States Department of Agriculture, panel discussion, Web.

4 Jacob Bunge, "Agriculture Giants Boost Cybersecurity to Shield Farm Data," *The Wall Street Journal*, Feb. 19, 2015, Web, Apr. 26, 2016.

5 Sheryl K. Maddux, Faye J. Feldstein, Todd M. Keil, and Clay Detlefsen, *Food and Agriculture Sector-Specific Plan: An Annex to the National Infrastructure Protection Plan 2010* (US Departments of Agriculture, Homeland Security, and the Food and Drug Administration, 2010), p. 13, Web.

6 LeeAnne Jackson, Josh Bornstein, Clay Detlefsen, Randy Gordon, and Caitlin Durkovich, *Food and Agriculture Sector-Specific Plan 2015* (United States. Departments of Agriculture, Homeland Security and the Food and Drug Administration, 2015), Web.

7 Loretta Schwartz-Nobel, *Starving in the Shadow of Plenty* (Lincoln: iUniverse.com, Inc., 2001).

8 James M. MacDonald, Penni Korb, and Robert A. Hoppe, *Farm Size and the Organization of U.S. Crop Farming*, ERR-152 (US Department of Agriculture, Economic Research Service, Aug. 2013).

9 John T. Hoffman, Andrew Huff, and National Center for Food Protection and Defense, *NCFPD Response to the NIST RFI for: Developing a Framework to Improve Critical Infrastructure Cybersecurity* (National Center for Food Protection and Defense, Mar. 10, 2013), Web.

10 Eugene Izhikevich, "Robots That Learn Will Shape the Future of Robotics Eugene Izhikevich of Brain Corporation Explains Why Programming Robots Is a Key Barrier to Their Success and Forecasts How Brain-inspired Learning Will Change the Game," interview by Vinod Baya and Bo Parker, *Technology Forecast: Future of Robots* (PWC, 2015), 3, Web.

11 Will Rodger and Kari Barbic, "American Farm Bureau Survey Shows Big Data Use Increasing, Big Questions Remain," *The Voice of Agriculture*, American Farm Bureau Federation, Oct. 21, 2014, Web.

12 Office of the National Counterintelligence Executive, *Foreign Spies Stealing US Economic Secrets in Cyberspace*, Report to Congress on Foreign Economic Collection and Industrial Espionage, 2009–2011 (Washington, DC, Oct. 2011), p. 9, Web.

13 Julia Edwards, "In Iowa Corn Fields, Chinese National's Seed Theft Exposes Vulnerability," Reuters, Apr. 11, 2016, Web, May 10, 2016.

14 Laurie Bedord, "Midwest Agriculture Is a Prime Target for Theft of Intellectual Property and Cyberattacks," *Agriculture.com*, Successful Farming, Apr. 5, 2016, Web.

15 Fred Gale, James Hansen, and Michael Jewison, *China's Growing Demand for Agricultural Imports*, EIB-136 (US Department of Agriculture, Economic Research Service, Feb. 2014).

16 Fred Gale, James Hansen, and Michael Jewison, *Prospects for China's Corn Yield Growth and Imports*, FDS-14D-01 (US Department of Agriculture, Economic Research Service, Apr. 2014).

17 Ted Genoways, "Corn Wars the Farm-by-farm Fight between China and the United States to Dominate the Global Food Supply," *New Republic*, Aug. 16, 2015, Web.

18 Jacob Bunge, "Chinese Citizen Pleads Guilty to Stealing High-Tech Seeds from U.S. Fields," *The Wall Street Journal*, Jan. 27, 2016, Web.

19 John Eligon and Patrick Zuo, "Designer Seed Thought to Be Latest Target by Chinese," *New York Times*, Feb. 4, 2014, Web.

20 Robert Pear, "U.S. Health Chief, Stepping Down, Issues Warning," *New York Times*, Dec. 4, 2004, Web.

21 Dean Olsen, "Agroterrorism: Threats to America's Economy and Food Supply," *FBI Law Enforcement Bulletin*, The Federal Bureau of Investigation, Feb. 2012, Web.

22 Lawrence Glaser and Rosanna Mentzer Morrison, *Ag and Food Sectors and the Economy* (US Department of Agriculture, Economic Research Service, Feb. 17, 2016), Web.

23 Joseph Marks, "ISIL Aims to Launch Cyberattacks on U.S." *Politico Pro Cybersecurity*, Dec. 29, 2015, Web.

24 Eliza Barclay, "Your Grandparents Spent More of Their Money on Food than You Do," *Food for Thought*, NPR, Mar. 2, 2015, Web.

25 Joseph Straw, "Food Sector Abandons Its ISAC," *Security Management*, ASIS International, Inc., Sept. 1, 2008, Web, May 10, 2016.

Section III

Crosscutting Issues in Cybersecurity

Twelve

The Evolving Role of Boards in Cyber-Risk Oversight

Ken Daly, CEO, National Association of Corporate Directors

Larry Clinton, President and CEO, Internet Security Alliance

O ne of the core roles of a board of directors in any organization is to oversee risk. This oversight has always encompassed physical assets, human capital, and the like. Over the last two decades, the nature of enterprise asset value has shifted away from the physical into the digital sphere. In the private sector up to 80 percent of total value of the Fortune 500 now consists of intellectual property and other intangibles.[1]

Along with the digitalization of enterprise assets comes a corresponding digitalization of enterprise risk. The explosion of cyberattacks now exposes organizations of every size, industry, and sector to threats such as loss of intellectual property, sensitive employee or customer information, purloined operating algorithms, data destruction, or alteration and potential disruption to critical infrastructure. Once realized, those threats result including loss of public confidence, harm to reputation, potential legal and regulatory sanctions, and even loss of ability to continue operations.

Oversight versus Management

Boards of directors are mysterious entities to many observers. As the National Association of Corporate Directors explains, outside of a set of defined board-level responsibilities such as CEO selection, evaluation and compensation, "The role of the directors is [primarily] advisory in nature, with specific day-to-day management functions and decision making delegated to the full-time officers and executive employees of the company." In other words, directors hold management accountable for the operation of the business in pursuit of the agreed-upon strategy and goals, but they are not themselves involved at an operational level. In publicly traded companies, this separation between the activities of the board and management is not just semantic: It is necessary if directors are to retain their independence as defined by—and required by—the stock listing exchanges, NYSE and NASDAQ. In cyber risk terms, this means that the company's executives, business and functional leaders, and employees are responsible for identifying, prioritizing, and managing cyber risks, while the board monitors execution through regular reviews and discussions with senior management.

Sidebar 12.1

In 2014, the National Association of Corporate Directors, in conjunction with AIG and the Internet Security Alliance, published the *NACD Director's Handbook on Cyber-Risk Oversight.* The handbook was unique in that it shifted focus away from the operational information technology issues that had traditionally dominated cybersecurity discussions and instead placed cyber risk in the strategic context that directors were most familiar with—including mergers and acquisitions, new product and service launches, strategic partnerships, and so on (see sidebar 12.1 for a discussion about board duties).

The handbook identified five principles all boards of directors ought to consider as the cyber-threat landscape continues to evolve. The first three of these principles focus on actions boards can take to improve their oversight capabilities. The final two principles address ways directors can challenge and test the adequacy of management's activities. While some of the handbook's content is aimed at corporate boards of directors (whether publicly listed or privately owned), the majority of its guidance is applicable to boards of not-for-profit organizations as well. This was intentional, because every organization is subject to cyber threats—and indeed, nonprofits, with their very valuable donor and member lists and potentially fewer staff resources to combat cyberattacks, may be especially vulnerable. The five principles are as follows:

1. Directors should approach cybersecurity as not just an IT issue but instead as an enterprise-wide risk issue.
2. Directors must understand the legal and liability implications of cyber risk as they apply to the company's specific situation.
3. Boards should have adequate access to cybersecurity expertise, and discussions about cyber-risk management should be given regular and adequate time on the board meeting agenda.
4. Directors should demand that management establish an enterprise-wide cyber-risk-management framework.
5. Board-management discussion of cyber risks should include which cyber risks to avoid, which to accept, which to mitigate, and which to transfer through insurance and specific plans associated with each approach.[2]

In the 2016 edition of its *Global State of Information Security Survey*, PricewaterhouseCoopers credited the handbook, by name, with contributing to significant improvements in how corporations were understanding, managing, and overseeing cyber risk. PwC reported that

guidelines from the National Association for Corporate Directors advise that Boards should view cyber risks from an enterprise-wide standpoint and understand the potential legal impacts. They should discuss cybersecurity risks and preparedness with management, and consider cyber threats in the context of the organization's over-all tolerance for risk.

Boards appear to be listening to this guidance. This year we saw a double-digit uptick in Board participation in most aspects of in-formation security. Respondents said this deepening Board involve-ment has helped improve cybersecurity practices in numerous ways. It may be no coincidence that, as more Boards participate in cyberse-curity budget discussions, we saw a 24% boost in security spending.

Other notable outcomes cited by survey respondents include identification of key risks, fostering an organizational culture of se-curity and better alignment of cybersecurity with overall risk man-agement and business goals. Perhaps more than anything, however, Board participation has opened the lines of communication be-tween the cybersecurity function and top executives and directors.[3]

As impressive as these early efforts have been, the director community—along with key stakeholders including regulators, lawmakers, investors, and the public—is seeking continuous improvement on board-level oversight of cyber risks. Three activities are essential:

- Understanding the specific cyber threats that are most material to the organization.
- Establishing board processes that support high-quality dialogue on cyber matters.
- Maintaining access to current information and expertise about cy-ber risks.[4]

UNDERSTANDING THE SPECIFIC CYBER THREATS THAT ARE MOST MATERIAL TO THE ORGANIZATION

Technology underpins nearly every aspect of a company's internal and external operations. As the handbook emphasizes, members of management and the board of directors must treat cybersecurity as an enterprise-wide risk issue, not a "technology issue" that can be relegated to an IT department. Organizations should establish a cross-departmental cyber-risk team with representation from business unit leaders, legal, internal audit and compliance departments, finance, and human resources, in addition to IT.[5]

The implications for boards of directors are twofold. First, directors should ask members of management to translate "cyber risks" into business and strategy risks, and assess them in the context of the company's overall risk appetite. Aspects of those risks will likely be very different among consumer retailers, biotech companies, traditional manufacturers, high-tech startups, utilities, law firms, and banks. Second, boards need to set the expectation with management that success is defined by how quickly the organization can detect—and respond to—cyberattacks and data breaches. When it comes to cyber threats, protection is essential, but total prevention is unrealistic.

Cybersecurity is a new breed of risk. Crisis response planning for major disruptive events such as natural disasters has long been a routine management activity (and oversight of those activities an important responsibility for directors). But cyberattacks have a number of unique characteristics that mean traditional contingency planning approaches may not apply. These include the following:

- The legal environment with respect to cybersecurity is extremely uncoordinated and in many cases nonexistent, especially at the international level. Some activities and cyber content that is outlawed in the United States are not necessarily illegal in other parts of the world. On the other hand, constitutionally protected speech here is in fact illegal in other parts of the world. This uncertain and at times conflicting legal environment substantially undermines the deterrent and investigative aspects of tracking criminal cyber behavior.
- The number and sophistication of cyber-law-enforcement agents and resources are miniscule in comparison to the extent of the

cyber threat. On a worldwide basis, analysts estimate that less than 2 percent of cyber criminals are successfully prosecuted.

- Many criminal enterprises in the cyber realm are actually supported by nation-states.
- Technology systems are now highly interconnected: every organization has myriad links to its suppliers, customers, partners, contractors, third-party vendors, and others. Some of these connections occur through "smart products" that open doors to the Internet without corresponding protection. Cyberattackers routinely target weaker links in a company's cyber ecosystem to successfully compromise even the best and most sophisticated enterprises. This means that companies literally cannot protect themselves—they must look beyond their own "borders" to assess others' defenses and develop coordinated approaches where needed.

ESTABLISHING BOARD PROCESSES THAT SUPPORT HIGH-QUALITY DIALOGUE ON CYBER MATTERS

The *Report of the NACD Blue Ribbon Commission on Risk Governance: Balancing Risk and Reward* recommended that risk oversight ought to be part of the duties of the full board.[6] However, boards take a variety of approaches to assigning specific risk oversight activities. For example, according to recent NACD survey findings, close to 44 percent of public company boards assign significant responsibility for risk oversight to the audit committee.[7] With respect to cyber-risk oversight, the handbook advises "Since cyber risks and threats can change quickly, committees with designated responsibility for risk oversight—and for oversight of cyber-related risks in particular—should receive briefings [from management] on at least a quarterly basis. The full board should be briefed at least semi-annually, or as situations warrant."[8] The allocation of cyber-risk oversight responsibilities should be clearly outlined in the board's governance guidelines and committee charters to avoid either duplication of activities or gaps in oversight.

Directors need to be clear in communications with management about their expectations regarding the scope, frequency, and format of cybersecurity-related information that is provided to the full board and key committees. Management should ensure that such information is presented in business terms and is free from jargon or complex "tech speak." And as noted earlier, board-level cybersecurity discussions should extend well beyond risk-related reports from the chief information officer, chief information security officer, or CEO. Cyber issues must be included in boardroom discussions about transactions, new market entry, new product development, legal and regulatory compliance, major joint-venture and partnership opportunities, and significant capital projects.

MAINTAINING ACCESS TO CURRENT INFORMATION AND EXPERTISE ABOUT CYBER RISKS

Directors do not need to be cyber experts to play an effective role in cyber-risk oversight. Like other significant business risks, cyber-risk oversight requires a thorough understanding of the company's business model, experience in strategy and leadership, sound business judgment, and the ability to constructively challenge management. In other words, the fundamental elements of high-quality board leadership.

Depending on their industry circumstances and threat profile (among other things), some organizations will choose to include a board member with specific cyber-related experience, and others will not. As the handbook notes, "Nominating and governance committees must balance many factors in filling board vacancies, including the need for industry expertise, financial knowledge, global experience, or other desired skill sets," as part of their role in maintaining a board composition that is appropriately diverse in terms of skills, backgrounds, and perspectives to suit the organization's current and future strategic needs.[9]

All boards can and should take steps to bring cutting-edge cyber expertise into boardroom discussions, by requesting briefings on a regular basis from independent advisors such as external audit firms and outside counsel, third-party consultants, or law enforcement. This information should be viewed as complementary to—not a replacement for or a signal of mistrust in—reports from management. In addition, directors seeking to stay informed and enhance their understanding about current and emerging cyber issues can take advantage of a wide range of board-focused educational programs offered by a number of providers, including NACD, and are doing so in ever-greater numbers.

Some commentators have raised the question of whether a third-party assurance model, similar to independent audits of financial reports, could be applied in the cybersecurity arena. At NACD and ISA's most recent Cyber Summit, held in Chicago in June 2016, participants noted that audits were by definition historical in nature, whereas cybersecurity assessments must include a forward-looking component. In addition, the notion that an organization's cybersecurity profile could be graded in "pass-fail" terms, similar to an auditor's opinion on financial reports, may be inappropriate because it could imply that there is a state of adequate security that an enterprise might reach. A new assurance model, one that is not exclusively backward-looking in nature, would need to be developed for use in the cybersecurity arena. Chapter 13 in this volume addresses this issue in more depth.

COORDINATION WITH GOVERNMENT
Individually and together, NACD and ISA have conducted a large number of roundtable dialogues with directors, senior executives, and leaders from government and law enforcement. Several themes have emerged from these discussions.

ONE-SIZE-FITS-ALL MANDATES FOR BOARD-LEVEL CYBER OVERSIGHT ARE NOT HELPFUL
In 2008, NACD, the Council of Institutional Investors, and the Business Roundtable developed a set of Key Agreed Principles for corporate governance "intended to assist boards and shareholders [in avoiding] rote 'box ticking' in favor of a more thoughtful and studied approach." They included the notion that (presuming compliance with all applicable legal, regulatory and exchange listing requirements) individual boards hold responsibility for designing the structures and practices that will allow them to fulfill their fiduciary obligations effectively and efficiently, and they are obligated to communicate those structures and practices to stakeholders in a transparent manner.[10]

Proposals aimed at requiring all boards to have a director who is a "cy-bersecurity expert"—even setting aside the fact that the severe shortage of senior-level cybersecurity talent, with hundreds of thousands of positions vacant in the United States alone, making such proposals impossible to implement—would take the important responsibility for board composition and director recruitment out of the hands of the only group with firsthand knowledge about a specific board's current and future skill requirements.[11] The *Key Agreed Principles* publication goes on to say, "valuing disclosure over rigid adoption of any set of [so-called] best practices encourages boards to experiment and develop approaches that address their own par-ticular needs."[12]

INFORMATION SHARING BETWEEN THE PUBLIC AND PRIVATE SECTORS IS HIGHLY BENEFICIAL

Directors and senior executives alike are interested in gaining a clearer understanding of what government agencies such as the departments of Homeland Security and Justice, the FBI, and the Secret Service do—and what they don't do—for companies in the cyber-risk arena, both in gen-eral and in the aftermath of a specific breach or attack. Because relation-ships with government and law enforcement are in management's domain, NACD has encouraged directors to ask the CIO, CISO, CEO, and other executives to provide the board with updates about those relationships and corresponding public sector–private sector communication activities related to cybersecurity. Expanding safe-harbor provisions related to infor-mation sharing is also important.

IDENTIFY OPPORTUNITIES TO COORDINATE AND STREAMLINE REGULATORY REQUIREMENTS

Current cyber regulations differ and in some cases contradict one another on multiple dimensions: from state to state, state versus federal, and do-mestic versus foreign jurisdictions, to name just a few. Industry-specific re-quirements add another layer of complexity. The associated cost burden is significant, especially for emerging-growth companies. More uniformity would enable management teams and boards to provide better information more efficiently. Another point of difficulty is that companies and boards are frequently faced with conflicting demands after a cyber breach: on the one hand, demand for prompt disclosure to satisfy requirements from the Securities and Exchange Commission and regulators for investor and consumer protection, and on the other hand, requests from law enforcement to refrain from going public in order to help an active investigation.

CONCLUSION

It has become an unfortunate truism that there are only two types of organizations: those that have been hacked and those that don't yet know they have been hacked. In such an environment, it is unrealistic to expect that any board of directors, or any management team, can prevent cyberattacks. Board members can and should play an active role in ensuring that their companies' cybersecurity processes, policies, and practices stay fit-for-purpose as the nature of the threat continues to evolve. This requires directors to stay informed about cyber risks, integrate cyber issues into a wide range of boardroom discussions, set clear expectations with management, and ask tough questions when necessary. The director community is rising to that challenge.

FOR FURTHER READING

NACD Director's Handbook on Cyber-Risk Oversight
NACD Advisory Council Brief: Emerging Trends in Cyber-Risk Oversight
NACD Advisory Council Brief: Cybersecurity, Internal Audit, and the Audit Committee
All publications are available for public download with free registration at NACD's Board Insights Portal

---

1 Tomo Ocean, "Intangible Asset Market Value," *OceanTomo.com*, Apr. 2011, Web, Jan. 14, 2014.

2 *NACD Director's Handbook on Cyber-Risk Oversight* (Washington, DC: NACD, 2014), p. 4.

3 PricewaterhouseCoopers (PWC), Turnaround and Transformation in Cybersecurity: Key Findings from the Global State of Information Security Survey 2016 (PWC, 2015), Web.

4 Adapted from Robyn Bew, "Cyber-Risk Oversight: Three Questions for Directors," *Ethical Boardroom*, Spring 2015.

5 *NACD Director's Handbook on Cyber-Risk Oversight*, p. 13.

6 *Report of the NACD Blue Ribbon Commission on Risk Governance: Balancing Risk and Reward* (Washington, DC: NACD, 2009).

7 *NACD 2015–2016 Public Company Governance Survey* (Washington, DC: NACD, 2015), p. 36.

8 *NACD Director's Handbook on Cyber-Risk Oversight*, p. 8.

9 Ibid, p. 11.

10 *Key Agreed Principles to Strengthen Corporate Governance for U.S. Publicly-Traded Companies* (Washington, DC: NACD, 2008 and 2011), pp. 1, 4, 5.

11 "Close the Talent Gap, Secure the Future," *MIT Technology Review*, May 23, 2016.

12 *Key Agreed Principles to Strengthen Corporate Governance for U.S. Publicly-Traded Companies*, p. 5.

Thirteen

Cybersecurity Assurance: A Comprehensive Approach

Center for Audit Quality

INTRODUCTION

The Center for Audit Quality's members are audit and consulting firms that perform financial-statement audits of public companies.[1] Because these firms provide a wide range of audit and consulting services across all industry sectors, they have the opportunity to observe cyber readiness in a variety of situations. Our contribution to *The Cybersecurity Social Contract* is focused on the observations and experience of our member firms with the current state of implementation of cybersecurity defenses, detection, and remediation by public companies. Accordingly, our observations in this chapter span many industry sectors. From that broad perspective, we have summarized a number of key observations with the current state of response by the public company community to cyber risks. Drawing from this breadth of observations to address cyber risks, we also describe our thoughts on a more comprehensive approach to assess and provide assurance over internal controls related to cybersecurity risk management. Work is currently being undertaken by the American Institute of CPAs and the CAQ to operationalize this new approach. We believe this new approach could be utilized by all industry sectors as companies continue to address the multiple threats from an interconnected cyber world.

KEY CONSIDERATIONS FROM THE AUDITOR'S VANTAGE POINT

In this section, we identify a number of key considerations with respect to the threats and responses by the corporate community to the evolving cybersecurity landscape. These considerations are based on our member-firm observations and feedback over time.

CYBERSECURITY IS FINALLY BECOMING ACCEPTED AS AN ENTERPRISE-WIDE RISK-MANAGEMENT ISSUE

Initially, all things "cyber" were relegated to the information technology department in most companies. Today, the trend has shifted and the C-suite and boards of directors are increasingly taking ownership of cyber risk. Breaches and hacks continue to generate attention-grabbing headlines and efforts by information technology personnel to protect, detect, respond to, mitigate, and recover from, on a timely basis, cybersecurity events. Senior management with oversight of the boards is taking on more of the unenviable job of developing a comprehensive cybersecurity internal control structure that is responsive to the identified and the evolving risk environment of cybersecurity. The expanded recognition by senior management and boards of their role with respect to this topic is a positive trend.

While There Continues to Be Considerable Discussion of What Management and Board Responsibilities Are Related to Cybersecurity and Corporate Cyber Readiness, Many Organizations Are Still Working to Find the Most Comprehensive Structure

Just a few short years ago, there were limited resources for management and boards to use as they approached designing a framework for risk identification, response, control design and implementation, assessment, and remediation. Now, there are a few leading frameworks but numerous standards, methodologies, and processes that have been put forth by federal and state governments, industry-specific groups, independent agencies, and other stakeholders. We applaud the efforts of each of these groups to provide a "common language" for management and boards to use when developing an enterprise-wide risk-management approach to cybersecurity. However, the vast number of players in this space dilutes the "common language" approach. We believe the options available to better manage cyber risks would benefit greatly from enhanced consistency across these myriad approaches.

Varying Legal and Regulatory Approaches also Impact the Ability of Companies to Have a Consistent Approach to Cybersecurity Risk Management and Response

The financial services industry, for example, operates under a regulatory regime that consistently monitors data privacy and protection, among other things. Other industries may not have the same level of monitoring. While we recognize that the level of oversight for certain industries should vary, the inconsistent approach to cybersecurity risk management and monitoring does not serve our interconnected marketplace well.

All Public Companies Are Required to Adequately Disclose a Variety of Business Risks to Shareholders, and Disclosures Related to Cybersecurity Can Pose Challenges

Disclosures around cyber risks are particularly complex to assess and to explain. For instance, it may be difficult for a shareholder to understand that even companies with strong cyber controls can experience a breach and not be able to detect it for several months. In addition, risk disclosures can themselves become a roadmap for bad actors who continue to demonstrate the ability to adapt to new system protections with amazing speed. We know that many cyber "incidents" do not represent an actual breach and that even some breaches have not resulted in the loss of data. However, a general lack of understanding of these concepts can make almost any disclosure seem far worse when reported without a proper context.

Regulatory and Law Enforcement Response to Cyber Incidents Is Uneven

While much of the existing regulatory activity has been directed at notification to potentially impacted stakeholders when there has been a cyber incident, often these disclosures add to the confusion and damage already realized—and may provide little improvement to forestall future events. Also adding to the confusion is the role of law enforcement and sequencing of notifying authorities and disclosing the breach to stakeholders.

The Marketplace for Cybersecurity Risk Management Tools Is Equally Splintered

Some products focus on hacker detection or development of incident response plans, while others provide a rating on an organization's cybersecurity maturity. While each of these tools focuses on important pieces of a risk-management strategy, there is no consistent way for companies to gain an independent assessment of their cybersecurity risk-management program and internal controls for a particular high-risk area, or entity-wide. In an environment where cybersecurity is not only a business issue but also a national security issue, we believe that such an independent comprehensive assessment would help management and boards take a more proactive approach to their cybersecurity risk oversight.

Any Organization That Transacts Business Today Is Susceptible to a Breach

Just a few years ago, most observers would not have made this bold statement. Thankfully, knowledgeable followers of the evolution of cyber threats have realized that total and absolute prevention from cyber intrusions is not a realistic goal. While this realization has not caused a shift away from protection of IT systems, it has significantly elevated the focus on timely detection and remediation and resiliency from cyber intrusions, which are positive developments.

Cybersecurity Threats Emerge from a Diverse and Growing Number of Sources

Some threat actors seek to steal data from companies and businesses that can quickly be criminally converted for financial gain. Companies also face the ideological nonstate actor and nation-state-affiliated attacks motivated by economic espionage or geopolitical objectives (or both). In addition, technology continues to evolve at a torrid pace, with the increasingly pervasive adoption of digitization and connectivity affecting the confidentiality, integrity, and availability of data and systems at almost all organizations. As companies have hardened their security defenses, adversaries have shifted to new tactics and targets, requiring companies to continuously evolve their cybersecurity-risk-management programs.

Threats Emanating from Internal Sources, Including Employees, Have Been and Continue to Be a Significant Challenge

Disgruntled employees are too often a source of compromised security access features. Even in companies with the best of intentions, unintentional lapses by employees using basic passwords, succumbing to phishing e-mails and other seemingly genuine correspondence have been found at the bottom of many significant breaches. These types of internal threats heighten the need for better internal controls, training and monitoring of compliance within an organizations own system.

The Impacts from Cyber Incidents Are Also Varied

Just as we have seen numerous sources of cybersecurity threats, there are also numerous ways that a cybersecurity threat can impact a company's operations, data, and reputation. These include events that

- result in unauthorized access to or acquisition of personally identifiable information of customers, employees, or other individuals;
- disrupt or compromise business operations (e.g., shut down of websites or e-mail systems);
- affect the integrity of key data, such as financial information and health records; and
- result in a major impact at the operational level and/or have a physical impact that creates safety issues. Such an event could, in the worst scenarios, lead to significant personal injuries, even loss of life.

As can be predicted from the list above, the nature of the cybersecurity event will impact the type of financial, legal, and regulatory exposure faced in the wake of that event. The consequences for stakeholders are also numerous and varied. For investors, they can include loss of business or public trust that can reduce the value of their investment. Customers and business partners may face denial of access to products and services because of an attack or have to grapple with disclosure of their confidential information. There can be little doubt that cyber risk presents a very broad range of implications and potential for negative outcomes. Accordingly, we believe that comprehensive, risk-based and enterprise-wide risk frameworks and validation are needed to more appropriately address this broad range of exposure.

DEVELOPING A MORE COMPREHENSIVE APPROACH

As we accumulated information about the challenges of dealing with cybersecurity risks from across the corporate community, we began to focus on possible additional audit efforts that would have the ability to be applied across all industry sectors. From the above summary of observations, we see a need for organizations to conduct ongoing, strategic, targeted and enterprise-wide assessments of their cyber risk and the adequacy of their programs and internal controls to address those risks. In other words, many of the actions being taken today are often reactive, piecemeal, or represent a "drill-down" on specific identified items within a broader risk profile. A comprehensive approach that is risk based and driven from the internal control structure of the company and that can be delivered with independence and objectivity offers a new approach for management and boards to bring to bear on cybersecurity risk.

To respond to the observations and challenges identified above, the American Institute of CPAs has begun the development of a new and comprehensive process to examine internal controls related specifically to cybersecurity risk management. This cybersecurity examination would be separate and apart from the existing financial-statement audit process. It could be performed by the external auditor or another audit firm. The existing financial-statement audit process and related internal control assessment do not extend to those controls specifically related to the cybersecurity procedures and controls of a company unless they impact the financial statements.[2]

To increase the confidence in the information companies communicate about the adequacy of their cybersecurity programs, boards and senior management request reports on the effectiveness of their programs from independent third-party assessors, including accounting firms. We believe this private-sector development is a positive one. It is important that information in these reports be presented in a consistent manner from company to company and year to year so that comparisons can be made, and the information is credible: that the stakeholders trust and have confidence in the reported information.

The objective of a cybersecurity report would be to provide the user with three key pieces of information about the entity's cybersecurity risk-management program: (1) a description of the entity's cybersecurity risk-management program, (2) management's assertion about whether that description is fairly presented and whether the controls are suitably designed and operating effectively, and (3) the practitioner opinion on fair presentation of the description and on the suitability of design and operating effectiveness of controls. These three elements taken together could greatly enhance the confidence that a user can place on the cybersecurity information provided by management.

The examination that the AICPA is contemplating would be entirely voluntary on the part of companies and audit firms. The criteria that are being developed are a customized version of the AICPA Trust Services Criteria that have been enhanced for cybersecurity considerations and closely aligned with the seventeen principles in the Internal Control-Integrated Framework, an internal control framework issued in 2013 by the Committee of Sponsoring Organizations of the Treadway Commission, known as COSO. The criteria will be mapped to the existing National Institute of Standards and Technology Cybersecurity Framework and the International Organization for Standardization Information Security Management standard (ISO/IEC 27001). In this way, companies can choose from among multiple cybersecurity internal control frameworks for their cybersecurity risk-management programs and not be required to move to different standards to avail themselves of an independent and objective assessment of their cybersecurity internal control environment. However, reports issued under this new approach would benefit from the consistency, rigor, independence, and objectivity of the practitioners. These new services would constitute an examination under the attestation standards of the audit profession and would not be a consulting type service.

THE AUDIT PROFESSION: A STRONG FOUNDATION TO BUILD ON

One of the cornerstones of such a new approach would be the application of the core elements of services from an independent auditor—independence and objectivity. An independent examination of a company's cybersecurity risk-management program, related to a specific risk area or enterprise-wide, would offer advantages in terms of identifying weaknesses and, by spotlighting the organization's cybersecurity strengths, enhance confidence in management's description of its security and protections against various cyber risks. This assurance could be valuable for investors, customers, business partners, regulators, and other stakeholders with an interest in the organization's cybersecurity and in the reliability of its efforts to secure sensitive information.

The audit profession has extensive experience providing independent, objective assessments. The most common example of an objective evaluation is the auditor's opinions on the audits of financial statements and internal control over financial reporting (ICFR). The Sarbanes-Oxley Act of 2002 added a requirement, applicable to most public companies, that management annually assess the effectiveness of the company's ICFR and report the results to the public. In addition, Sarbanes-Oxley requires most large public companies to engage their independent auditor to audit the effectiveness of the company's ICFR.

The audit profession, through performing ICFR audits, has further honed existing expertise in evaluating the design and implementation of internal controls. As part of the ICFR audit, auditors look at a flow of transactions and ask, "What could go wrong?" They critically assess whether management has a control in place that is sufficiently designed to timely prevent or detect a potential material misstatement. The auditor then tests those controls to determine whether they operate effectively to address the assessed risk of misstatement. For some flows of transactions, there may be more than one control that addresses the risk of material misstatement, or there could be one control that addresses a risk in several flows of transactions. The auditor exercises judgment in determining which controls to test.[3]

The auditor also has experience in performing independent, objective assessments of an entity's privacy and security practices through other attest engagements that are already trusted in the capital markets. The audit profession brings a multidisciplinary skill set and approach to these engagements, involving subject-matter expertise in cybersecurity and information technology. The proposed service would be an extension of this existing knowledge and experience.

A first step toward recognition of the importance of addressing cybersecurity controls within an organization's internal control framework has already been taken. In 2013, COSO, an initiative of accounting-related organizations with an interest in effective internal control, replaced its 1992 framework with an updated framework to assist companies in structuring and evaluating controls that address a broad range of risks. That new framework was expanded to better address operational controls beyond financial-statement preparation. Those expanded operational areas addressed for the first time internal controls related to cybersecurity. In 2015, COSO also released *COSO in the Cyber Age*, which outlines considerations for performing a COSO-focused cyber-risk assessment.[4]

While the expansion of the internal control areas addressed in the COSO framework now include reference to operational areas such as cybersecurity, assessment of internal controls in these areas are not required for public companies. As indicated earlier in this chapter, the proposed new approach of a comprehensive examination and report on a company's internal controls for cyber that the AICPA is developing would not be a required service.

In developing this new approach to perform a comprehensive assessment of cybersecurity internal controls for a specific risk or enterprise-wide, the AICPA is drawing upon the fundamental principles and standards of performance that have defined the auditing profession for over 125 years:

- Auditor attestation services involve an independent and objective evaluation of controls or information that is the responsibility of another party, and provide a level of assurance on those controls or information. Attestation services can provide management, or the board or audit committee, or others an unbiased measure of confidence in the reliability of those controls or information.
- The professional requirements for an attest service require a rigorous, methodical, and consistent approach to fieldwork and reporting. In addition to other requirements, the auditor must adequately plan the work and properly supervise any assistants. She or he must also obtain sufficient evidence to provide a reasonable basis for the conclusion that is expressed in the report and prepare and maintain attest documentation.
- An auditor must have adequate technical training to perform the attest engagement.
- Audit personnel must have adequate knowledge of the subject matter.
- The auditor must have reason to believe that the subject matter is capable of evaluation against criteria that are suitable and available to users. In this regard, the new approach being developed is intended to be neutral with respect to any particular set of existing cybersecurity frameworks.
- The auditor must also exercise due professional care in the planning and performance of the engagement and the preparation of the report.
- The auditor or practitioner performing the attest engagement must comply with an established professional code of conduct.

Attestation services applied to the cybersecurity environment can also provide a level of consistency in application given the common standards used when performing an attestation service, and consistency allows for measurement, comparability, and creates accountability. Such an assessment would assist management, boards, and other users in objectively assessing a company's cybersecurity risk-management program for a specific risk area or entity-wide. These services would not prevent a cybersecurity threat or breach—nor are they intended to do so. These services could demonstrate a proactive and consistent approach by management and boards to protect information and data and increase consumer confidence.

Today, companies are bombarded with advice and services to help address the risks of cybersecurity. While the information is helpful, it does not provide a common framework for companies to use to address enterprise-wide cybersecurity risk management, or allow for a common approach or professional standard for providing security assessment services related to a company's cybersecurity posture. While each audit firm or professional in public practice currently can craft individual strategies for providing attestation services related to cybersecurity, the audit profession can best meet the needs of report users if the profession adopts a consistent, profession-wide approach to providing cybersecurity attestation services that meet the informational needs of a broad range of potential report users.

PRINCIPLES FOR BETTER CYBERSECURITY OUTCOMES

Whether one is considering the potential benefit from a comprehensive examination of a company's cybersecurity process and internal controls or any of the other sound recommendations included in other chapters of *The Cybersecurity Social Contract*, we believe there are several overall principles that must be acknowledged for the suggested improvements to produce better outcomes. We believe that the following principles must be embedded in the public-policy dialogue around these and future enhancements to adequately address cybersecurity.

AVOID BLAMING THE VICTIM

To date, the prevailing attitude when a breach has been discovered and disclosed is to see the customers and shareholders as the only victims of the incident. The reality of the complex world of cyber preparedness is that even in the very best companies with the very best protections, there will be breaches. The bad actors are just that smart. Therefore, we must change the dialogue around cyber incidents to recognize in some situations that the company that has been breached is in fact a victim as well.

THE REGULATORY SYSTEMS THAT COME INTO PLAY IN BREACH SITUATIONS SHOULD ALLOW FOR AN APPROPRIATE ASSESSMENT OF CYBER DEFENSES DEPLOYED BY MANAGEMENT, INCLUDING THE TIMELINESS OF REMEDIATION AND THE RESILIENCY OF THE COMPANY

Without positive reinforcement for good actors, there may not be sufficient incentives for companies to step up to the costly process of maximizing their protections. Our regulatory and legal processes should never act as a disincentive to installing appropriate internal controls necessary to protect the company and its stakeholders. In other words, if a company sees the regulatory and legal downside of a security breach as being no different whether they make a good faith effort to prevent, detect and remediate for such exposures or not, then some companies will do less and "hope" that nothing bad happens. That would not be the best public-policy outcome for our market-based system. A cybersecurity examination report could be one way to demonstrate good faith effort on the part of management and the board.

IMPROVEMENTS DRIVEN BY THE PRIVATE SECTOR SIGNIFICANTLY INCREASE THE OPPORTUNITY TO PRODUCE MEANINGFUL AND TIMELY IMPROVEMENTS IN CURRENT PRACTICE

Although the AICPA has begun development of a new attest service, we believe that the decision to utilize such a service should rest with each individual company and its board and management and should not become a regulatory requirement.

We appreciate this opportunity to share the views of the CAQ on behalf of the audit profession about the need to find better ways to enable organizations to enhance their cybersecurity-risk-management programs for the benefit of all stakeholders. We thank the ISA for providing the platform to gather views from a broad range of interested parties.

---

1 The Center for Audit Quality (CAQ) is an autonomous public-policy organization dedicated to enhancing investor confidence and public trust in the global capital markets. The CAQ fosters high-quality performance by public-company auditors, convenes

and collaborates with other stakeholders to advance the discussion of critical issues requiring action and intervention, and advocates policies and standards that promote public-company auditors' objectivity, effectiveness, and responsiveness to dynamic market conditions. Based in Washington, DC, the CAQ is affiliated with the American Institute of CPAs. For more information, visit www.thecaq.org. This chapter represents the observations of the CAQ but not necessarily the views of any specific firm, individual, or CAQ Governing Board member.

2 A financial-statement auditor's primary focus is on the controls and systems that are in the closest proximity to the applications and data of interest to the audit—that is, systems and applications that house financial statement–related data. Therefore, systems and data in scope for most financial-statement audits usually are a subset of the totality of systems and data used by companies to support their overall business operations.

3 Public Company Accounting Oversight Board Auditing Standard 2201, *An Audit of Internal Control Over Financial Reporting That Is Integrated with an Audit of Financial Statements*, paragraphs 39–40.

4 Mary E. Galligan and Kelly Rau, *COSO in the Cyber Age* (COSO Committee of Sponsoring Organizations of the Treadway Commission, Deloitte, Jan. 2015), Web.

Fourteen

The Role of Cyber Insurance in Promoting Cybersecurity

Tracie Grella, Head of Cyber Risk Insurance, AIG

INTRODUCTION

The insurance industry has a very strong interest in working with the federal government to improve the state of US cybersecurity. An existing partnership, formed under the auspices of the Department of Homeland Security National Protection and Programs Directorate, brings together academia, infrastructure owners and operators, insurers, chief information security officers, risk managers, and others to find ways to expand the cybersecurity insurance market's ability to address emerging risks.

This chapter aims to build on past discussions and provide an overview of market challenges and recommendations. Cyber insurers have the capacity to assist the government in accelerating broad adoption of leading practices, which will dramatically improve the general level of US cybersecurity.

In the following pages, we provide an overview of the cyber insurance market, the underwriting process applied by insurers, and the ongoing benefits of working through this process. Additionally, we provide a perspective on challenges to the growth of cyber insurance and recommend solutions that will improve and expand access to valuable and affordable cyber insurance.

In summary, we recommend strengthening the partnership between insurers and the federal government, and working jointly on the following:

- Encouraging widespread adoption of cybersecurity best practices and incentivizing companies to intelligently invest in better security.
- Enhancing intelligence gathering, data collection, and information sharing and disseminating such information through Information Sharing and Analysis Centers.
- Expanding technical education in information technology and cybersecurity to build a robust pool of talent to protect the nation's digital infrastructure.
- Continuing to pursue offensive and defensive protections that assist companies in addressing high-powered attacks from state-sponsored actors or nation-states.
- Clarifying the application of the Terrorism Risk Insurance Act to cyber events, as well as circumstances that would constitute a cyber war.
- Expanding funding for research that will foster the development of leading technologies and enhance the security of emerging technologies created by the Internet of Things.

The insurance industry looks forward to partnering with the federal government to share its risk-management expertise and dramatically improve the state of cybersecurity.

MARKET OVERVIEW

Insurance exists to help companies and individuals manage the financial impact of unexpected events. Most businesses today purchase a suite of policies that include property, general liability, and workers' compensation. Companies are increasingly adding a new insurance product to this list: cyber insurance.

Cyber insurance exists to provide financial reimbursement for unexpected cybersecurity losses. This may include accidental disclosure of data, such as losing an unencrypted laptop, or malicious external attacks, such as phishing schemes, malware infections, or denial-of-service attacks. When a cybersecurity incident occurs, most cyber insurance products offered today provide coverage for one or more of the following:

- Costs to address an incident (forensics, network repair, data restoration, victim notification, credit monitoring services, public relations, etc.).
- Lost profit and additional expense associated with an interruption to a company's computer network.
- Costs to respond to a cyber extortion demand including extortion payments, lost profit, and related expense.
- Third-party claims, including damages, legal defense, settlement, and regulatory fines and penalties.

Demand for cyber insurance is rapidly increasing. In 2015, one in five US companies purchased a cyber insurance policy, a 27 percent increase from 2014 and a doubling from 2012.[1] The increase is attributable to several factors:

- High-profile events including those at Anthem, Inc., JPMorgan Chase, Sony Pictures Entertainment, Target Corporation, and The Home Depot.
- Increased board of director and executive focus on cybersecurity and significant costs associated with security failures.
- Established and emerging regulatory reporting requirements from state governments, the Federal Trade Commission, the Financial Industry Regulatory Authority, the Securities and Exchange Commission and others.
- Advances in technology that have increased the criticality of networked systems such as mobile devices, cloud computing, big data analytics, and the Internet of Things.[2]
- Insurer product enhancements and broker marketing, which is increasing awareness and take-up of cyber insurance products.

Take-up rates vary on the basis of company size, industry sector, value of data assets, and regulatory requirements. The influence of mandatory regulatory reporting requirements is particularly evident in healthcare, where roughly half of all companies purchase a cyber insurance policy.

Demand for insurance differs greatly between large and small companies. Nearly half of companies with revenues greater than $1 billion have cyber insurance, a percentage far greater than the rate of 20 percent for all US companies (figure 14.1).[3] This suggests that large and publicly traded organizations are more actively protecting against attacks in response to internal expectations and external pressures.

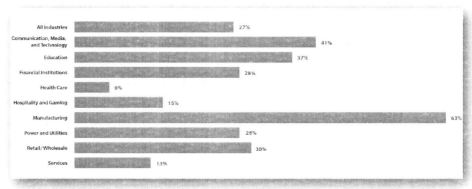

Figure 14.1. Cyber insurance growth rates by industry
in 2015. (From March Global Analytics.)

Companies that purchase cyber insurance generally are buying modest limits. A recent survey of risk managers suggests that nearly 60 percent buy less than $20 million of coverage.[4] For large companies, insurance may only cover a portion of total cybersecurity event costs. For example, Target Corporation reported in its 2015 annual report that "breach costs totaled $291 million, partially offset by expected insurance recoveries of $90 million."[5] In sum, Target retained two-thirds of costs related to its security incident.

Large companies can buy up to $500 million of cyber insurance, but the largest purchases generally range from $200 million to $400 million.[6] In most cases, demand is met by the market, but there is a small subset of large companies (we'd estimate about 150) whose demands exceed available market supply. Many of the shortfalls relate to the limited size of buyer insurance budgets and insurer limits on single-account capacity given uncertainty about systemic catastrophe loss potential.

Marsh & McLennan Companies note that, on average, media and technology (around $90 million) and financial institutions ($60 million) purchase the largest limits of all sectors. Chemical, utility, and oil and gas companies are seeking large limits to protect against business interruption losses and property damage associated with attacks on industrial control systems. Manufacturers have a strong interest in insuring against espionage and the theft of intellectual property, but to date insurance does not cover these hard-to-value losses.

To meet market demands, there are more than fifty insurers offering cyber insurance. Statistics on the size of the market vary, but most sources suggest that insurers collected between $2 billion and $3 billion of premium in 2015.[7] A recent PricewaterhouseCoopers study estimates that the market will grow three-fold by 2020 to $7.5 billion.[8] That said, market growth is somewhat constrained by a lack of data, actuarial models, insurer concerns that a single attack could affect many companies at the same time and the speed of technological change (figure 14.2).

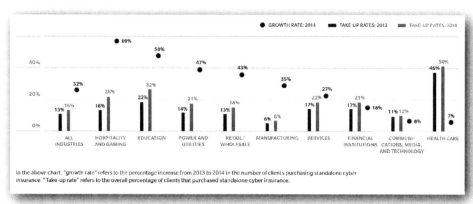

In the above chart, "growth rate" refers to the percentage increase from 2013 to 2014 in the number of clients purchasing standalone cyber insurance. "Take-up rate" refers to the overall percentage of clients that purchased standalone cyber insurance.

Figure 14.2. Cyber Insurance Take-Up and Growth Rates by Industry. (From March Global Analytics.)

Insurers are working to address these challenges by collecting more data from insureds in the underwriting process, leveraging external data, building more advanced models, and strengthening technical knowledge of network security. The supply of insurance should increase as these models mature and pricing stabilizes on the basis of historical loss costs. We estimate that this will take several years given the current pace of data collection and investments in modeling.

Given the uncertainty, most insurers are operating cautiously. Generally speaking, large insurers offer a single insured up to $25 million of coverage, and smaller players offer $5 million or $10 million. This makes it difficult to negotiate the needed capacity for large manufacturers or financial institutions, which might require up to fifteen different insurance companies. Insurance brokers specialize in assembling a panel of insurers for these large accounts.

Large losses have also led to supply shortages in certain pockets of the market. For example, several cyber insurers stopped offering insurance to retailers following a run of high-profile consumer data breaches. Insurers are approaching other high-risk sectors with caution, for example, hospitality and hotels, universities, and healthcare companies, as those industries also experienced a recent string of data breaches. Utilities seeking large limits for cyber terrorism and business interruption may also face tight supply as insurers are still working to properly model such risks. Pricing in these areas will reflect supply shortages and, in some cases, may be higher than companies are willing to pay.

CYBER INSURANCE—PRODUCT AND SERVICE

The insurance industry has created a system to help companies plan, prepare for and respond to incidents. Insurers frequently conduct in-depth reviews of company cybersecurity frameworks during the underwriting process. In partnership with technology companies, law firms, public relations companies, and others, insurers also offer a suite of ex-ante and ex-post services that minimize the likelihood and impact of a breach. Companies that use these services report significant progress in improving their prebreach security posture and postbreach response and resilience.

THE UNDERWRITING PROCESS

Before writing a policy, insurers review the quality of each company's cybersecurity framework. For smaller companies, underwriting may be more automated and based on a standard set of questions. For larger companies, the underwriting process involves more in-depth questions and discussions with management to better understand the procedures in place to defend against an attack. For the largest accounts, insurers may also partner with external security experts to test the strength, integrity, and resiliency of the insured's network.

Information from the underwriting process informs pricing decisions. Insurers have built models that combine historical quantitative and qualitative data to determine a price for coverage. Pricing variables include prior loss experience, cybersecurity strength ratings, industry sector, data type and volume, annual revenue, reliance on IT systems, among other factors. Each account is priced individually to reflect its risk relative to other accounts in the portfolio.

Insurance pricing can be a strong signal that helps companies understand their cybersecurity strengths and weaknesses. Information from the underwriting process can be used to inform decisions about future cybersecurity investments and mitigation efforts. Companies that invest and show improved resiliency are rewarded with lower insurance premiums. In this way, insurance is highly important to driving widespread cybersecurity resilience.

Cybersecurity Consultative Services

Once a policy is bound, the insured often has access to a valuable set of services. Larger insurers have partnered with leading technology companies to make available a battery of preventative measures that help an insured prepare for an attack. This includes cybersecurity framework review and governance, vulnerability scanning, Internet protocol address blacklisting, and consultative security services. Additionally, some insurers provide insureds a cybersecurity report card from an independent third party. This information is objective, on the basis of data collected about the insured's network, and can point to areas needing improvement and investment.

Some insurers also assist company executive teams in planning for breaches. This involves active cross-departmental discussions about roles, responsibilities and actions when a breach occurs. The discussion involves the board of directors to ensure that all relevant parties are aware of the potential for disruption and prepared when it occurs. The output of this process is a cybersecurity action plan that codifies the firm's strategy for addressing security events. The plan is a living document that is updated as the company enhances its framework.

All attacks cannot be prevented. As such, the insurance product provides contingent capital when it is most needed, as well as a suite of support services to address and remediate the breach.

THE CLAIMS PROCESS

Insurers maintain claims departments that are experienced in responding to security events. A sophisticated insurer's claims department has developed knowledge and expertise over many prior events. It can provide insight and support that is needed to determine whether coverage applies to loss, how to get needed support services quickly and address critical issues.

Event Response Services

Many insurers also maintain a panel of partner companies to assist clients in the critical days following a breach. These partner companies provide forensic investigation, incident response, legal, public relations, and other services. This panel of services minimizes the time to remediate a breach and dramatically reduces the overall cost and impact.

MARKET CHALLENGES

While the market is advancing quickly, there are several inhibiting factors that constrain its full capacity.

DISPARATE COMPANY PREPAREDNESS AND INVESTMENT

Company preparedness and investment in cybersecurity vary greatly. Larger publicly traded companies generally invest more than midsized and smaller companies. This partially relates to a lack of awareness and education about the damaging impact of a cybersecurity event. It may also stem from lower expectations of internal and external stakeholders such as the board of directors, customers, and regulators. This disparity is highly challenging as a network is only as strong as its weakest link. The nation's cybersecurity depends on significantly increasing the knowledge base and investment across all companies, particularly smaller and midsized companies.

UNCERTAINTY ABOUT FUTURE ATTACK METHODS AND OUTCOMES
Predicting future attacks and outcomes is difficult. The technology landscape changes constantly with new devices added, software reconfigured, and expanding networks. The community of external attackers continues to grow as large profits are made. Attackers continually shift targets and attack modes, rendering past attack data of questionable use. It is essential to have a platform for timely and detailed information sharing on attack modes, trends, and fixes to drive ongoing improvements in cybersecurity. This platform should minimize the time between discovery of a trend or issue and its dissemination.

GEOPOLITICAL FACTORS SUCH AS TERRORISM AND WAR
Companies need to protect against geopolitically motivated attacks from sophisticated nation-states. Such attacks can be well funded, highly engineered, and powerful. It is difficult for even the most sophisticated companies to defend against these attacks. The federal government can play an important role by investing in and strengthening national defenses to minimize the potential for successful attacks on US companies. This may include strong diplomatic efforts, as well as expanding cybersecurity resources at the Federal Bureau of Investigation and National Security Agency.

Additionally, insurers need greater certainty about what constitutes an official act of terrorism and war in cyberspace. Acts of war are generally excluded from insurance coverage. Terrorist attacks may be covered, and certain coverages qualify for federally funded reinsurance through the Terrorism Risk Insurance Program Reauthorization Act of 2015. It is unclear when, and if, cyberattacks would be deemed acts of terrorism, thus triggering TRIA. The nature of cyberattacks complicates this, since the origin may be impossible to pinpoint with certainty. The insurance market needs more clarity about when TRIA would apply to cyber events and actions that would constitute cyber war.

LACK OF SUITABLE DATA FOR MODELING

Insurers use data from past events to model the potential for future losses. Cyber risk is particularly challenging to model for two reasons: a short time series of data and attack heterogeneity. Cyberattacks are a relatively new phenomenon, and data have only been collected for a handful of years. Attack modes and vectors constantly shift, diminishing the value of past data for predicting future attacks. While data collection is most appropriately managed by insurance companies, the federal government can assist by providing timely and detailed information on its latest intelligence gathering efforts.

Insurers are also challenged by companies that limit the data they are willing to share following a security event. It's quite common for companies to provide the minimum amount of information required and withhold the full forensics report. Companies should be incentivized to share the full details of these reports with their insurers to facilitate proper claims adjusting and allow for data and trend analysis across data breaches. Greater information sharing between compromised companies and insurers will lead to lower cost and wider availability of cyber insurance.

CHALLENGES OF RISK AGGREGATION AND CORRELATION

Correlation and aggregation of risk also presents a difficult challenge to insurers. Insurance is based on the law of large numbers, which suggests that expected losses for a pool of homogeneous, independent risks can be estimated based on average losses in past data. This principle breaks down for risks that are highly dependent or connected to one another. This is true in cybersecurity because many companies could be subject to the same loss. An example is the potential for a cloud breach subjecting many companies to loss at the same time.

WEAK PUBLIC UNDERSTANDING OF CYBERATTACK IMPORTANCE

Cyber insurance is also constrained by a general lack of understanding and awareness of the importance of cybersecurity. Large attacks grab headlines, but the staying power of their warning is limited. It is essential to have a coordinated campaign to sustain a level of awareness and engagement that fosters continual focus and investment in cybersecurity. It would be beneficial to design a campaign that could be rolled out broadly, targeting midsized and small businesses, as well as individuals.

COMPETING PRIORITIES AND OPPORTUNITY COSTS OF INSURANCE PURCHASES

Insurance is generally perceived as a low-value product, at least before a loss occurs. Generally speaking, most companies would spend their next dollar to increase sales rather than protect against a potential cybersecurity loss. It is essential to change thinking in this area and demonstrate the very real value of investing in cybersecurity. Incentives, such as tax credits, for companies that invest in cybersecurity and purchase cyber insurance would dramatically improve the general level of security.

SHORTAGE OF QUALIFIED TALENT TO ADDRESS THE RISK

Cybersecurity is a highly technical field that blends concepts of information technology, computing, security, economics, and psychology. Individuals with the requisite skill set are in short supply. It is essential to increase the number of professionals trained in security and institute standards for such education. This effort should be an ongoing collaborative effort between business, universities, and the federal government. An organized program that attracts, trains, and launches individuals into information technology careers is critically needed.

RAPID GROWTH OF THE INTERNET OF THINGS AND RESULTANT RISKS

The Internet of Things is rapidly advancing and increasing the number of devices connected to the Internet. Additionally, IoT is connecting assets of significant economic importance to systems that could be targets of attack. For example, power systems are increasingly digital. Additionally, attacks on newly connected transportation methods (cars, trucks, and airplanes) could lead to bodily injury or death if compromised by a hacker. This is an area where more research is needed on the potential risks of such technologies and standards need to be in place to protect human life. The insurance industry has a strong interest in leading this research and would like to invite the federal government to participate and contribute to this effort. Federal funding for research in this area would be beneficial to ensure that the issue is properly studied, understood and addressed.

Additionally, it is very important to encourage companies to build security into the design phase of products rather than treat it as an afterthought. Industry groups should work jointly to establish common security standards particularly for products that are critically important to human health, safety and stability. Examples of such products might include industrial control systems, networked medical devices, transportation vehicles, and financial transaction systems. The insurance industry is prepared to partner with manufacturing companies to advance collective knowledge in this area.

RECOMMENDATIONS

Federal and state governments can play a role in advancing the state of cybersecurity. The insurance industry is very interested in partnering with the government to advance the quality and resilience of national security.

TAX INCENTIVES FOR CYBERSECURITY INVESTMENT

Companies should be incentivized to invest in cybersecurity. Investments will benefit all citizens—they will ensure that data and networked physical assets are kept safe and secure. The federal government should consider economic incentives that accelerate company investment in security. This could take the form of tax incentives for such investments or the purchase of cyber insurance. The latter would ensure that more companies are subjected to an independent review of their cybersecurity framework. Companies that partner with cyber insurers also have strong economic incentives to continually improve security practices that raise the overall level of national preparedness.

GOVERNMENT INTELLIGENCE SHARING

Government intelligence sharing currently happens through industry-based Information and Security Analysis Centers. Some ISACs are more effective than others, and it would be beneficial to enhance all of them to ensure a consistent level of information and engagement across industry sectors. While participation in such groups is voluntary, the federal government can incentivize strong participation by using these forums to deliver timely and highly valuable intelligence on emerging cybersecurity threats. Information sharing should be expedient—it is essential that information is shared quickly to maintain its relevance to receiving organizations.

SCENARIO PLANNING WORKSHOPS
The insurance industry is prepared to facilitate cross-industry cyber scenario workshops. These would involve federal government agencies, universities, corporations, and other participants. The workshops would focus on designing and implementing scenario analysis to better understand the types of attacks that could impact the private and public sector. Scenarios could range from data theft and destruction, to extortion, hacktivism, terrorism, and other such events. The workshop content could be shared with companies and individuals to better inform them of the risks and take steps to prevent against such attacks. These workshops could be aligned or integrated with DHS' current C-Cubed programs.

CYBERSECURITY EDUCATION
It is essential that the country highly prioritize and accelerate the education and preparation of cybersecurity professionals. The government's program to certify universities and provide loan forgiveness to students who major in cybersecurity and work for the government is a very good start. We recommend continuing to invest in such programs to ensure that a suitable pool of talent is filled and that companies can draw on this pool. Federal funding for research at nonprofits and universities would also dramatically improve the level of knowledge in the field.

PUBLIC SERVICE CAMPAIGN
We also recommend creating a public campaign similar to the "Say No to Drugs" campaign. This would be highly effective in raising the general level of awareness for cybersecurity and raising the issue to national attention. Additionally, educational materials should be developed and delivered to

midsized and small businesses through various channels such as the Small Business Administration and other governmental programs. We recommend that the federal government partner with leading universities to develop the content for the campaign and the release of such materials.

GEOPOLITICAL RISK MANAGEMENT

It is essential that government take an aggressive stance on protecting the nation against attacks from geopolitically motivated sources. Companies are incapable of protecting against sophisticated, well-funded nation-state attacks. As such, the DHS, FBI, and NSA need to take the lead in protecting the country against such attacks through appropriate offensive and defensive means. Further, intelligence gained from such actions should be shared openly with the private sector to enhance understanding of threats and allow for preparedness. This is particularly important to help protect highly valuable trade secrets and intellectual property of US companies.

CLARIFY THE TERRORISM RISK INSURANCE ACT

The insurance market needs greater clarity on the applicability of the Terrorism Risk Insurance Act and declarations of war for cyberattacks. Large-scale terrorist attacks launched by cyber means should qualify as certified acts of terrorism and trigger TRIA for covered lines. Additionally, greater clarity on what constitutes an act of cyber war would be helpful to ensure that all parties are clear if, and when, an event occurs. Most importantly, it is essential that the federal government do everything in its power to avoid cyber terrorism and war to preserve the nation's social and economic strength and security.

LEGAL AND REGULATORY IMMUNITY

The federal government should consider legal or regulatory immunity for companies that develop products to prevent and address cyberattacks. This includes manufacturers of antivirus software, network devices and equipment, and other new technologies. It is essential that legal concerns do not stifle innovation and new technologies that will better protect our society and economy. The federal government should also consider extending the

SAFETY Act to include liability limitations for certified products and services that are designed to prevent or mitigate loss from cyber terrorism and cyber-criminal activity.

SOFTWARE AND HARDWARE SECURITY STANDARDS
The insurance industry also supports the creation of an independent organization that would be tasked with certifying the security of commonly used software and hardware devices. This initiative would be equivalent to standards developed under the Underwriter Laboratories for the introduction of new electronic devices and components. The development of standards and testing would uncover security weaknesses and dramatically improve the overall state of cybersecurity.

CONCLUSION AND NEXT STEPS
The insurance industry is a strong partner to the federal government in advancing the state of cybersecurity. Insurers are actively meeting with companies, applying a standard underwriting process to assess cybersecurity and connecting companies with valuable pre- and postbreach services. Additionally, insurance pricing represents a valuable indicator that can be used to incentivize companies to enhance their framework.

The cyber insurance market is growing, but there are factors that are slowing its growth. These include opportunity costs of investing in cybersecurity, as well as the challenge of accurately modeling frequency and severity of attacks. Insurers are advancing on this latter item and have developed standard data collection procedures and are building more advanced models. We expect that the supply of cyber insurance will expand and price will stabilize as insurers advance in these areas.

We recommend several areas where government can assist the market in addressing cybersecurity. First, information dissemination and sharing is essential and can be fostered through ongoing interaction with ISACs. Second, government policy should institute incentives for cybersecurity investment to expand the base of companies that are planning and prepared for an attack. Third, government can participate in raising the level of awareness and understanding of attacks through partnering with the private sector in scenario workshops. Fourth, federal funding is needed to continue research into new technologies and the evolving risks associated with the Internet of Things. Finally, it is paramount to continue government investments in cybersecurity, anti-terrorism and diplomatic solutions to cyber war. This is an issue of national security, and clarity is needed to better understand how the nation would respond to a large-scale cyber terrorism event or war. This includes the applicability of TRIA, as well as conditions that would lead to declarations of cyber war.

The insurance industry looks forward to continuing its partnership with the government in these areas and bringing its knowledge to bear on the tremendous challenge of managing cybersecurity.

---

1 Marsh, *Benchmarking Trends: Operational Risks Drive Cyber Insurance Purchases* (Marsh Risk Management Research, Marsh & McLennan Companies, Marsh LLC, Mar. 2015), Web.

2 Aon Risk Solutions, *Cyber-Risk Solutions* (Financial Services Group, Professional Risk Solutions, Aon Risk Solutions, Aon Plc, 2016), Web.

3 RIMS: The Risk Management Society, "74% of Risk Professional without Coverage Are Considering Purchasing Cyber Insurance within Two Years," *RIMS Newsroom*, Jan. 8, 2015, Web; Marsh, *Benchmarking Trends*.

4 RIMS, "74% of Risk Professional."

5 "Annual Report Pursuant to Section 13 or 15(d) of the Securities Exchange Act of 1934: Commission File Number 1-6049," 10-K. U.S. Securities and Exchange Commission, Web.

6 Marsh, *Benchmarking Trends*.

7 Willis, *Marketplace Realities 2016: Bringing the Pieces Together* (Willis North America Inc., 2016), Web.

8 PWC, *Insurance 2020 & Beyond: Reaping the Dividends of Cyber Resilience* (PWC, 2015), Web.

Fifteen

Deploying a Voluntary Cyber-Resilience Program: A Strategic Imperative

Andrea Bonime-Blanc, JD/PhD, CEO, GEC Risk Advisory

A HOLISTIC APPROACH TO CORPORATE CYBER RESILIENCE

This chapter makes the case that to be cyber resilient, businesses of any kind, shape, or form should design, develop, and implement a voluntary internal cyber governance, risk, and compliance/culture program ("Cyber-GRC program").[1]

Developing and adopting a Cyber-GRC program will allow a company to gain better and more sustainable cyber resilience, benefitting the entity itself (in terms of preparedness, crisis management and business continuity), its key stakeholders (in terms of value preservation and creation), its communities and society as a whole (in terms of safety and protection of people and assets), and regulators (who will have fewer cases of enforcement). A holistic, strategic approach to corporate cyber resilience developed voluntarily, internally, and customized to the specific needs of a company also obviates the need for unnecessary, bureaucratic, inapplicable, or otherwise extraneous and costly laws and regulations. Figure 15.1 depicts a holistic approach to Cyber-GRC.

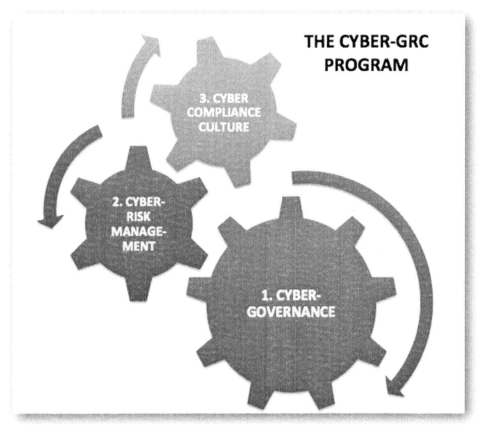

Figure 15.1.

The cyber-resilient company will have the following three general categories of Cyber-GRC in place:

1. **Cyber governance** is a framework that includes oversight, strategy, and a plan for implementation of the overall company approach and philosophy on cybersecurity as articulated by the board, the C-suite, and the top cyber-focused executives. Cyber governance is the first and most important step that a company should take as it develops its overall posture, strategy and tactics necessary to address the company's specific cyber-threat profile.

2. **Cyber-risk management** integrated with an enterprise-risk-management system refers to the system of risk management in

place for managing cyber risk, a leading example of which is the NIST Cybersecurity Framework. Having a robust and evolved risk-management system that addresses the cyber risks applicable to a particular company and its sector, footprint, products, services, and "crown jewels" is a necessary second step in building cyber resilience, which will help to determine the best shape for the third major element, the Cyber-GRC program.

3. **Cyber Culture** zeroes in on how the cyber-governance strategy and risk-management framework can best be implemented throughout the organization and at the front lines, especially focusing on people (employees and third parties), and providing them with the practical and cultural tools and resources necessary to meet the particular cyber challenges the company faces.

Most mature or advanced companies who are proactively addressing their cybersecurity already have some form of cyber governance in place as well as cyber-risk management, although in many cases even these elements are still under development given the relatively novel, superchallenging, and constantly changing nature of the cyber threat. Some may also have identified but have not yet fully integrated into their overall Cyber-GRC culture. Companies that fully integrate these three elements into their cyber-resilience strategy will become more robust and capable of managing crises.

A ROBUST CYBER-RESILIENT CULTURE TRUMPS THE LAW

There is, however, another great benefit to the deployment of an internal Cyber-GRC program. By building internal resilience into the governance, risk, and culture of your company—people and assets—there is less need for regulatory and government involvement in legislating the minutiae of cyber management at the company level. This is a win-win for both the private and public sectors as companies pursue what is truly useful for their particular sector, footprint, and overall profile, and regulators don't spend time and taxpayer money spinning unnecessary and expensive wheels trying to regulate too much or the wrong things at the expense of effectiveness.

A key postulate is that if companies build robust cyber resilience, the need for additional and potentially costly and ineffective laws and regulations will be obviated. Part of the purpose of this chapter is to show both private- and public-sector decision makers what a robust, voluntary Cyber-GRC program looks like so that each can identify and understand when a company has such a profile when and if things go wrong from a cybersecurity standpoint.

I use a powerful precedent to the idea of a voluntary internal Cyber-GRC program: the experience of companies over the past three decades in building effective ethics and compliance programs to meet their legal, compliance, and integrity risks. Drawing heavily on this enlightening precedent, later sections provide the case for more internal resilience and less external regulation through the deployment of a Cyber-GRC program and a roadmap to accomplish more holistic, strategic overall cyber resilience.

A PARADIGM FROM ANOTHER TIME: THE DEFENSE INDUSTRY INITIATIVE AND THE RISE OF THE EFFECTIVE E&C PROGRAM[2]

INTRODUCTION

The paradigm is the result of a period of decades of collaboration between companies, professional associations, research and academic sources, and, yes, lessons learned from challenging examples, mistakes, and scandals unfolding in the marketplace with concomitant waves of prosecutions, legislation, and regulation.[3] In this chapter we refer to this paradigm as the "E&C paradigm."

However, an important distinction needs to be made upfront on the use of this paradigm. As cyber threats have increased exponentially over the past few years, it is important to note that cyber risk is quite different from the average ethics and compliance challenge. Cyber mostly happens not because of "bad actors," negligent or reckless leaders, a toxic culture or pervasive unethical conduct. Cyber events happen mainly because of the barrage of technological, geopolitical, and economic changes that have so quickly evolved and the exponential growth of the cyber underworld that is overwhelming the global marketplace.

In other words, unlike ethics and compliance challenges, companies do not fully control cyber challenges—and because of the nature of the cyber threat, neither should corporations be held as being fully responsible for it. Cybersecurity is a challenge that requires a broad set of solutions and one of them is the adoption by all companies of a customized, voluntary Cyber-GRC program that will in turn obviate the need for unnecessary and largely inapplicable and ineffective new laws and regulations.

THE DEFENSE INDUSTRY INITIATIVE

The origins of the E&C paradigm can be traced back to the launch of the Defense Industry Initiative in 1985. The DII emerged in the wake of several waves of corruption and fraud involving the defense industry, starting with the foreign bribery scandals of the 1970s that led up to the adoption of the Foreign Corrupt Practices Act of 1977 and the defense procurement fraud cases of the early 1980s (involving many of the same defense industry companies) that triggered congressional investigations and the creation in 1985 of the Packard Commission to investigate fraud in the defense industry.

While the Packard Commission investigated what appeared to be industry-wide fraud and abuse, Jack Welch, then CEO and chairman of General Electric, started an industry initiative—eventually named the DII—calling for the collaboration of eighteen other major defense contractor CEOs. The DII developed in tandem with the Packard Commission investigation to such a point that when the commission report was published in 1986, the DII principles (the defense industry's voluntary code of conduct program to establish internal guidelines for each company to address and promote ethical and compliant behaviors within their companies) were attached as an exhibit to the report.

Chapter four of the Packard Commission report starts with this statement: "In our view, major improvements in contractor self-governance are essential," underlining the need for voluntary change to meet the ethical and legal challenges of the industry.[4] The report then lists five key components of defense contractor self-governance, or what would eventually be considered elements of an effective E&C program:[5]

1. Creating well-defined risk-based codes of conduct.
2. Developing a system that tracks and vets conflicts of interest.
3. Developing an employee instructional and communications system.
4. A system to monitor compliance and internal controls.
5. An independent audit committee.

Over time, the DII became both the harbinger and a major contributor to the larger debate about, and development of, the E&C paradigm. The DII was the principal precursor to a key governmental initiative—Chapter Eight of the United States Sentencing Guidelines, first published in 1991 and amended several times since then. The USSG is a hybrid animal. It is neither law nor regulation but provides a series of guidelines for prosecutors and judges to help them determine whether a company with an underlying civil or criminal allegation or conviction has an effective E&C program. If a company is found to have such a program, it can derive very substantial financial and reputational benefits (lower or no fines, deferred or no prosecution, less or no media and social-media-driven brand damage, etc.).[6]

THE EVOLUTION OF THE E&C PARADIGM
Over the decades following the creation of the DII and the USSG, a number of other factors both nationally and internationally have helped to sculpt what is increasingly acknowledged to be an "effective" E&C program within the private and public sectors, with board directors and corporate executives on the one hand and prosecutors, legislators, and regulators on the other, acknowledging their importance in determining whether a company is acting with or without integrity and whether or not it deserves investigation, prosecution, or other legal sanction.

Among the key trends over the past two decades are the following:

- **Industry codes:** market-based code of conduct initiatives in the healthcare, pharmaceutical, electrical, extractive, and other industry sectors, nationally and internationally.

- **NGOs:** the long-term lobbying, pressure, and research of international nongovernmental organization Transparency International being one of the first and still leading examples of such an NGO working against corruption worldwide.
- **International conventions:** the passage of international anticorruption conventions, the first and most notable of which was the Organization of Economic Cooperation and Development Anti-Bribery and Anti-Corruption Convention of 1997.
- **High court decisions:** the first and most important of which was the Caremark decision of 1996 in which the Delaware Court of Chancery made a landmark decision expanding the duty of care of boards of directors in overseeing ethics and compliance programs.
- **Regional and national initiatives:** regional anticorruption conventions and agreements (including, notably, the United Nations Global Anti-Corruption Convention, similar regional anticorruption initiatives in Latin America, Africa and Asia, as well as programs at the World Bank and similar institutions).
- **Professional associations and think tanks:** the tireless work of professional and corporate member associations in helping to develop these ethics and compliance national and global standards also requires much acknowledgment.[7]

These and other developments have had a major effect on the global debate and development of what we could now call a global E&C paradigm. While there was always a to-and-fro between the private sector and the public sector on the development of E&C programs, most governmental initiatives (other than anticorruption laws) have focused on providing guidelines to the private sector.

This has included, most notably, in the United States in the last few years, the Department of Justice and Securities and Exchange Commission soliciting private-sector compliance officer input, listening to, analyzing, and incorporating what the private sector had developed voluntarily in terms of E&C programs. In these cases, the DOJ and SEC have adopted the private sector's best practices E&C paradigm to the point of even hiring a private-sector compliance officer to review the compliance programs of companies under investigation or prosecution to determine whether or not they are "effective" and whether or not such companies deserve a break from the full weight of the law.[8]

THE EMERGENCE OF THE USSG

It should be emphasized that, at the time of the creation of the DII in mid-1986, there were no other notable incentives in place for the creation of an internal system of business ethics or governance other than the existence of specific federal, state, and local laws forbidding all manner of wrong-doing. Constructive incentives to do the right thing from a preventative compliance standpoint did not exist until the USSG indirectly created such a framework through Chapter Eight several years later.[9] When adopted in 1991, Chapter Eight of the sentencing guidelines provided the first cross-industry set of government incentives for corporate wrongdoers or po-tential wrongdoers to create an internal system of business conduct and compliance.

In essence, Chapter Eight mimics many of the tenets of the DII prin-ciples. Table 15.1 summarizes the many areas of equivalency and similarity of the respective elements of a sound E&C program as set forth under each document.

Table 15.1

Comparison of DII Principles of 1986 to US Sentencing Guidelines of 1991

DII Principle[10]	Chapter Eight of the US Sentencing Guidelines[11]
Principle 1: Written code of business ethics and conduct	Code of conduct and system of policies
Principle 2: Employees' ethical responsibilities	Training and communications programs
Principle 3: Corporate responsibility to employees	Anonymous and other reporting without fear of retaliation
Principle 4: Corporate responsibility to the government	Internal compliance risk assessments, monitoring, and auditing
Principle 5: Corporate responsibility to the defense industry	

Principle 6: Public accountability	
	Effective, comprehensive, and fair system of internal discipline
	Delegation of approval authority (system of internal controls)
	Establishing and supporting proper internal resources in the form of an ethics and compliance officer and other personnel

THE EMERGENCE OF A GLOBAL E&C PARADIGM

Fast forwarding over the next two decades, it is possible to articulate the key elements of an "effective" E&C program, or what we are calling the E&C paradigm. Figure 15.2 provides a breakdown of the nine elements of an effective E&C program as it exists as of now.[12]

The Elements of an Effective Ethics and Compliance Program

E&C Risk Assessment	Conduct a periodic and targeted E&C risk assessment.
Code & Policies	Adopt a code of conduct and related system or framework of policies.
CECO Resources	Create an Office of the Chief Ethics and/or Compliance Officer (CECO) with sufficient resources and budget.
Board and C-Suite Access	Give the CECO access and report to highest levels of the organization including to management and the board.
Training and Communications	Provide appropriate E&C training and communications at all levels of the organization.
Internal Controls Alignment	Implement a system of internal controls and proper delegation of approval authority.
Helpline/Hotline System	Devise a system to solve concerns and problems including anonymous reporting options.
Consistent Discipline	Implement a consistent system of internal discipline.
Audit, Monitor, and Evaluate	Periodically audit, monitor and evaluate your E&C program.

Figure 15.2.

The most recent salvo in this long ongoing private-public debate was just issued in mid-2016 by the Ethics and Compliance Initiative (ECI, successor to both the ECOA and the ERC), consisting of a more succinct but powerful series of principles as follows:

- Principle 1: ethics and compliance is central to business strategy.
- Principle 2: ethics and compliance risks are identified, owned, managed, and mitigated.

- Principle 3: leaders at all levels across the organization build and sustain a culture of integrity.
- Principle 4: the organization encourages, protects, and values the reporting of concerns and suspected wrongdoing.
- Principle 5: the organization takes action and holds itself accountable when wrongdoing occurs.[13]

BUILDING AND DEPLOYING A VOLUNTARY AND EFFECTIVE CYBER-GRC PROGRAM: A ROADMAP

What can we learn from the evolution and emergence of the E&C paradigm that might be applicable to the creation of a robust and voluntary Cyber-GRC program within companies? As we articulated at the beginning of this chapter, there are three basic elements of a strong cyber-resilience or GRC Program: governance, risk management, and culture.

RISK GOVERNANCE

This means that the company board, C-suite, and top enterprise risk and technology managers are all on the same page about how strategic risk, including cyber risk, is handled at the company. Do they follow the strategic risk governance best practice of applying a triangular approach to key strategic risks such that:

- The board exercises effective strategic risk oversight.
- The C-suite prepares the business strategy and strategic plan taking key risks into account and providing the necessary budget, resources, and management for the company to meet these challenges.
- The key executives and management in charge of implementing the business plan and strategy are both talented and equipped with the necessary tools, budgets, and strategic guidance to accomplish the board and CEO vision.

Figure 15.3 is a depiction of the triangular cyber-risk governance approach I advocate in another piece I wrote for the Conference Board in 2015.[14]

Figure 15.3.

The ten key takeaways of the Conference Board report on "Emerging Practices in Cyber-Risk Governance" are summarized in figure 15.4 and provide a sense of some the key practices that make for a robust cyber-risk-governance deployment.

1. Develop a triangular governance approach to cyber risk management
2. Understand the reputation risk consequences to strategic cyber risk management gone wrong
3. Know who your cyber risk actors and stakeholders are
4. Have a deep understanding of the organization's "crown jewels"
5. Engage in a relevant cyber risk public-private partnership
6. Develop a cross-disciplinary approach to cyber risk management
7. Develop a cross-segmental/divisional approach to cyber risk management
8. Make cyber risk governance an essential part of your organization's resilience approach
9. Choose one of the three effective cyber risk governance models
10. Transform effective cyber risk governance into an opportunity for better business

Figure 15.4.

INTEGRATE CYBER INTO ERM AND OTHER KEY RISK-MANAGEMENT INITIATIVES

Integrate Cyber-Risk Management into ERM

Companies that have solid risk-management infrastructure in place will be much better off integrating cyber risk into their framework than those who take a haphazard approach to risk management, or worse, look the other way. Figure 15.5 is an evolutionary view of types of risk management that may or may not be in place at an organization—clearly those tending toward the right-hand side of this evolutionary spectrum are more likely to be able to successfully address and integrate their cyber risk into their ERM portfolio.

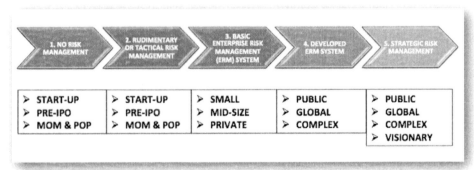

Figure 15.5.

230

The challenge of cyber risk for the average business is, arguably, greater than any other risk they have faced before. Even for highly evolved companies with sophisticated ERM systems, it is a challenge. Let alone for those companies that hide their head in the sand when it comes to cyber risk, taking a "wait and see" or "it won't happen to me" approach to cyberattacks. They must not have heard the FBI Director's admonition several years ago that there are two kinds of companies: those that have been hacked and know it and those that have been hacked and don't know it.

Understand That Cyber Risk Is More Often than Not a Strategic Risk

Not every risk is a strategic risk—many are operational, financial, technological, legal, environmental, and the like. But some risks are, whether because they directly affect the organization's strategy or because of their high likelihood or severe impact.

Cyber risk can be a strategic risk mainly under two sets of circumstances: instantaneously, when it can seriously and deleteriously affect a business strategy or plan all of a sudden (witness the Sony Pictures Entertainment case),[15] or over time, when a situation affecting a company's and its stakeholders' well-being has been brewing slowly, persistently, and eventually surfaces with high impact and strategic consequences (e.g., the Target case).[16]

When a company has good strategic risk management and governance in place, integrating cyber risk is relatively speaking easier, compared of course to companies without such capabilities.

Understand Cyber-Reputation Risk as It Relates to Your Company

In 2007, the Economist Intelligence Unit published a study in which it identified reputation risk as "the risk of risks."[17] No one had taken a serious look at this issue in quite the same way before. Since then, reputation risk has become one of the top five to ten strategic risks that most concern boards and C-suites globally.[18] Additional work has been done on understanding the full meaning of reputation risk—in one study, reputation risk is defined as follows:

Reputation risk is an amplifier risk that layers on or attaches to other risks—especially ESG risks—adding negative or positive implications to the materiality, duration or expansion of the other risks on the affected organization, person, product or service.[19]

Under this definition, any risk, including cyber risk, qualifies as an underlying risk onto which reputation risk may layer and attach itself, "adding negative or positive implications to the materiality, duration or expansion...on the affected organization, person, product or service." It depends heavily on whether the company in question has prepared properly for that specific risk.

The full implications of cyber reputation risk are only now beginning to be understood and have been underscored in several important industry surveys, including from Marsh and AIG, which underline that "cyber-reputation risk" may be the "risk of risks" turbocharged.[20] Here are the findings from the June 2016 AIG survey:

- More than two out of three executives and brokers believe that the reputational risk from a cyberattack is far greater to a company than the financial risk.
- More than seven in ten executives and brokers say legal compliance issues are making companies think more about cyber risks.
- The vast majority of brokers and executives believe hackers are the primary source of cyber threats, though nearly three-quarters of those surveyed also perceive human error as a significant component of cyber risk.[21]

Know Your Cyber Stakeholders and Their Crown Jewels

Companies have stakeholders, from shareholders and employees to customers and regulators. Each stakeholder has one or more interests or "stakes" in the company. In the case of shareholders, it's the protection and growth of their investment. In the case of employees, it's the preservation of jobs, opportunity for growth and advancement. In the case of customers, it's the protection of personal data and other entrusted customer "crown jewels." In the case of governments and regulators, it's the protection of lives and assets.

Governments, at the end of the day, are focused on the common threat: how to manage it and protect society. Companies should be focused on how to manage their own risks and threats in a manner that builds resilience, sustainability, and protection of stakeholder interests, and externally, collaborating and benchmarking within the private sector (developing good practices with other companies), and societally (learning from and contributing to applicable public/private partnerships). The extent and depth of such private and public collaboration will be determined by the company's business, strategy, cyber-threat exposure, and the volume and sensitivity of its cyber-crown jewels.

Knowledge of your stakeholders and their crown jewels will go a very long way to understanding what your top cyber-risk priorities are.

Create a Robust Cyber Culture

It's important to create an internal system of learning among employees and third parties about the cyber risks that they may be exposed to. This includes providing helplines/hotlines, unplanned trainings and communications modules that will help them learn the lessons that need to be learned and get accustomed to the type of threats and attempts that are most likely to occur in your business (phishing, social engineering, spoofing, etc.).

Integrate cyber-risk learning and teachable moments into your ethics and compliance or human resources or learning center scheduled and unscheduled trainings and take it all the way up to the boardroom on a regular and periodic basis.

Taking a page from the E&C paradigm, table 15.2 provides both an overview of the nine E&C paradigm elements and their cyber equivalent or similar program as well as several additional cyber-specific activities that a company should consider integrating into their Cyber-GRC program most specifically targeting the building of a cyber-resilient culture.

Table 15.2

Robust Cyber-GRC Program and Its Comparison with E&C Paradigm

E&C Paradigm Element	Similar Elements within a Cyber-GRC Program
1. E&C risk assessment	• Cyber-risk assessment (NIST/Other)
2. Code & policies	• Integrate cyber risk as a key issue into existing code of conduct • Develop/integrate all necessary supporting policies & procedures
3. Chief ethics & compliance office resources	• CISO/CIO/CRO cyber resources, budget
4. Board & C-suite access	• Board & C-suite access & reporting lines for CIO/CISO/CRO periodically (quarterly) & under crisis conditions
5. Training & communications	• Integration of cyber training & communications into company learning systems/HR/E&C regular & exceptional training
6. Internal controls alignment	• Close collaboration with audit, risk & compliance to ensure all internal controls & other systems are aligned, tested & monitored

7. Helpline/hotline system	• Ensure that cyber issues are part of any helpline/hotline/concern line system within the company
8. Consistent discipline	• When cyber incidents occur internally—from employees or third parties—ensure coordination with HR, legal, compliance of any follow-on disciplinary or other action
9. Audit, monitor & evaluate	• Ensure that there are several audit, monitoring, or evaluation initiatives customized to the company's needs that take place periodically
• Different/Additional Cyber-Code Program Elements	
10. Engage in private/public partnerships	• Engage in private/public partnership—ensure that appropriate contacts and connections are made with relevant law enforcement and regulators
11. Integrate cyber into resilience system	• Integrate cyber deeply into your company's crisis, business continuity & data protection/recovery systems
12. Cross-disciplinary & cross-divisional collaboration	• Have a cyber working group of necessary and desirable cross-disciplinary and cross-divisional experts

13. Know your cyber jewels & cyber actors	• Roadmap the company's crown jewels & engage in cyber actor/perpetrator analysis
14. Cyber-reputation risk & stakeholder analysis	• Engage in cyber-stakeholder analysis—prioritize who they are and prepare for reputation risk management
15. Integrate cyber into third-party/supply-chain management	• Extend cyber program to third parties and supply chain as necessary or required by law

CONCLUSION: CYBER RESILIENCE BEGINS AT HOME

Cyber resilience begins at home. If companies build it, regulators should respect it. The key is to create cyber resilience through the deployment of an appropriate Cyber-GRC program that is customized to the needs and profile of a company (just like in the example of the evolution of the E&C paradigm) and that both the private and public sectors alike can recognize as such.

The development of a Cyber-GRC program paradigm doesn't have to take as long as the development of the E&C paradigm for several reasons. We live in a quicker time, when cyber-risk management cannot wait and the wrong kind of regulatory or legal imposition can actually hinder rather than help. Additionally, in the case of cyber risk (as contrasted with E&C risk issues), companies are largely not at fault, and a good relationship between the public and private sectors on this topic is critical and benefits all stakeholders—the company, the community, and society.

To wrap things up, figure 15.6 is a typology of Cyber-GRC resilience, a bird's-eye view of the categories of cyber-risk readiness that exist at companies on the basis of two critical criteria: (1) whether their leadership (management and board) is taking a proactive and informed approach to Cyber-GRC as it relates to their specific business and sector, and (2) whether the specific organization operates in a medium/high to very high risk environment, sector, or footprint.[22]

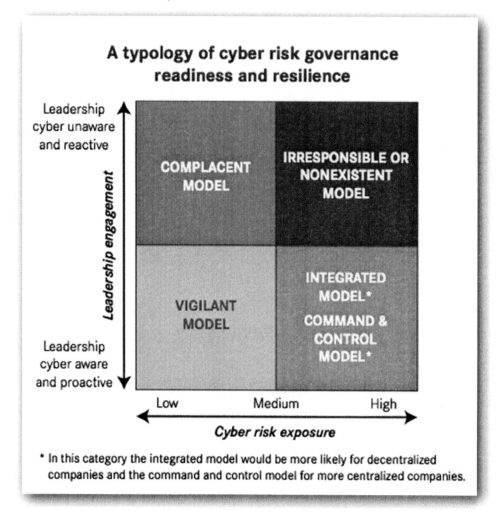

Figure 15.6.

If we display this typology along an "evolutionary" spectrum (figure 15.7), we can see that only three out of the five categories would provide what we would call "effective" Cyber-GRC resilience. Companies that find themselves on the left side of this spectrum would do well to get their cyber act together, and regulators and govern-ment agencies that deal with companies in the middle to right side of this spectrum should be grateful for the investment of time, resources, talent, and care that such companies are devoting to this singularly challenging risk.

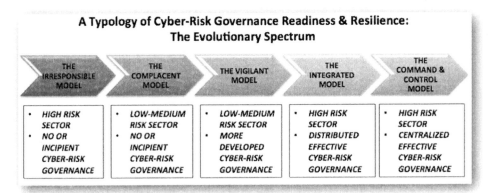

Figure 15.7.

Companies that are able to deploy a proactive and robust Cyber-GRC posture will in the process (a) comply with laws and regulations that exist for their sector better, (b) establish and deploy successful standards of be-havior and cyber culture within their organizations, (c) protect themselves better and in a more informed way from cyber threats, (d) help to shape and influence the development of industry-wide frameworks for the tack-ling and handling of such new threats and challenges, and (e) maybe even find opportunity within their cyber risk to add value either through process improvements or even enhancements within their portfolio of products and services.[23] See figure 15.8.

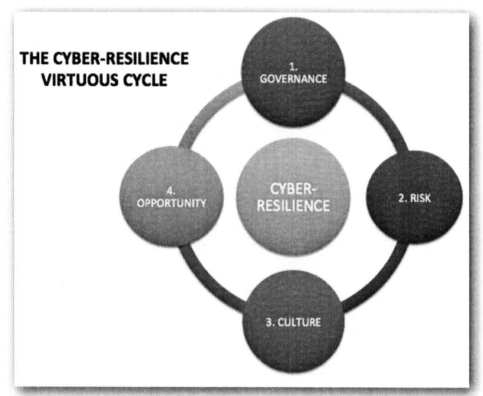

Figure 15.8.

---

1 While this chapter focuses on corporations and business, the suggestions made throughout this chapter are organizationally applicable to any other form of entity including nonprofits, universities, and even governmental agencies, national and international.

2 Much of this section is adapted or directly excerpted from Andrea Bonime-Blanc, "The Defense Industry Initiative: From Business Conduct Program Innovator to Industry Standard?" chap. 4 in *Globalization & Self-Regulation: The Crucial Role that Corporate Codes of Conduct Play in Global Business,* ed. S. Prakash Sethi (Basingstoke: Palgrave Macmillan, July 2011).

3 The bribery scandals of the 1970s (leading up to the passage of the US Foreign Corrupt Practices Act in 1977 (FCPA); the US savings and loans scandals of the 1980s; the healthcare fraud scandals of the 1990s; Enron et al. at the turn of the century (leading up to the passage of the Sarbanes Oxley Act in 2002); the financial scandals and meltdown of 2008 (leading up to the passage of the Dodd Frank Act in 2010); etc.

4 President's Blue Ribbon Commission on Defense Management, *A Quest for Excellence: Final Report to the President by the Blue Ribbon Commission of Defense Management* (June 30, 1986), pp. 81–83.

5 Ibid, p. 84.

6 Though in this chapter we stress the voluntary nature of the E&C paradigm, it is important to note that when a company strays into alleged or actual illegal conduct, it is investigated and/or prosecuted by the government; if the prosecutors find that the company did not have an effective E&C program in the first place, short of prosecution, the government may impose a monitorship (an external expert to oversee the company's E&C and other operations, sometimes for years), a deferred prosecution agreement (DPA), and/or corporate integrity agreement (CIA) on the company, which for all intents and purposes, will require it—involuntarily—to create an effective E&C program. If it is found that, at the end of such monitorship, DPA, or CIA, the company has not complied with the creation of an effective E&C program, the prosecution may come down with its full prosecutorial force on that company and be far less compromising on any fines, settlements, or jail terms for executives. Thus the E&C paradigm, when adopted in advance of actual or alleged E&C illegal behaviors, will not only act as a risk mitigant or preventer but also provide the company with a shield and defenses (almost like an insurance policy) in the event of a violation. There is growing body of evidence that the E&C paradigm, when properly developed within a company, will be seriously taken into account by prosecutors when they investigate a company for alleged wrongdoing.

7 Today, several major organizations exist in the United States and Europe that are devoted to the issue of building internal organizational business conduct programs. Among them are the original associations of this kind: the Ethics Resource Center (ERC) and the Ethics & Compliance Officer Association (ECOA)—which merged in 2015 and are now known as the Ethics and Compliance Initiative (ECI); a number of other US and non-US-based organizations such as the Society for Corporate Compliance and Ethics, the Open Compliance and Ethics Group, the Institute for Global Ethics, the UK-based

Institute of Business Ethics, the French- and Belgian-based Cercle D'Ethique des Affaires/Cercle Europeen des Deontologues; and a number of national associations such as the Association of Compliance Officers of Ireland or regional associations such as the Australasian Compliance Institute and the European Business Ethics Network. None of these organizations, except for the ERC, which in turn, played a major role in the creation of the DII, existed before 1992 when the ECOA was founded.

8 *The FCPA Resource Guide* of 2012 made heavy reference to the *Ethics and Compliance Handbook* published in 2008 by the Ethics and Compliance Office Association (now ECI) in which fifteen leading chief ethics and compliance officers deliberately developed each of the major elements of an effective E&C program on the basis of the USSG. A very recent development at the DOJ involved its fraud division hiring a member of the private sector, an ex-chief compliance officer of several leading companies, as an in-house expert to determine whether companies under investigation or prosecution had "effective E&C programs" in place, which might give them a break from prosecution or on the amount of fines or settlements that might otherwise be applicable under the law.

9 Chapter 8 specifically provides that organizations that are found to have committed a crime and do not have compliance and ethics program elements in place to prevent or detect such crime may not get the benefit of reductions in fines, jail terms, and other penalties. Refer to US Sentencing Guidelines Manual Section 8B2 at www.ussc. gov/2007guid/8b2_1.html.

10 See the original DII Principles at www.dii.org/resources/dii-charter.pdf.

11 See the US Sentencing Guidelines at www.ussc.gov/2007guid/8b2_1.html. The Sentencing Guidelines were amended in 2004 and again in 2010. This summary adds all amendments through 2004.

12 Chart from Andrea Bonime-Blanc and Martin Coyne II, "The Life-Cycle Guide to Ethics & Compliance Programs," *NACD Directorship Magazine*, Dec. 2014.

13 The Ethics and Compliance Initiative, *Principles and Practices of High-Quality Ethics & Compliance Programs* (Washington, DC, 2016).

14 Also see Andrea Bonime-Blanc, *Emerging Practices in Cyber-Risk Governance* (New York: Conference Board, 2015).

15 Bonime-Blanc, *Emerging Practices in Cyber-Risk Governance*.

16 Ibid.

17 The Economist Intelligence Unit, *Reputation: Risk of Risks*, white paper, *Economist*, Ace, Cisco Systems, Deutsche Bank, IBM, and KPMG, Dec. 2005, Web.

18 See Deloitte and Eisner Amper surveys quoted in Bonime-Blanc, *The Reputation Risk Handbook*, and Aon and Allianz surveys available at http://www.aon.com/forms/2015/2015-global-risk-management-survey.jsp and http://www.agcs.allianz.com/assets/PDFs/Reports/AllianzRiskBarometer2016.pdf respectively.

19 Andrea Bonime-Blanc, *The Reputation Risk Handbook: Surviving and Thriving in the Age of Hyper-Transparency* (Sheffield, England: Greenleaf Publishers, 2014).

20 Andrea Bonime-Blanc, "Cyber-Reputation: Risk Turbo-Charged," *Ethical Corporation*, Mar. 2016.

21 "Cyber Threats Reputational Risk Top Concerns: AIG," *Business Insurance*, June 2016.

22 Bonime-Blanc, *Emerging Practices in Cyber-Risk Governance*.

23 Two out of the five proactive Cyber-GRC companies profiled in *Emerging Practices in Cyber-Risk Governance* not only had effective programs in place but also developed and deployed cyber-related products and services (cyber-risk software and cyber-risk insurance) for sale to their customers. Bonime-Blanc, *Emerging Practices in Cyber-Risk Governance*.

Sixteen

The Digital Equilibrium Project: Balancing Cybersecurity and Privacy

James Kaplan, Partner, McKinsey & Co
Salim Hasham, Partner, McKinsey & Co
Chris Rezek, Senior Expert, McKinsey & Co

Y ou might feel more secure knowing your government can listen to conversations between terrorists. But are you comfortable with the idea that your smart TV can listen to conversations in your living room? You're probably glad that your increasingly intelligent car might someday save your life or another traveler's. But are you aware that it can be hacked and cause a fatal accident? You are likely relieved that your doctor can use advanced algorithms to help diagnose your illnesses. But are you concerned that corporations can use advanced algorithms to deny you healthcare?

These are the realities of the connected world, which grows deeper every day. From 2011 to 2015, the percentage of US adults owning a smartphone nearly doubled, from 35 percent to 68 percent.[1] From 2010 through 2015, average daily Internet consumption similarly doubled worldwide.[2] And this is only the beginning. We are building billions of intelligent devices with embedded applications that will run our power grids, our bodies, our automobiles, our thermostats, our kids' new playthings.

Our amazing technologies may be planting the seeds of disaster, even as they make tremendous improvements in our quality of life. The blinding pace of digital adoption has far outrun the laws, social norms, and diplomatic constructs that we painstakingly developed over centuries. The result of that gap is a growing tension between privacy and security—not only in our digital world but also in the physical world that has become intimately and inextricably bound to it.

We see the results daily. Cybercrimes unpunished. Loss of trust in governments and corporations. Undeterred sovereign-directed attacks, without effective response. We are all digital citizens, but our digital society is a global and nearly lawless one.

To avert this, we cannot rely on new technology. Instead we need to reimagine our collective experience with social problems as old as human culture itself—breaches of the privacy and security that are essential to the smooth functioning of the physical world and perhaps even more crucial in the digital world. Without some set of norms of behavior and standards for privacy and security, we will not know how to tell our devices to behave appropriately in this interconnected digital world, any more than we know how to tell ourselves or our children.

This is indeed the defining problem of the digital age. Whether we solve it will determine whether we are its masters or victims. The only ones benefiting from today's status quo are those who are the biggest threats to the privacy and security of all of us: criminals, hacktivists, and rogue nations.

PRIVACY AND SECURITY IN THE DIGITAL AGE: A NEW APPROACH

For several years, privacy advocates have waged a two-front battle. First, they contest what they see as overly intrusive, even illegal, efforts by the United States and other governments to gain information about citizens and noncitizens in pursuit of national security. Second, they fight corporations who they believe are collecting massive amounts of information on consumers, often without their informed consent, to use for economic gain.

At the same time, the intelligence community has harnessed the technologies' collection and analytics power to gain new advantages in support of their missions. In the commercial sector, organizations have poured hundreds of billions of dollars into technologies and services designed to secure their digital infrastructures, even as outsiders, comprised of state and nonstate actors, have extracted billions of dollars in value from unprotected or poorly protected corporate digital infrastructure.

Most Americans would argue they feel less safe and enjoy less privacy than just a few years ago. For example, less than 10 percent of Americans polled in 2015 were "very confident" that either the government, landline telephone companies, or credit-card companies would ensure both the privacy and security of their records.[3] The continued theft of intellectual property, financial data, and personal information from organizations is echoed by the concerns of information security practitioners who feel the task of defending their enterprises is harder than ever.

Even as we slide backward in our pursuit of both security and privacy, the light-speed evolution of technology nears an inflection point that makes today's problems pale by comparison to what may come. By 2020, according to many estimates, we will see approximately twenty to thirty billion intelligent devices in use, all connected to our digital networks and systems. These devices will be capable of collecting data on nearly every aspect of our lives. The total economic impact of the Internet of Things could range between $3.9 and $11.1 trillion by 2025.[4]

This explosion of devices will create an exponential challenge both for privacy (nearly every device will be a source of data for some provider) and security (the digital attack opportunities will be literally a hundred times the level of risk we see today).

SETTING THE STAGE: HOW WE GOT HERE

Concerned that today's polarized approaches to privacy and security are resulting in the erosion of both, a group of cybersecurity, government, and privacy experts banded together as part of the "Digital Equilibrium Project" to foster a new, productive dialogue on balancing security and privacy in the connected world. This chapter contains our foundational thoughts on how to advance the discussion past simple binary propositions about security and privacy.

In the past decade, processing power has increased by greater than twenty times, while its cost has fallen to a small fraction of what it was.[5] With billions of transistors on a single chip, the Internet of Things is now possible and affordable. Internet traffic has increased by greater than thirty times.[6] Storage capacities have increased by greater than ten times making collection—and retention—of information nearly free.[7]

Each of these improvements is individually comprehensible. Taken together, the systemic change these technologies are driving is remarkable and unpredictable.

Today, the very definitions of what it means to be human are being called into question by advances in genetics and artificial intelligence. Is it any wonder that our definitions of privacy, on the basis of our experiences in the physical world over hundreds of years, are no match for the scenarios emerging daily?

Consumers are worried that corporations are eroding privacy and that their personal information can be stolen in cyberattacks, while the disclosures of Edward Snowden and others stoke additional fear, uncertainty, and doubt. The result is a society worried, frustrated, and unsure how to respond.

A similar set of factors play out in the relationships between nations. The interconnectedness of the digital world has blurred the definition of national sovereignty even as it creates new vectors for espionage, theft of intellectual property, and even destruction of property and infrastructure. Classic definitions, rules, and agreements fail in this new environment. At current course and speed, we should expect catastrophic digital conflicts between nations, with physical consequences. Perhaps even more frightening, nonstate actors, terrorist groups, and even individuals will find it easier to acquire and use these destructive capabilities.

Our path—fast, rocky, and contentious—is not sustainable. Technology is about to enable a step-function increase in the ubiquity of digital infrastructure and how deeply it pervades our lives.

CROSSING THE CHASM: THE FUSION OF THE DIGITAL AND PHYSICAL WORLDS

The billions of new intelligent devices add new urgency and new complexity to the need to resolve the security/privacy debate. Why? Because they represent a tipping point where our physical and digital worlds become irrevocably fused, as do our risks and social issues.

Why such dramatic consequences? There are three reasons:

1. The increasingly critical role of these devices in our lives, coupled with limited abilities to manage or secure them, will add entire new categories of risk, both digital and physical. This will not go unnoticed by nation-states and nonstate actors alike who will explore both the defensive and offensive implications and opportunities created by the extraordinary increase in attack surface.
2. The intimate role of these devices in our lives, coupled with their ability to collect and share all manner of information about their (and our) status and behavior, will render some of our most basic constructs of privacy obsolete.
3. The ability of these devices to lower costs and create value for corporations, while adding convenience and new services for consumers, will make their rapid proliferation inevitable, even as angst over both the security and privacy of our world becomes more acute.

Economies worldwide will be increasingly based on digital foundations, resulting in increasing sensitivity to the risks and opportunities for their wealth and safety that are already seen in more digitally advanced economies.

THE IMPLICATIONS

This path threatens to turn our nation-level digital glass houses into a global house of cards. The increasingly powerful and essential digital infrastructure will sit on an ever-less-capable or relevant set of social, legal, and diplomatic constructs that are unable to ensure the security and privacy of individuals, organizations, and nations.

As the social and legal underpinnings of our integrated physical and digital world become increasingly unstable and ineffective, the costs potentially are incalculable. Since economic trade depends on trust, we can expect increased friction in global trade as trust between nations erodes. The erosion of wealth in the form of intellectual property theft, for example, already costs the United States more than $300 billion annually.[8]

If the return on investment in innovation falls because of piracy and theft, we can expect enterprises to either rethink their investment strategies or pressure their government for increased intervention in forms that could foster embargoes, tariffs, and other forms of trade war. As our digital devices "cross the chasm" and become intertwined with our physical world, the likelihood of physical harm arising from compromises to digital devices becomes nearly certain. Digitally connected cars, trains, power grids, medical devices, and so on create opportunities to reduce many of today's risks, but all represent opportunities for new forms of calamities. Already we see isolated examples sensationalized in the media. History shows that we can expect today's "proof of concept" hacks to turn into tomorrow's weapons.

The risk that comes from a lack of new norms and constructs for digital privacy and security will fall into three categories:

- **Economic**: Increased friction in the global economy could cost at least $1 trillion to 2 trillion annually in just a few years. The longer-term threat to trade and globalization and its economic consequences are indeed incalculable, but tens of trillions of dollars are at stake.
- **Existential**: As digital exploits increasingly cause physical and economic harm, the risk of existential catastrophe become very real, either directly (exploiting flaws in digital security to disable power grids for example), or as second-order effects (digital attacks or conflicts between nations escalate into traditional kinetic conflicts).
- **Societal**: Even if we are able to avoid existential catastrophes, the loss of trust between consumers and providers or citizens and their

governments, driven by continued erosions in privacy, will reduce our willingness to use digital technologies freely in communication, collaboration, and innovation in every aspect of society.

THE FAILURE OF TODAY'S DEBATE

Unfortunately, when it comes to privacy and security, we cannot even begin to claim success. The polarization of the discussion, the vested self-interest of parties on all sides, and the challenges that come from creating lasting consensus in a rapidly changing world have conspired against practical discussion.

WHAT WE PROPOSE

- A new balanced approach, not based on creating detailed polices or legislation but a framework for creating those instruments. A constitution, not a book of laws. This framework must embody basic beliefs and guiding principles that will be meaningful beyond any evolutions of technology so that it can guide our laws and policies as technology changes.
- A set of structures for continued dialogue and problem solving, so that continued rapid changes can be understood and incorporated into policy, law, and public discourse.
- A framework that builds on successes and finds and leverages analogies to today's world in free trade, diplomacy, law enforcement, and social norms, while embracing the unique characteristics of speed, scale, and change that mark our new digital age.

We thought of the problem along four dimensions: privacy and security relationships within organizations, between consumers and providers, citizens and their governments, and between nations themselves. We asked ourselves, and others, a fundamental question about each of those four areas.

We believe that cutting the Gordian knot of the privacy and security debate into these constituent parts can make dialogue more achievable.

Eventually of course, these threads will need to be knit back together into a strong fabric that unifies the varied points of view and challenges represented in each, since each domain has implications for the other.

QUESTION 1: WHAT PRIVACY MANAGEMENT PRACTICES SHOULD ORGANIZATIONS ADOPT TO ACHIEVE THEIR GOALS WHILE PROTECTING THEIR CUSTOMERS?

On its face, this question would seem simple to resolve. In an open market, consumers could choose to do business with providers who managed personal information in ways the consumer could accept. Market forces would strike the natural balance between privacy and convenience.

However, those market forces can only work when there is transparency, when both sides know what they are trading and open communication can enable the market to settle on its "natural" level. When it comes to personal information and its potential uses, many elements work against that transparency.

Technology changes so fast that every element, from the ways information can be collected and what information is possible to collect, to the ways it can be leveraged for profit or organizational gains, is in constant flux. Consumers can't anticipate all the ways information about them can be collected and used, and organizations can't predict all the ways they may wish or need to capture and use information in the future. Legislators can't write laws that target specific technology, collection techniques or uses of information that remain relevant for long, or for societies to avoid unintended consequences from legislation.

Even if organizations could predict their own needs, the competitive advantages of unlimited access and use of information are massive. Many organizations use customer information to deliver more value. So organizations are inherently motivated to seek new ways to use that information and are usually rewarded for their efforts by increased revenues or more satisfied customers.

Massive differences in national laws that regulate collection and use of digital information can, over time, create significant imbalances in the abilities of organizations to compete against better-informed, faster-moving rivals. Commercial organizations in particular will be tempted to look globally for the lowest bar to privacy and assume any higher bar they adopt will inhibit their ability to compete.

Despite those challenges, we believe that elements of an open market can improve relationships between consumers and providers of goods and services. What follows are proposals we believe are illustrative of the broader discussions that need to take place.

STARTING HYPOTHESIS

While perfect transparency is impossible, organizations could make significant progress by clarifying and simplifying privacy statements. Consumers who understood information collection practices could make informed choices, even automatically if privacy policies are machine-readable, and help establish a more market-based approach to establishing norms. So far, most machine-readable privacy policies have failed, but they should not be discarded as technology advances.

Limits on the use of personally identifiable information, such as one-time use of health information, may be embedded in policy, but it would be a major source of friction, preventing rapid advances in everything from healthcare to economic productivity. However, privacy statements could embrace broad categories of use that consumers could choose to accept or deny, on the basis of their willingness to contribute their information to the organization. Choice and notice themselves are not new, but more transparency will allow consumers to make more intelligent choices and ensure privacy by design.

Some forms of a "transactional model" could allow for a more continuous negotiation of privacy agreements between consumers and providers. Moreover, we might change the balance of power: rather than force consumers to navigate complex legal language with every service, why can't they set the parameters and require the service providers to demonstrate they can honor them? Machine-readable parameters set by consumers, if made practical, could enable a more fluid transaction-based approach to negotiating privacy between these parties.

We submit that the major focus on certain kinds of information collection, mostly related to consumers, could hamper massive progress in areas such as health, medicine, and education. Inadvertently creating constraints on possibly well-meaning, well-governed practices could put short-lived and potentially ineffective restraints on corporations in unrelated fields that might reduce significant prospective benefits at this stage in our nascent digital history.

Companies need a commercial incentive to be more transparent toward their customers and better stewards of their privacy, and at the same time, it should be easier for organizations in regulated sectors to sort out overlapping or conflicting regulations, including on data retention and usage. The concept of private/public space (with varying expectations of privacy) needs to be extended to the digital world, and commercial relationships need to evolve to match changing expectations. Any successful solution will need to be able to account for changes in technological and behavioral norms as our society evolves, and to help reconcile the view of those who consider privacy an absolute right with others who consider it obsolete.

QUESTION 2: HOW CAN ORGANIZATIONS CONTINUE TO IMPROVE THE PROTECTION OF THEIR DIGITAL INFRASTRUCTURES AND ADOPT PRIVACY MANAGEMENT PRACTICES THAT PROTECT THEIR EMPLOYEES?

Let's take the second part first. Employees work for their companies, and companies have an incentive and obligation to protect their assets and reputations, including gaining information about their employees. Background checks for example, are an accepted part of the application process for a range of roles.

As to the initial part of the question, the exploding capabilities of the digital world offer powerful new ways for organizations to defend themselves, even as those capabilities give attackers new means of attaining their nefarious goals. Protecting digital networks is not simply a function of building walls and barriers to hide behind (or, to use the language of the information security world, implementing firewalls and intrusion prevention systems). As digital infrastructures become more fluid and software based, organizations will be left with only two constants upon which they can focus: their users and their users' applications. While scrutiny of users and quality of applications is a must, security also will require deeper insight into the behavior of systems and information, so subtle, anomalous behaviors that are signs of compromise can be spotted and remediated. However, in many nations worker privacy laws prevent collection of the very kinds of information that are essential to performing that monitoring task.

Those challenges cannot be addressed at a technical level alone. Boards of directors could play a far larger role in developing policies for privacy and security. They would need to understand digital risks as well as they understand financial and operational risks and be able to assess the competence of their information security programs. Most boards are woefully unprepared on both accounts. Board-level governance would need to mature quickly to provide context for technical investments and policy creation, or security and privacy practitioners will be caught in the cross fire between employee demands and their respective job requirements.

The immaturity of corporate governance related to digital issues is not the only challenge. The following are even more acute:

- Organizations face a quagmire of contradictory or outdated laws and regulations; laws to protect worker privacy, for example, can make use of new behavior-based security technologies that help protect that privacy, actually illegal to implement.
- Personnel for both policy creation and security program management are hard to find. The current skills gap in information security alone is estimated at three hundred thousand to one million workers and will only worsen as the landscape evolves. Without talented and trained professionals to help solve this problem, we will fall further and further behind.
- The complex nature of organizational supply chains, partnerships, and business relationships makes the surface area of risk that must be defended nearly infinite in scope.

It's no wonder security teams often feel helpless or unequipped to meet their challenges no matter how much they spend. While Gartner predicts global IT spending on security to top $100 billion by 2017, a study of IT and risk professionals by IT security company RSA shows that even the largest and best funded of security teams feel their defenses are immature and inadequate in the face of the risks they confront.

STARTING HYPOTHESIS

Business-, academic-, and public-sector partnerships could help create a larger flow of qualified cyber professions, both in the technical and policy/leadership domains.

Boards of directors could add new members who offer the new skills they need and can collaborate to create more shared knowledge and perspectives.

Employees in privacy-oriented nations could recognize that they have more to lose by not empowering their security professionals than they do to gain through inflexible postures on privacy. Enterprises could do a better job of providing transparency so their employees know how their information is being collected and protected in the workplace.

The quality and security of applications, networks, and identity management programs could be held to a level closer to that of automobiles, foods, and other products where risk of flaw or compromise can lead to significant harm.

Information-sharing partnerships could continue to grow, built around mutual shared-interest such as supply chains, leveraging maturing models for sharing indicators of compromises, and the evolving tools, tactics, and procedures of adversaries. See the Finance Services Information Sharing and Analysis Center as a model of progress in this area.

Integral and increased investment in new security capabilities as applications or services are developed will be required and needs to be considered as essential to digital innovation as HVAC systems are to buildings.

Governments could borrow from the nuclear industry and others to create and clarify a government role to help corporations protect their critical infrastructure from attack while managing privacy and security interests. We need to find a way to rework the compliance versus cyber balance so that companies spend more time on value-added cybersecurity strategy and less on compliance-related work, while creating a forcing function or criteria for strong application, networks, and identity management pro-grams to ensure corporations are adequately protecting their employees and customers.

QUESTION 3: WHAT PRACTICES SHOULD GOVERNMENTS ADOPT TO MAINTAIN CIVIL LIBERTIES AND EXPECTATIONS OF PRIVACY, WHILE ENSURING SAFETY AND SECURITY OF ITS CITIZENS AND CRITICAL INFRASTRUCTURE?

This question has been at the heart of much of the debate in recent years, spurred by the release of classified documents by former intelligence work-er Edward Snowden and accusations of impropriety against the National Security Agency for collection and use of digital information. The underly-ing privacy relationship between citizens and their government is as old as societies themselves and has often been uneasy. However, in the digital world, the ability to collect and analyze massive amounts of information without transparency takes the issue into new dimensions. And the issue will become more explosive through refinement of technologies such as facial recognition.

In terms of our collective physical safety, this question is the most press-ing to make progress on, but perhaps the most difficult. Terrorist organi-zations use the Internet (and offshoots such as the so-called dark web), for recruitment, planning, and coordination activities. Cybercrime costs the world's economies over more than $445 billion annually.[9] But as individu-als, corporations, nations, criminals, and terrorists all increasingly roam the Internet together, enabling governments to protect their citizens without compromising the privacy and trust of those citizens is increasingly diffi-cult. Here is where the most dogmatic lines seem to be drawn between privacy advocates and security professionals (including military and law enforcement).

Interestingly, in this regard the challenges faced by enterprises and governments have many parallels. Just as organizations are adopting new approaches to information security in the face of eroding perimeters and increasing connectivity, government must find ways to defend their citizens in the face of porous national borders, increasing global flow of individuals, and the democratization and ubiquity of communication. Increasingly, that strategy will rely on even more information and better analytics, which, without proper governance, will further exacerbate the concerns of privacy advocates and citizens. The dearth of skill and expertise in the commercial world for cybersecurity will be a factor here as well, as governments seek to protect critical infrastructures.

STARTING HYPOTHESIS
Government could play a bigger role in helping define the "how," not just the "why," of protecting critical infrastructure, building on the National Institute of Standards and Technology Cybersecurity Framework.

Government could provide proper incentives for corporations to invest in cybersecurity for critical infrastructure.

Governments could develop and enforce safety standards for software used in critical infrastructures.

Governance and transparency could be strengthened for intelligence agencies, so that citizens can have confidence that those agencies are working within the existing laws and guidelines.

Government could communicate more clearly both the intentions and realities of intelligence gathering efforts. The Snowden disclosures and ensuing outcry saw little to no clear, productive communications response by the White House or Congress. We need rational, fact-based debate and deliberation that result in clear action.

Legal limits to domestic military involvement can be rethought: digital tools can now create kinetic actions to cause real physical harm to our infrastructure, as demonstrated by the Stuxnet-based damage to Iranian nuclear centrifuges. The role of the military in defending US citizens could be redefined to extend to cyber defense on US soil, without running afoul of legal and constitutional constraints, or increasing the worry of citizens as to their privacy and basic freedoms.

Governments need to find an approach for attribution and retribution to find and punish culprits of cybercrime, even across national borders. At the same time, private companies may need to be allowed to "hack back" and retrieve their stolen information before it's gone for good, given the challenges of relying on law-enforcement and the intelligence community.

We have to ensure transparency over law-enforcement and defense activities without unduly compromising their missions and effectiveness.

Spending and information resources should be pooled between governments to, for example, improve prosecution rates for cyber criminals (now at 2 to 3 percent), and governments need to be more proactive, not just reactive and defensive postattack.

QUESTION 4: WHAT NORMS SHOULD COUNTRIES ADOPT TO PROTECT THEIR SOVEREIGNTY WHILE ENABLING GLOBAL COMMERCE AND COLLABORATION AGAINST CRIMINAL AND TERRORIST THREATS?

As long as there have been nations, there has been espionage. Spying on enemies (and sometimes friends) has been a known responsibility and undertaking of all governments.

Signals intercepts have been a part of those efforts since the days of the horse-mounted courier. In the digital world of course, espionage takes on a whole new complexion. Spying on communications has never been easier for governments with the proper skills, and as more information of every form has become digital, more governments have gotten into the business of spying on behalf of their local corporations, in the form of intellectual property theft and communications intercepts.

When these campaigns become public, the outcry is understandably great. Action is typically far more subdued. That is because the digital age makes the crimes of espionage at once more intimate and more difficult to prosecute. Intimate because the world largely shares one digital infrastructure, and a host of deep, complex trade relationships that make commerce, communication, and collaboration across national boundaries an absolute necessity. These crimes are more difficult to prosecute because the acts are committed remotely, through networks that make attribution difficult and evidence both ambiguous and highly technical. The perpetrators are nameless, faceless, and abstract to the average citizen.

STARTING HYPOTHESIS

We believe this situation will change. As the world becomes increasingly digital, the playing field will become more level. As more nations have more to lose by aggressive cyber activity against their allies and trading partners, pressure will mount to address this issue. Just as nations finally concluded that the long-term benefits of free trade outweighed the short-term benefits of capturing or sinking each other's ships on the high seas, nations will eventually come together to create digital rules of engagement. But why wait?

The risks in the meantime will remain high. Cyber intrusions that cause significant economic or physical damage create the possibility of escalation into traditional armed conflict. Even absent direct escalation into a shooting war, cyberattacks will increasingly cross over from bits to atoms, and become kinetic in the damage they cause as we connect more of our devices to the Internet. It is nearly inevitable that cyberattacks by nation-states or terrorists will kill people at some point. Keeping those incidents isolated and containing their escalation into armed conflict is essential.

This is where nations must come together, to recognize the mutual interests in promoting clear rules of engagement and international law for the digital world. These agreements are not easy, but they are possible. We know nations are capable of reaching agreement on difficult and complex topics, as evidenced by the recent climate accords in Paris.

We need to limit cyber espionage, the targeting of individual corporations or organizations for economic or political motives. We believe that espionage will continue, but the current practices of many governments to use their national power to attack private institutions or other nations creates a dangerous imbalance and tips us toward broad-scale cyber conflicts.

We need to create "arms control" mechanisms to limit the spread of increasingly sophisticated malware tools. Unlike traditional weapons, cyber weapons spread rapidly, are quickly reproduced and modified, and are cheap.

We need to address the issues of nonstate actors who may target governments, enterprises, or individuals across national borders. These actors often have multiple roles, working for their own goals as well as providing services to governments or other nonstate actors.

We need to ensure that digital tools (software and systems) can be created free from nation-state interference either overt or covert so that these tools can be trusted by users globally.

THE NEXT STEPS ARE UP TO US

It is up to us to create the constructs that enable the digital age to mature into the force for good it has shown us it can be.

Today, cutting-edge cancer research happens at the intersection of technology, biology, physics, and mathematics. The impact of thousands of potential new drugs is modeled in computer simulations that would take years each to conduct using clinical trials. Massive data sets, not crowded hospitals, are the source for knowledge and the proving ground for advances that will perhaps save millions of lives in the years ahead.

Today we communicate, collaborate, buy, sell, trade, and chat about everything in our lives using digital technologies that are already so ubiquitous that we don't even notice them, but that are destined in short order to become exponentially more intimate parts of how we live—and how we can die.

The digital age that's dawned for us promises the most rapid gains in wealth, health, culture, and global collaboration we have ever witnessed. It is an adolescent at best, with physical attributes and energy that far outstrip its wisdom, experience, and mature sense of right and wrong. It is up to us to create the constructs that enable the digital age to mature into the force for good it has shown us it can be. And to start on that path, it is up to us to form a new kind of dialogue, on the basis of shared long-term interests and mutual trust between ideologies, economic interests, and national agendas. Only by doing so can we create the same sort of constitution for the digital world that has served our nation so well in its history.

This chapter is adapted from a paper by the Digital Equilibrium Project. Contributors included Stewart Baker, Tim Belcher, Jim Bidzos, Art Coviello, Dr. Ann Cavoukian, Larry Clinton, Michael Chertoff, Richard Clarke, Edward Davis, Brian Fitzgerald, Kasha Gauthier, J. Trevor Hughes, Michael McConnell, Nuala O'Connor, and JR Williamson, in partnership with McKinsey & Company.

---

1 Monica Anderson, "Technology Device Ownership: 2015," Pew Research Center, Oct. 29, 2015, Web, Jan. 14, 2016.

2 Jason Karain, "We Now Spend More than Eight Hours a Day Consuming Media," *Quartz*, June 1, 2015, Web, Citing Optimedia survey.

3 Mary Madden and Lee Rainie, "Americans' Attitudes About Privacy, Security and Surveillance," Pew Research Center, May 20, 2015, Web.

4 James Manyika, Michael Chui, Peter Bisson, Jonathan Woetzel, Richard Dobbs, Jacques Bughin, and Dan Aharon, "Unlocking the Potential of the Internet of Things," McKinsey Global Institute, June 2015, Web.

5 Growth in number of transistors per commercially available microprocessors for 2005–2015, using the Pentium D Smithfield from 2005 (169 M transistors) and the Intel 18-core Xeon Haswell-BP (5 B transistors)."SIN Graph–Micro Processor Cost per Transistor Cycle," *The Singularity Is Near*. Web.

6 Arielle Sumits, "The History and Future of Internet Traffic," *Cisco Blogs*, Aug. 28, 2015, Web, Jan. 14, 2016; 1.3 exabytes/month from 2004 to 42 exabytes/month in 2014.

7 "IBM SONAS Enterprise NAS: A Comprehensive Review–Wikibon," n.p., Mar. 17, 2010, Web, Jan. 14, 2016; extrapolated from International Data Corporation showing data storage capacity growth of 9x from 2006 to 2012.

8 The Commission on the Theft of American Intellectual Property, *The IP Commission Report: The Report of the Commission on the Theft of American Intellectual Property* (National Bureau of Asian Research, May 2013), Web.

9 Center for Strategic and International Studies and McAfee, *Net Losses: Estimating the Global Cost of Cybercrime. Economic Impact of Cybercrime II* (Intel Security, June 2014), Web.

Seventeen

Best Practices for Cybersecurity Public-Private Partnerships

Larry Clinton, President and CEO, Internet Security Alliance

INTRODUCTION

Shortly after taking office in 2009, President Barack Obama called for a comprehensive review of the nation's approach to combating cyber threats. The president said,

> The federal government cannot succeed in securing cyber space if it works in isolation. The public and private sectors interests are intertwined with a shared responsibility for ensuring a secure, reliable infrastructure upon which businesses and government depend...Only through such partnerships will the United States be able to enhance cybersecurity and reap the full benefits of the digital revolution.[1]

This chapter is an attempt to review the nation's approach to combating cyber threats and how "best practices" for public-private partnerships may help ameliorate—to some degree—growing cyber threats. The first section describes a brief history of the evolution of cyber-focused public-private partnerships, followed by a discussion of case studies in how such partnerships have demonstrated effective results in enhancing cybersecurity through a robust assessment process. The chapter concludes with twelve best practices generated by that analysis for more effective management of cyber-partnership activities. Ideally, partnerships would continue to evolve to share leadership, appreciate differing perspectives, and develop shared goals and priorities. The digital economy increasingly requires this kind of collaborative environment to continue to flourish, encouraged by the meaningful cybersecurity accomplishments of public-private partnerships.

A BRIEF HISTORY OF THE PUBLIC-PRIVATE PARTNERSHIP FOR CYBERSECURITY

When the first National Strategy to Secure Cyberspace was written in 2003, the mutually shared nature of the Internet led to the proposition that cyberspace would best be secured through a partnership of mutual benefit.[2] It was assumed that industry's natural interest would lead it to develop adequate technologies and practices to secure the expanding cyber systems.

Government's role was initially thought to be primarily securing its own systems. With respect to the private sector, government's role was largely confined to education, international coordination, and assisting with research and development. Market efficiency was assumed to be sufficient to drive adoption of adequate protective measures.

By the time the first National Infrastructure Protection Plan (known as the NIPP)[3] was written in 2006 and updated in 2013,[4] a more sophisticated understanding of digital economics made it apparent that the public and private sectors had "aligned, but not identical, interests" with respect to cybersecurity.

Experience demonstrated that commercial security levels were generally lower than those required for national security and other governmental purposes. The NIPP clarified that a voluntary partnership model that could respond to the quickly changing cyber environment was in the nation's national and homeland security interests. However, for this voluntary model to succeed, government would need to do more than just rely on naked market forces or traditional regulation to prompt the private sector to elevate its security spending to meet national security needs.

The updated NIPP articulated the notion that, to create a sustainably secure cyber system, government could not rely on the private sector to

continually make substantial investments that were commercially uneconomic. Instead, an incentive system similar to those used to achieve social
needs in sectors such as agriculture, environment, transportation, and others would have to be evolved and applied to the cybersecurity partnership:

> The success of the partnership depends on articulating the mutual
> benefits to government and private sector partners. While articulat-
> ing the value proposition to the government typically is clear, it is
> often more difficult to articulate the direct benefits of participation
> for the private sector...In assessing the value proposition for the
> private sector...government can encourage industry to go beyond
> efforts already justified by their corporate business needs to assist
> in broad-scale CI/KR [critical infrastructure/key resource] protection
> through activities such as...supporting incentives for companies to
> voluntarily adopt widely accepted security practices.[5]

There were periodic efforts to redefine the partnership model to secure cyberspace in such a way as to mimic the traditional government-industry regulatory model. The most prominent of these efforts was legislation, which
combined efforts of the Senate Homeland Security and Commerce committees in 2012. This combined bill, drafted under the auspices of Senate
majority leader Harry Reid and generally referred to as Lieberman-Collins,
would have empowered the Department of Homeland Security to set cybersecurity mandates for large portions of the private sector and grant DHS
compliance authority backed by substantial penalties for noncompliance. It
defined this new partnership in the following way:

> This bill creates a dynamic partnership between government and
> the private sector in which the private sector is responsible for en-
> hancing security of the nation's most critical infrastructure while the
> government ensures effective oversight and compliance.[6]

Not surprisingly, industry found this construction of the partnership somewhat strained.

The idea that the private sector would fund national defense needs, including defending against potential nation-state attacks against critical infrastructure, was both naive and impractical. Busch and Austen Givens pointed out in one of the few academic analyses of public-private partnerships, "Any business executive who suddenly announced he was increasing security spending by 25 percent for the good of the nation would almost certainly be fired."[7]

This is not to say that industry is unwilling to spend on cybersecurity. In fact, industry spending on cybersecurity has more than doubled in recent years and is now over $100 billion a year.[8] By comparison, DHS spending on cybersecurity is just over $1 billion annually and total federal government spending is under $15 billion.[9]

In addition to the financial issues that undermine the attempt to define a traditional regulatory approach as a partnership, there were numerous other reasons why the regulatory approach to cybersecurity was ill founded, which have been detailed elsewhere.[10] These include the generally unfounded assumption that the primary reason for successful cyberattacks is corporate malfeasance by underfunding security as opposed to the inherent weakness in the technology and the sophistication of the attackers. There has also been notable lack of success for the regulatory approaches that have been tried in this area, such as HIPPA (healthcare) and Gramm-Leech-Bliley (financial services), and the enormous negative economic impact that imposing a government-centric regulatory regime would have on goals as desirable as security such as innovation, economic growth, and job creation.[11] As a result of all these problems and despite holding a strong majority in the Senate, the Lieberman-Collins bill couldn't drum up enough support even to make it to the floor.

Following the collapse of the regulatory effort to impose cybersecurity mandates on critical infrastructure, President Obama issued Executive Order 13636 in February 2013, which was accompanied by Presidential Decision Directive 25. Both documents embraced the voluntary model of industry-government partnership for cybersecurity and more fully defined several of the elements that would be necessary for it to succeed. The president's executive order largely followed the "Cybersecurity Social Contract" paradigm that had been proposed by a coalition of industry and privacy groups.[12]

This renewed and more fully articulated partnership model called for industry to work collectively with government through the National Institute of Standards and Technology to identify industry-based standards and practices worthy of voluntary adoption by critical infrastructure owners and operators. This framework was to be voluntary, scalable, cost effective, and prioritized. The administration pledged not to seek additional regulatory powers for cybersecurity and to promote voluntary adoption of the targeted standards and practices through the deployment of market incentives.[13]

In a rare case of bipartisanship, the social contract model was also embraced by the House GOP Task Force on cybersecurity that had been appointed by Speaker of the House John Boehner.[14] By 2015 there had been such a consensus developed that cybersecurity would best be addressed through a voluntary industry-government partnership process that independent assessors were reporting that it was difficult to find anyone in the nation's capital who disagreed with the wisdom of the voluntary partnership model.[15]

HOW TO MAKE PUBLIC-PRIVATE PARTNERSHIPS FOR CYBERSECURITY WORK: CASE STUDIES

Realizing that frustration with the partnership model was building in 2011, the IT Sector Coordinating Council wrote to DHS undersecretary Rand Beers and requested that DHS join with the IT SCC in a process to develop a set of collaborative guidelines for operating effective partnerships for cybersecurity. Working together, the Government Coordinating Council for IT and the industry sector coordinating council devised a three-step program using an adaption of critical-incident methodology.

First, leaders from the SCC and GCC would select a sample of six programs that had sought to use the partnership as spelled out in the NIPP. Second, since it was understood that government and industry could look at the same program and come to different conclusions as to its effectiveness, the GCC and SCC were asked to independently analyze the programs by accessing planning documents and interviewing key participants.

The goals of the interviews were to assess the participant's judgment as to whether the programs were successful or unsuccessful in meeting their goals and to identify characteristics of the programs that would explain why the programs were labeled as successful or unsuccessful. Finally, the independent GCC and SCC leadership teams jointly analyzed all the results from step two and attempted to identify common elements that were used in successful and unsuccessful programs. Both government and industry independently agreed which programs fit into the successful and less successful categories and were able to identify a dozen "best practices" that were found to have been commonly used in the successful projects and not in the less successful ones. The results of the study were presented at the annual 2012 IT/Comms Government-Industry "Quad" conference in 2012. A summary of this analysis and its results follows.[16]

A PARTNERSHIP SUCCESS STORY: THE 2006 NATIONAL INFRASTRUCTURE PROTECTION PLAN

Development of the 2006 NIPP was the result of a collaborative process that reflected multiple rounds of stakeholder review and comment during which the department received thousands of individual comments. The private sector was given the opportunity to participate in the NIPP 2006 drafting process and reported that DHS made a genuine effort to include them in its development. The final 2006 NIPP recognized that partnership is the appropriate model for coordination between industry and DHS. In addition, existing cross-sector organizations or their predecessors (like the Partnership for Critical Infrastructure Security) participated and provided a valuable cross-sector viewpoint to the 2006 NIPP. Both the government and industry leadership teams agreed that the process used to create the 2006 NIPP was an example of partnership success.

What Was Successful and Unsuccessful in This Effort

Early involvement by industry in the 2006 NIPP development was judged to be a key to a successful product. The opportunity for industry to provide inputs as the document was being developed was judged by both DHS and the IT SCC as fundamental to the success of the final document. Among the characteristics praised by both industry and the government were the following:

- **Codrafting**: Reflection of private-sector comments in the final language demonstrated that DHS respected and was listening to its partner.
- **Personal commitment by DHS**: DHS assistant secretary for Infrastructure Protection, Robert Stephan, owned the NIPP 2006 process and was committed to partnership with all the stakeholders, including the critical infrastructures, in drafting it. He frequently showed his engagement and leadership by engaging directly in draft language–related discussions with stakeholder groups in calls or in person.
- **Personal commitment by industry**: The leaders of industry's sector coordinating councils and information sharing and analysis centers and other bodies were equally engaged.

A PARTNERSHIP SUCCESS STORY: THE IT SECTOR BASELINE RISK ASSESSMENT

The IT Sector Baseline Risk Assessment was developed as part of the sector's implementation of the sector-specific plan. The risk assessment departed from the traditional physical risk assessments, which focused on identifying critical assets, and instead identified six "critical functions" that the IT sector provides. The goal of the assessment was to identify high-consequence/high-likelihood events to prioritize risk-mitigation resources and efforts.

More than seventy subject-matter experts from industry and government participated in the development of the IT Sector Baseline Risk Assessment. The IT SCC and IT GCC each appointed a cochair to the committee that developed the assessment, thereby providing joint authority and accountability. The cochairs met regularly to develop and map timelines, plan future meetings, track ongoing initiatives, and resolve any conflicts. The committee of industry and government subject-matter experts met two to four times a month to develop the risk assessment methodology. Both industry and government judged this program a successful partnership.

What Was Successful and Unsuccessful in This Effort
Among the characteristics praised by both industry and the government were the following:

- Having industry and government cochairs ensured joint account-ability and authority, with defined roles and responsibilities for each cochair.
- Committee decisions were made on a consensus basis, with exten-sive efforts to accommodate all reasonable considerations. Support staff captured action items and impartially drafted meeting materi-als on the basis of committee discussions, as opposed to any pre-determined or hidden agenda.

A PARTNERSHIP SUCCESS STORY: THE CYBERSPACE POLICY REVIEW

Shortly after taking office, President Obama assigned staff of the National Security Council to conduct an intensive review of our nation's cyber read-iness, public and private. This process led to the publication of the ad-ministration's signature document on cybersecurity—"Cyberspace Policy Review." The task was a "clean slate review" assessing all US policies and structures for cybersecurity. The review team of government cybersecurity experts actively engaged and received input from a broad cross section of industry, academia, the civil liberties and privacy communities, state govern-ments, international partners, and the legislative and executive branches. The review team systematically reached out to the specifically designated elements of the public-private partnership as identified in the NIPP, such as the SCCs and the ISACs. The process was multifaceted including both public and private meetings of substantive nature, and an active effort was made to solicit written input from stakeholders. Both industry and govern-ment assessed this program as an example of a successful partnership.

What Was Successful and Unsuccessful in the Effort
Among the characteristics praised by both industry and the government were the following:

- Starting with a "clean slate." The review team did not betray a bias toward a particular ideology or approach but rather sought to openly solicit perspectives of all elements of the partnership and then integrate them into a coherent volume.
- Broad stakeholder involvement. The review team of government cybersecurity experts actively engaged and received input from a broad cross section of stakeholders. The drafters clearly had listened to the various inputs, as is evidenced in the numerous quotations from these inputs cited in the review.
- Utilizing the NIPP. The review team systematically reached out to the specifically designated elements of the public-private partnership as identified in the NIPP.
- Input. An active effort was made to solicit written input from stakeholders.
- Early engagement with the private sector.

A LESS SUCCESSFUL PARTNERSHIP EFFORT: INDUSTRY INTEGRATION INTO THE NATIONAL INFRASTRUCTURE COORDINATION CENTER

Building a joint industry-government cyber operations center had been a long-standing goal of both industry and government. Although this initiative was not technically a joint SCC and GCC initiative, it did involve open operational collaboration and engagement between industry and government. Specific *National Security Telecommunications Advisory Committee* members created a concept of operations for the joint operations center, and it was subjected to a pilot program. Members of the pilot program agreed to the concept of operations, providing binding partners to the same program rules and operations. A common portal was used so that participating organizations could share information and see what others submitted, and "cross-sector analysts" were responsible for doing additional correlation and analysis. Both industry and government assessed this program as an example of a less successful partnership.

What Was Unsuccessful in This Effort

While DHS used elements of the above program to attempt to build an integrated capability, the program was not developed in collaboration with industry. As a result, analysts from both the IT SCC and the GCC identified various shortcomings with this program. See the following for example:

- There was no common governing document or framework for the program.
- Participants were not told who else was participating in the program, so they did not know who else was receiving the information they shared.
- There was no clarity or transparency on the criteria used to determine who qualified for this program.
- Instead of building situational awareness among participating organizations by providing access to the shared information on a common portal, only DHS analysts had access to the information shared by program participants.

A LESS SUCCESSFUL PARTNERSHIP EFFORT: INFORMATION TECHNOLOGY SUPPLY-CHAIN–RISK-MANAGEMENT COLLABORATION

Both industry and government had agreed to develop cohesive policy to manage cybersecurity supply-chain risk. Unfortunately, the private sector felt blocked in its efforts to collaborate due to the lack of information sharing regarding DHS efforts. The private sector felt the lack of information sharing was undermining the public-private partnership as well as fueling the proliferation of multiple, uncoordinated efforts to address supply-chain risk-management issues within the US government. Both industry and government assessed this program as an example of a less successful partnership.

What Was Unsuccessful in This Effort

Overall, the general lack of communication by government to industry was mutually judged to be unproductive and had the potential to breed misinformation, which exacerbated the challenge of building an effective public-private effort. Specifically, the following was found:

- DHS did not share details or specific supply-chain risk-management assessment or evaluation criteria and other practices and policies that they were considering applying to the private sector.
- DHS declined to engage in a substantive discussion regarding current IT supply-chain risk-management practices and standards or potential policies and regulations, when requested by the private sector.

A LESS SUCCESSFUL EFFORT: BLUEPRINT FOR A SECURE CYBER FUTURE—THE CYBERSECURITY STRATEGY FOR THE HOMELAND SECURITY ENTERPRISE PROGRAM AND FUNDAMENTALLY ALTERING THE PUBLIC-PRIVATE PARTNERSHIP

Although the National Infrastructure Protection Plan and Cyberspace Policy Review both articulated the need for a voluntary public-private partnership, and government officials publically pledged their support for this effort, DHS launched a series of policy programs inconsistent with this direction.

Prominent examples were the so-called Blueprint and Enterprise programs. The policy papers accompanying those programs argued that the voluntary partnership was not working and that there was a need to alter the voluntary public-private partnership and fundamentally change it into a traditional regulatory model. At no point did DHS or any other federal agency engage the partnership model to explain why this change in philosophy had been reached, or what the evidence was that problems related to cybersecurity issues were the result of market failures. When the existence of these efforts came to light, elements of the partnership were asked for only limited input and advised they would be engaged only at the implementation stages. Both industry and government assessed this program as an example of a less successful partnership.

What Was Unsuccessful in This Effort

Many in the private sector found it disingenuous for elements at DHS to advocate for a fundamentally different structure of the partnership model (switching from voluntary to a government mandate system) without ever engaging the partnership model to discuss the reasons for this dramatic change. The lack of trust these efforts engendered was magnified as DHS publically espoused the benefits of the partnership model. The papers created ill will and undermined the ability for the partnership to function in the national interest. As a result, the Partnership for Critical Infrastructure Security, which represented all critical industry sectors, formally protested these nonpartnership activities to Homeland Security secretary Janet Napolitano and noted that the mistrust these programs engendered truncated partnership programs as DHS eventually acknowledged. Specific items cited as problematic in the "Blueprint" effort were as follows:

- While it is clearly stated in the NIPP that economics is a central issue in developing a sustainable cybersecurity partnership with the private sector, DHS never produced any economic analysis. As a result, the "blueprint for the cyber ecosystem" failed to even consider one of the most central elements of that economic system. Analyses from both the government and industry agreed in retrospect that this critical omission would not have occurred if a more inclusive process had been used.

CYBER STORM AND NATIONAL LEVEL EXERCISE

The Cyber Storm Exercise series and the National Level Exercise series have been opportunities to leverage the partnership to help manage risks. National Level Exercises: NLE 2012 was the first tier-one exercise on cyber and was an opportunity to leverage the partnership to enhance prevention, detection, and operational and policy response. Many of the lessons learned through the Cyber Storm series, however, were not leveraged for NLE 2012. The exercise series has received mixed reviews with some notable successes and sustained criticism for the lack of follow-through from the exercises.

What Was Unsuccessful in This Effort

Analysts reported both successful and unsuccessful elements of the series. Among the successful items were the following.

Early Strategic Engagement

- Integrating participating communities in a joint coordinated planning process.
- Enabling participating organizations and sectors to identify objectives and ultimately harmonize those so that *all* participants gained value and exercise play was appropriately synchronized and coordinated via a core scenario.
- Establishing a National Private Sector Working Group to engage the participation and expertise of a wide range of private-sector stakeholders.

Room for Improvement

- While NLE 2012 raised awareness about cyber risks to a broader community and examined intergovernmental coordination to some degree, the insights could have been greater for all participants if the partnership had been more fully leveraged.
- The findings and recommendations in NLE 2012 were notably similar to many recommendations from previous exercises, including the Cyber Storm Exercise series. Marginal improvements occurred, but meaningful and substantial progress to coordinate and enhance the collective cybersecurity response capability between government and industry was not made.

BEST PRACTICES GENERATED BY THE JOINT DHS PRIVATE-SECTOR CASE STUDIES

On the basis of joint government-industry analysis of the six partnership projects summarized above, a set of a dozen best practices that consistently generated successful partnership programs on both a substantive and operational maintenance level were agreed to. Subsequently the PCIS, which at the time was the body designated in the NIPP to represent all the critical industry sectors, endorsed the best practices and urged DHS to officially embrace them as well. As of this writing, DHS has proposed a memorandum of understanding to the PCIS that will embrace these principles for operating future partnership programs. These best practices are as follows:

- Senior-level commitment to the partnership process communicated to staff and upper echelons.
- Involvement at the priority, goal, and objective phases of projects, not just implementation.
- Use of the process identified in the NIPP for involving industry.
- Reaching out to stakeholders early on, ideally at the "blank page" stage.
- Continuous and regular interaction between government and industry stakeholders.
- Providing adequate time for stakeholder review (equivalent to government review).
- Establishing coleadership of programs.
- Consensus partnership decision making.
- Communicating genuine interest in stakeholder input (e.g., via codrafting).
- Adequate engagement from federal agencies beyond DHS.
- Government follow-through on partnership-related decisions.
- Adequate and competent support services.

FOLLOWING BEST PRACTICES IN REGULATED AND UNREGULATED INDUSTRIES: MORE SUCCESS STORIES

THE NIST CYBERSECURITY FRAMEWORK

Executive Order 13636 instructed NIST to launch a collaborative process with industry designed to develop a framework for critical infrastructure cybersecurity. Rather than impose the subsequent framework by seeking additional regulatory authority, as it had done previously through the Lieberman-Collins bill, the administration pledged to retain a voluntary approach supplemented by the deployment of a set of market incentives.

This NIST process embodied virtually every one of the best practices identified in the IT Sector–DHS partnership study. The president himself launched the process via the executive order, and senior officials regularly reemphasized commitment to the process. NIST made every effort to involve industry and make the framework an "industry framework not a government framework." This included an extensive process of six national workshops across the country that brought in hundreds of stakeholders. This process was complemented by an extensive series of private meetings with interested stakeholders. NIST regularly updated drafts of the framework with adequate time for industry review and comment and embraced comments and made substantial and clearly evident changes as the process matured. NIST also did not display the sometimes-pernicious tendency of government agencies to claim "ownership" of the process. Perhaps, in part because of the clear direction directly from the president, NIST comfortably folded in adequate engagement from other government agencies.

Feedback has been nearly unanimous in praising the process. Michael Daniel, White House special assistant to the president and cybersecurity coordinator, called industry's response to the framework "phenomenal." A second White House official, Ari Schwartz, until recently a senior director for cybersecurity, added that business support for the framework has "exceeded expectations." Such recognition is constructive and helps keep the private sector engaged in using the framework and promoting it with business partners.[17]

From the industry side, the US Chamber of Commerce—which had vehemently opposed the Obama administration's earlier efforts on cybersecurity—now echoes the administration's assessment of the NIST process:

The Chamber believes that the release of the Framework for Improving Critical Infrastructure Cybersecurity has been a remarkable success. The Chamber, sector-based coordinating councils and associations, companies, and other private and public entities collaborated closely with NIST in developing the framework since the first workshop was held in April 2013. Critical infrastructure sectors are keenly aware of and supportive of the framework.[18]

The financial services industry, one of the sectors most targeted and most severely affected by cyberattacks, also expressed strong support for the NIST process:

> Regarding the framework development process, it was a success due in large part to its transparency and because it sought to harmonize various views into a cohesive whole. We applaud that NIST's process for developing the Framework engaged these other sectors during the Framework's drafting. NIST's successful approach at inclusion of so many essential parties are reflected in how broadly embraced the Framework has become across so many sectors.[19]

However, a process that generates a positive effect is inadequate if the larger public-policy goals are not met. Here again, the NIST process seems to be generating commitment and advancement to improved cybersecurity. In the words of the Financial Services Roundtable:

> With respect to the framework, its true value is that it synthesizes a process for cyber-risk management that is accessible from the boardroom to the operations floor, across not only individual enterprises but also entire sectors. It relies on international standards and is consistent with the regulatory requirements that have been in place for our sector for more than a decade. It is a "Rosetta Stone" in that it provides a common lexicon for categorizing and managing cyber risks across sectors and enterprises for various unifying risk management jargons and creates a common understanding around various risk management terms, methodologies, ideas and language.[20]

As a result, we have heard from member financial institutions that, in terms of internal enterprise usage, chief information security officers are using the framework to communicate ideas and achieve "buy-in" for various cybersecurity initiatives. Externally, firms are beginning to use it to communicate "expectations and requirements to vendors."[21]

CSRIC WORKING GROUP 4 (FCC AND COMMUNICATIONS SECTOR)

The Department of Commerce has no regulatory authority, and hence its bureau, NIST, might be expected not to utilize a more traditional regulatory model when seeking to promote improved cybersecurity behavior in the private sector. By contrast, many elements of the telecommunications sector come from a strong and varied regulatory history. Hence, when the Federal Communications Commission undertook the task of engaging the industries under its authority to promote improved cybersecurity practices, it might have been expected that they would resort to a legacy model of federal regulations supplemented by adapting historic state and local authorities. However, FCC chairman Tom Wheeler chose instead to call for a "new paradigm" to address the unique challenges of digital technology and asked industry and commission staff to utilize the Communications Security, Reliability and Interoperability Council (CSRIC Working Group 4) process to find a new way to implement the NIST Framework within the communications industry.

CSRIC Working Group 4 launched a six-month process to operationalize the "new paradigm" sought by Chairman Wheeler. The process embraced virtually all of the previously identified best practices. And much like the NIST process, the reviews from both government and industry have been starkly positive.

In a featured speech at the 2015 RSA Security Conference, Chairman Wheeler said that Working Group 4

> developed a range of activities intended to provide transparent assurances to the FCC, to DHS, to industry, and to consumers. These visible assurances should provide confidence that companies throughout the sector are actually taking effective steps to manage cyber risk...I believe that CSRIC's assurance model will provide much-needed accountability for network security, while avoiding top-down prescriptive regulation of industry practices. A cooperative and collaborative approach is the FCC's preferred means of engagement. I have every reason to be confident the industry will live up to its commitments and deliver meaningful action.[22]

CONCLUSION

Cybersecurity is one of the areas of public policy where substantial consensus has emerged. There is broad agreement that the security problem is severe and growing and that the traditional regulatory model does not fit well with unique characteristics of the Internet and the conscious and sustained attacks on it. Instead, a novel, voluntary, and economically sustainable partnership between industry and government needs to evolve. Early efforts at partnership met with inconsistent success.

More recently, industry and government have collaborated and identified a set of practical guidelines or "best practices" for managing cyber-partnership activities. This more sophisticated notion of partnership departs from having critical functions decided unilaterally by government, with industry's role confined to comment, implementation, or compliance. Instead, the new partnership model requires, among other things, that the partners share leadership, appreciate each other's differing perspectives, and develop partnership priorities, goals, and objectives together.

Notwithstanding the mounting evidence that these partnerships, properly managed, are generating success in an extremely challenging arena, government agencies may be reluctant to depart from the traditional regulatory model for a model that requires more time and collaboration on the front end and less traditional enforcement on the back end. However, the digital economy of the twenty-first century may demand an evolution away from the legacy independent regulatory model developed in the nineteenth century. When utilized, this approach has, at least initially, driven meaningful cybersecurity accomplishments.

---

1 Executive Office of the President of United States, "Cyberspace Policy Review: Assuring a Trusted and Resilient Information and Communications Infrastructure," *WhiteHouse.gov*, 2009, Web.

2 President's Critical Infrastructure Protection Board, *The National Strategy to Secure Cyberspace* (Washington, DC: President's Critical Infrastructure Protection Board, 2002).

3 Department of Homeland Security, *National Infrastructure Protection Plan: 2006* (Washington, DC: Department of Homeland Security, 2006).

4 Department of Homeland Security, *National Infrastructure Protection Plan: 2013* (Washington, DC: Department of Homeland Security, 2013).

5 Ibid, p. 15.

6 Cybersecurity Act of 2012, S. 3414, 112th Cong. (2012).

7 Nathan E. Busch and Austen D. Givens, "Public-Private Partnerships in Homeland Security: Opportunities and Challenges," *Homeland Security Affairs* 8 (Oct. 2012): 18, Web.

8 Ponemon Institute, "Cybersecurity Incident Response: Are We as Prepared as We Think?" *Lancope*, Jan. 2014, Web.

9 *Annual Report to Congress: Federal Information Security Management Act* (Office of Management and Budget, Executive Office of the President of the United States, the White House, Feb. 27, 2015), p. 83, Web.

10 Larry Clinton, "A Relationship on the Rocks: Industry-Government Partnership for Cyber Defense," *Journal of Strategic Security* 4, no. 2 (2011): 97–112.

11 Ibid.

12 Internet Security Alliance, "Improving our Nation's Cybersecurity through the Public–Private Partnership," white paper, Mar. 8, 2001.

13 Exec. Order 13636, Section 7(d).

14 Office of US Representative Thornberry, "Recommendation of the House Republican Cybersecurity Task Force," Oct. 2011, Web.

15 Jarno Limnell, "Cybersecurity Is a Team Sport," *Politico*, May 15, 2015, Web.

16 Information Technology Sector Coordinating Committee, *Best Practices for Partnership* (Internet Security Alliance, 2012).

17 Steven Chabinsky, "What Is the Most Influential Cybersecurity Team?" *Security Magazine*, Sept. 1, 2013, Web.

18 US Chamber of Commerce, Comments on the NIST Request for Information on the Cyber Framework, Oct. 10, 2014, Web.

19 Ibid.

20 *Testimony of Paul Smocer on Behalf of BITS/Financial Services Roundtable before the United States Senate Committee on Commerce, Science and Transportation Hearing on "Building a More Secure Cyber Future: Examining Private Sector Experience with the NIST Framework,"* 114th Cong. (2015) (testimony of Paul Smocer on behalf of BITS/Financial Services Roundtable).

21 US Chamber of Commerce, Comments on the NIST Request.

22 Tom Wheeler, FCC Chairman, prepared remarks for RSA Conference, San Francisco, Apr. 21 2015.

Appendix A

Ten Cybersecurity Items for the President's First One Hundred Days

Some of the recommendations in this volume are tonal (act with greater urgency) and hard to immediately measure, while others clearly could take substantial time to implement (government reorganization). Here is a short list of items that the new administration can announce in its agenda for the first one hundred days and can be accomplished within the first year or sooner:

- Leverage existing partnership structure in the National Infrastructure Protection Plan to begin pilot testing the NIST Cybersecurity Framework for cost effectiveness and prioritization for small companies.
- Require all federal agencies to demonstrate cost effectiveness for all cybersecurity regulations programs promulgated on the private sector.
- Initiate reform of the cyber-compliance model to reflect cyber-maturity improvements as opposed to pass-fail compliance.
- Using the same model that created the NIST framework in conjunction with federal agencies, develop menus of market-incentive programs for cybersecurity, as called for in Executive Order 13636.

- Federal agencies shall coordinate among themselves and with states and localities and eliminate duplicative cyber regulations among jurisdictions.
- Initiate public awareness program on law-enforcement cyber roles and responsibilities by leverage private-sector associations.
- Initiate a cybersecurity education program for senior government officials modeled on the program run by National Association of Corporate Directors.
- Require federal agencies operating cyber-partnership programs to follow best practices for private-sector engagement as reported in the *Journal of Strategic Security* in Winter 2015.[1]
- Reform clearance process allowing for ability to transfer the holding of clearances to different government agencies and retaining them with US-based employment changes.

---

1 See Larry Clinton, "Best Practices for Operating Government-Industry Partnerships in Cybersecurity," *Journal of Strategic Security* 8, no. 4 (2015): 53–68.

Appendix B – Briefing Memos

One

A Brief History of the Cybersecurity Problem and Policies That Have Attempted to Address It

Larry Clinton, President and CEO, Internet Security Alliance

THE PROBLEM: IT'S REALLY BAD—AND ABOUT TO GET MUCH WORSE

The Internet was designed in the '70s and '80s to be an "open" system, not a secure system. The core protocols that the Internet is based on are insecure by design. In addition, new software services and applications tend to be built on these core protocols, and so modern innovative products inherit the original vulnerabilities. This trend will be exacerbated by the explosion in mobile devices and the Internet of Things.

THE ATTACK COMMUNITY IS GROWING MUCH MORE SOPHISTICATED

Nearly a decade ago, the National Security Agency coined the term "advanced persistent threat." APT was originally used to describe the ultra-sophisticated, multistaged cyberattacks we had begun to see between nation-states and the defense establishment. We are now seeing these same sorts of attacks being launched throughout the cyber ecosystem. The advanced persistent threat has now become the *average* persistent threat.

ALL THE ECONOMIC INCENTIVES IN CYBERSECURITY FAVOR THE ATTACKERS

When one considers the economic balance—the cost benefits of cybersecurity—it quickly becomes apparent that the economic balance overwhelmingly favors the attackers. Cybercriminals have an extremely attractive business model. Unlike many traditional illicit enterprises that require the use of a large, unreliable workforce, and long supply chains, cyberattacks require comparatively small workforces that can be safely located far from disruptive civil forces. Attackers generally have first-mover advantage in deciding who, when, and how to attack, often on the basis of stealthy reconnaissance. Defense is historically a generation behind the attacker. Complicating the economic imbalance, many of the technologies and business practices that are required for enterprises to operate successfully in a worldwide competitive market tend to undermine cybersecurity.

WHY TRADITIONAL MECHANISMS ARE FAILING TO PROVIDE SECURITY

THEY WERE DESIGNED FOR A DIFFERENT TYPE OF PROBLEM

Traditional mechanisms such as independent regulatory agencies, consumer lawsuits, and government regulation are proving ineffective in adequately bolstering our security in light of the modern threats. Much of our traditional regulatory processes and judicial enforcement are designed to address malfeasance. However, the core problem with cybersecurity is not that the technology is poorly constructed or companies are unwilling to invest in reasonable security. It's that the technology is under attack.

GOVERNMENT DOESN'T HAVE THE CREDIBILITY NEEDED TO REGULATE FOR CYBERSECURITY

There is no evidence that government has attained that degree of expertise in cybersecurity. In fact, the data suggest the opposite. Greg Wilshusen, director for info security at the Government Accountability Office, explained in congressional testimony some of the reasons why. Among them is this: "Government agencies follow what IT pros call a policy-based approach to cybersecurity where agencies check off a list of requirements set by law-makers and regulators that they have to follow."

GOVERNMENT IS NOT PROPERLY STRUCTURED TO DEAL WITH THE DIGITAL AGE

A Bank of America Merrill Lynch 2015 report found that "The US government is still in the process of determining who will have jurisdiction in cyberspace. As the Department of Defense, DHS, and their subordinate organizations like the Air Force, Navy, Army, Defense Agencies and Commands battle for jurisdiction and funding. The result is a fragmented system muddled with a political agenda which hinders the development of a more secure system."

EVEN IF GOVERNMENT WERE UP TO THE TASK, THE REGULATORY MODEL DOESN'T FIT THE PROBLEM

The expert agency regulatory model, wherein an elected body empowers a regulatory agency to specify requirements for the private sector, essentially attempts to locate a static standard that assures safety wherever producers are in compliance. Technology and attack methods change constantly and quickly. The traditional regulatory process cannot keep up with the evolution of what constitutes the required cybersecurity at any given time.

There is a role for regulation in certain spaces, such as requirements to notify citizens when their personal data have been compromised, or in industries where the core economics of the industry are already intimately involved in regulation, such as municipal water services. But traditional regulation generally falls short as an effective sustaining private-sector cybersecurity, because of the nature of government and the nature of the problem itself.

OTHER INDUSTRIAL-AGE CONTROL MECHANISMS ARE NOT WORKING, ARE INAPPROPRIATE, AND MAY BE COUNTERPRODUCTIVE

Disclosure Models Don't Fit the Digital Age

While citizens have an obvious right to know if their personal data have been compromised (as virtually every state now demands), disclosure as a motivator for improved security is too blunt an instrument to achieve our broader goals.

Court Action Is Proving Ineffective

Notwithstanding the hype from the plaintiff's bar, the predicted (for ten years) avalanche of lawsuits by consumers harmed by cyberattacks and the resulting improvements in security to avoid such suits has not materialized. One of the main reasons for this mechanism's failure to promote the needed security upgrades is that the suits are usually unsuccessful.

THE PATH FORWARD: THE CYBERSECURITY SOCIAL CONTRACT

The concept of the social contract initially focused on the relationship between the individual and the state and what each would exchange with the other in order to achieve broader social order and benefit for the community. In the early twentieth century, the social contract was adapted to the exchange between corporations and the state in order to achieve mutual and greater benefit for the social order.

At the time, the hot technologies were telecommunications (phones) and distributed electricity. Initially these services were provided where the economies justified them: urban and affluent areas. The policy makers of the era understood that universal service of these technologies would have broad social benefit but also realized government couldn't accomplish this on its own. Moreover, compelling the private sector to provide the services without adequate compensation would be an unsustainable model.

So, a "social contract"—essentially an economic deal—was developed. Private companies agreed to provide universal service at regulated rates. In exchange, the government agreed to guarantee a substantial rate of return on their investments. Thus was born rate-of-return regulation and the private-investor-owned public utility.

Critical to understanding the social contract as applied to infrastructure development in the United States is the realization that not only did it enhance the greater public good but there was also an economic exchange in return for this societal benefit. Moreover, the infrastructures, adequately supported by the economic incentives imbedded in the contract, were continually made more sophisticated and innovative. The rapid development of these infrastructures provided the foundation for accelerated industrialization, job creation, and innovation.

In publications printed in 2008 and 2009, ISA argued that a similar situation exists today with respect to cybersecurity. In the ensuing years, we have seen substantial progress at the conceptual level as the private sector and both political parties have gravitated toward embracing the Cyber Social Contract model.

President Obama's signature policy paper on cybersecurity, "Cyberspace Policy Review," authored by Melissa Hathaway, made ISA's 2008 "Cyber Security Social Contract" publication it's first and most frequently cited reference. In 2013, the president issued an executive order on cybersecurity that also embraced the principles of the cyber social contract. The president abandoned the traditional regulatory approach and instructed the National Institute of Standards and Technology to identify the appropriate standards and practices that ought to be voluntarily adopted by the private sector and reinforced by the development of market incentives.

Although we have now developed a broad consensus on the conceptual approach, we need to stimulate progress on implementation. As we turn to a new administration and Congress, there is still a great deal of work to be done, at both the macro- and microlevel, to build on the consensus that has been developed and implement a secure cyber system that is both technologically responsive to the evolving threat and economically sustainable.

Two

A Twelve-Step Program
for Implementing the
Cybersecurity Social Contract

Larry Clinton, President and CEO, Internet Security Alliance

1. WE NEED TO ATTACK THE CYBERSECURITY PROBLEM WITH MUCH GREATER URGENCY

Compared to the speed with which our information technology systems are being compromised, federal policy making has moved at a glacier pace, because of bureaucratic processes and constant turf battles. A new president can do a lot to set the proper aggressive tone to address the issue. Cybersecurity needs to figure prominently in the new president's first hundred-day agenda.

2. GOVERNMENT NEEDS TO RECOGNIZE THE IMPORTANCE OF ECONOMICS IN CYBERSECURITY

The critical factor for addressing cyber risk is cost. Economics is the driving force for private-sector behavior, yet in cybersecurity virtually all economic incentives favor the attacker. Government must integrate cybersecurity issues into its broader infrastructure programs. In recent years, government has appropriated billions of dollars for innovative digital programs without properly apportioning funds to assure these new systems are secure. Cybersecurity is more of an economic issue than an IT issue, yet government policy ignores the economics. The new administration needs to expand the focus on cybersecurity beyond the IT silo, embrace the broader nature of the problem, and rebalance the economic-incentive structure.

3. GOVERNMENT NEEDS TO DRAMATICALLY INCREASE FUNDING FOR CYBERSECURITY

The private sector spends twice as much on cybersecurity than the entire departmental budget for DHS. Improving cybersecurity will cost money, and government funding needs to increase in order to improve security for the entire system. In a digital environment where systems are shared, government must partner with industry, even spending public monies to support private systems whenever the latter are vital to the national interest.

4. GOVERNMENT NEEDS TO BE ORGANIZED TO REFLECT THE CURRENT DIGITAL REALITIES

The chaotic and disorganized governmental structures are inefficient, and most of government's organizational problems emanate from the lack of responsiveness to the digital age. All current and future government cybersecurity programs need to have clear objectives that are subject to a cost-benefit analysis. The incoming administration and Congress need to seize the opportunity to reorganize for the digital age, and government needs to fully integrate the private sector into its cybersecurity planning and operations.

5. WE NEED TO FOCUS MORE ON CYBERSECURITY FROM A LAW-ENFORCEMENT PERSPECTIVE

Law-enforcement efforts for cybercrime are minimal. Law-enforcement agents are vastly overmatched in terms of scope of the problem compared to resources available. Plus, the legal structure, particularly internationally, has not adapted to deal with modern cybercrime. The new administration should engage in a multitiered program to bolster cyber law enforcement, review legacy law-enforcement spending, and help create a practical, operational international legal structure to address international cybercrime.

6. TEST PILOT THE NIST CYBERSECURITY FRAMEWORK

One of the most positive and popular cybersecurity initiatives of the Obama administration was the creation of the NIST Cybersecurity Framework in 2013. We need to test the NIST Framework for effectiveness, cost effectiveness, and prioritization. These elements are called for in Executive Order 13636, yet virtually nothing has been done on them. No private-sector organization launches a new product or service without testing it, yet three years into the NIST Framework and still no single objective piece of evidence exists to show it has changed behavior, or if such change has been for the better and at what cost.

7. GOVERNMENT PRIORITY FOR WORKING WITH THE PRIVATE SECTOR SHOULD BE REVERSED TO EMPHASIZE SMALLER COMPANIES INSTEAD OF LARGE ONES

We need to focus more on smaller companies. Smaller companies are more vulnerable than larger ones, understand the issue less, are investing less, and are probably the segment that most needs government help. Small companies are used as access points for sophisticated attacks on larger firms. We cannot develop a sustainably secure system by focusing exclusively on large companies. While government must continue to work with larger companies, it must also increase emphasis on smaller companies, and make cybersecurity easier and cheaper for SMBs.

8. WORKFORCE DEVELOPMENT: AWARENESS YIELDS TO UNDERSTANDING AND MAKING CYBERSECURITY COOL

We need to be much more creative in terms of workforce development. We need to leverage the private sector far more, use the gaming community to attract kids, and integrate cybersecurity into existing programs rather than treating them like separate issues. We need an integrated, multifaceted, and targeted program with research-based messaging. Career influencers, such as high-school, community-college, and university guidance counselors, need to be targeted with proper messaging so they can assist in cyber career development. The new administration should prioritize coordination of outreach programs with the private sector, facilitate partnerships, and allow the private sector to lead workforce-development programs.

Government should focus on training at the top. The National Association of Corporate Directors operates a highly successful (independently verified) program to train corporate boards about cybersecurity. We need a similar training program for members of Congress, agency heads, and cabinet officials.

9. MODERNIZE AND STREAMLINE REGULATION

The explosion of cyber regulations has occurred regardless of policies promoting voluntary usage of the guidance like the NIST Cybersecurity Framework. Companies now often face multiple inconsistent regulatory and quasiregulatory systems that more likely hinder cyber efforts than help. Security professionals are routinely diverted away from actual security to compliance, making regulations counterproductive to security efforts. Governmental turf battles and bureaucratic inertia have stymied any significant measures to streamlining the regulatory process. The new president ought to charge the Office of Information and Regulatory Affairs with developing a cross-government program for streamlining regulations. Congress should aggressively require federal agencies to reduce duplicative regulations and eliminate those that have not been proven to be cost effective as a condition of their annual appropriations.

10. DEVELOP MARKET INCENTIVES TO PROMOTE SOUND CYBERSECURITY BEHAVIOR

Policy makers have not thought through the incentive discussion broadly or creatively. Most view incentives as taxes or tax breaks. However, taxes are too limited in perspective. Some may even incentivize innovation by the attack community, while disincentivizing corporations to improve cybersecurity. Altering the assessment and compliance process and moving away from a "pass-fail" audit model to a more useful maturity model can create incentives without increasing government spending. The private sector has offered multiple proposals for consideration including liability incentives, procurement incentives, insurance incentives, and good actor benefits such as streamlined regulation, patent or trademark preferences, forbearance, and streamlined auditing.

11. ARTICULATE CLEARLY THE ROLE FOR GOVERNMENT WHEN INDUSTRY FACES A NATION-STATE ATTACK

Many cyberattacks are affiliated with nation-state actors. Virtually no private institution can adequately defend itself from a concentrated nation-state attack. Legal precedent going back decades in the nuclear industry by virtue of the design-basis-threat theory provides that private entities are not responsible for securing themselves from nation-state activity, but rather the federal government is. However, there is no clear policy or systemic assistance private companies can expect from the federal government when dealing with nation-state cyber threats. The federal government should offer (on request) equivalent federal assistance to private companies that suffer a cyberattack by a nation-state as if it were a physical attack.

12. GOVERNMENT AND INDUSTRY NEED TO PARTNER TO RETHINK THE CYBERSECURITY COMPLIANCE MODEL

The traditional regulatory model is ill-suited to the cyberspace. Instead of the current backward-looking, finance-based, pass-fail, blame-the-victim model, we need to create a forward-looking, risk-management model powered by growth and incentives, not penalties and compliance. The new administration must work collaboratively with the private sector to develop this model.

Three

Cybersecurity in the Defense Industrial Base

Jeff Brown, Vice President and Chief Information Security Officer, Raytheon
JR Williamson, Director and Deputy Chief Information Security Officer,
Northrop Grumman

WHAT MAKES THE DIB SECTOR UNIQUE

The defense industry has a different economic model than most industries, and investing in cyber protection is not a function of traditional economic risk management. Top-tier defense companies sell to national governments with few alternatives, and the Pentagon is unlikely to opt for lower cost products from rival nations, especially should the design suspiciously resemble American-made technology.

The defense industry invests in cybersecurity, despite the lack of traditional economic interest, out of a fundamentally patriotic sense of responsibility to our warfighters and because strong data and network security are essential to brand credibility when doing business with the military.

However, small- and medium-sized companies lower in the defense supply chain have a greater proportion of commercial business than defense business. The greater the commercial component of a business, the more the traditional economic risk-assessment calculations predominate. Financial conditions facing SMBs do not afford them the luxury of uneconomic investments in cybersecurity.

Differences in incentive structures have created a two-tiered defense ecosystem. One tier contains the large, well-funded system integrators and the other everyone else. Into this mix, DoD has introduced new compliance requirements, in an attempt to artificially influence traditional economic-based risk-management calculations.

CHALLENGES FACING THE NEW ADMINISTRATION

Modern weapons systems are built via a supply chain hundreds of companies long, spanning multiple countries and subject to cyber manipulation. Defense developers and innovators are at risk of intellectual property theft through cyber espionage. Second-level nations skip generations of research development, becoming competitive with US weaponry, and the economic losses portend negative downstream effects on future investment and innovation.

Government reporting and information-sharing requirements are confusing and divert resources away from security to compliance. New regulations have significantly increased costs of doing business with the government and shifted cybersecurity focus from incentives, as called for in Executive Order 13636, to compliance with standards. These increased costs dwarf information technology budgets for small businesses. However, compliance alone will not generate security and must not be confused with it.

The collaboration process codified in the Defense Industrial Base Framework Agreement has been successful but is labor-intensive. Cyber threats have expanded to attack the defense supply chain, an ecosystem of smaller, less cyber-capable companies, ill-suited for such processes.

Cybersecurity policies assume US-based companies operating on American soil. Yet, reductions in defense spending led many companies to expand their presence overseas, creating a very different set of dynamics for cyber defense in the sector. The requirements levied by the International Trafficking in Arms Regulations drives the defense industry into maintaining two distinct networks—one for US persons and one for non-US employees—making a unified cyber defense both difficult and expensive. Privacy laws of many of countries also make a unified monitoring environment difficult.

Most countries now require coproduction or offset suppliers. As the demand for coproduction rises in the value chain, so does the need to defend the networks of suppliers, resulting in policy challenges to the defense industry in two areas: first, current information-sharing policies preclude open sharing of information with foreign partners; second, the Defense Federal Acquisition Regulation Supplement rules on safeguarding defense information mandate application of NIST controls to overseas suppliers anytime covered information is involved. But few foreign companies are likely to submit themselves to DoD-imposed standards, leaving defense companies to choose between continuing with a foreign supplier who is out of compliance or abandoning the supplier and failing to meet contractual offset requirements.

RECOMMENDATIONS

INSTITUTE A TIERED MODEL FOR GRADING CYBERSECURITY COMPETENCY

The current regulatory compliance model is binary—either comply with everything or fail. Turn it into an incentive model with different tiers of compliance, where each level represents a concrete improvement in security. Companies will then prioritize efforts, and the government and larger defense contractors could tailor contract requirements to a certain level of security, incentivizing suppliers to move to the next tier to gain eligibility for larger contracts. This would transform the compliance environment to a competitive one, which will then incentivize defense companies to advance tiers in order to set themselves apart from their peers or gain market share. A maturity model would also allow small- and medium-sized defense contractors to realistically participate.

INFORMATION SHARING BEYOND THE ELITES

Current close-hold information-sharing methods are designed for companies with the infrastructure and staff capable of manually receiving complex threat data, evaluating these data for their environment, and applying them to any number of defensive systems. Small companies cannot do this.

Instead, sharing with small companies requires a passive model where the company can accept threat data in an automated system and have these data applied to their network. The Pentagon needs to work with industry to create a broader information-sharing environment that is affordable and passive. Defense can allow large system integrators to share DoD-provided, unclassified threat indicators with defense contractors in their supply chain via automated monitoring systems. Extending to the supply chain can have a high payoff at a low cost.

DOD SHOULD MOVE TO BETTER ACCOMMODATE A GLOBAL DEFENSE INDUSTRIAL BASE

Defense needs to work with industry to develop operating concepts for cyber defense in an increasingly global market. Compliance regimes and information-sharing processes must both be modified to accommodate overseas suppliers and coproduction agreements. They must also work to develop a way to share cyber-defense information with foreign suppliers of critical items. DoD should work with NIST to find an acceptable international standard that can serve as an overseas substitute for defense-controlled-information cybersecurity controls.

THE PENTAGON NEEDS TO INCREASE ITS FOCUS ON SMALL BUSINESSES

Defense depends on small businesses to support its missions, spark innovation, and develop technologies to support soldiers. While the Office of Small Business Programs has acknowledged that cybersecurity is an important and timely issue for small businesses, it has not identified or disseminated any cybersecurity resources in its outreach and education efforts to defense-sector small businesses. The next administration should ensure cybersecurity is a part the OSBP outreach and take steps to stabilize the office's performance and leadership team.

Four

Cybersecurity in the Healthcare Industry

Dustin Wilcox, Vice President and Chief Information
Security Officer, Centene

WHAT MAKES THE HEALTHCARE SECTOR UNIQUE

Patient data are uniquely valuable to criminals. The cost of purchasing stolen patient records on the cyber black market is approximately ten times the cost of purchasing that same individual's stolen credit-card data and includes all data elements necessary to impersonate the victim. Hackers further monetize health records by compromising weaknesses in the healthcare system, billing fraudulent claims to Medicaid and Medicare, potentially prescribing narcotics, and even filing fraudulent tax returns.

Perhaps the most interesting evolution in the cyber threat facing healthcare industry is the rise of the nation-state threat. Governments of other countries direct their cyber warriors to hack into hospitals and health insurers to steal medical records. It's likely that nation-state actors are stealing patient data to build databases on American citizens for espionage activities.

Insider threats are particularly insidious in the healthcare sector. Healthcare data processors say malicious insiders account for just about 10 percent of data breaches but are the root cause of double the percentage of medical-identity thefts. Accidental insiders cause more, albeit smaller, breaches.

The number of individuals who have access to data during a healthcare transaction represents another point of vulnerability. Even a routine visit to the doctor exposes medical data to a dozen people or organizations as diagnostic and billing information makes its way through various systems. Each hand represents another potential point of vulnerability or attack.

CHALLENGES FACING THE NEW ADMINISTRATION

Two major laws governing healthcare cybersecurity practices are not functioning as intended. The massive 2013 omnibus rule updating HIPAA, mandated by the HITECH Act, has failed to have the desired effect of making the healthcare industry more secure. In the years since its implementation, massive health-payer data breaches have occurred.

Moreover, the regulations take a retributive approach to cybersecurity, punishing organizations that get breached. Breaches spawn audits, and audits spawn punitive outcomes in the forms of substantial fines and other penalties, regardless of how much time and money was put into trying to prevent a breach.

The cost of security is a great obstacle for healthcare organizations. Large organizations have the ability to fund teams dedicated to both implementation of security best practices and regulatory compliance. Small practices have minimal resources. While all organizations must abide by the same rules and regulations, not all have equivalent access to the financial resources and expertise necessary to comply. The high cost of compliance, and the higher cost of failure, further exacerbates the problem.

The doctor-patient relationship is unique—patients are unlikely to abandon their medical provider over a data breach, so there is little incentive beyond regulatory consequences to spend time and effort defending against potential breaches.

The proliferation of technology in healthcare is another obstacle. Like most disruptive technologies, the uses for mobile-enabled practice management systems multiplied long before any serious thought was given to securing the technology.

Escalating ransomware attacks on the healthcare industry creates another challenge. For now, ransomware attacks appear unconnected to data theft. But given the real value of patient data—in its theft for exploitation or resale—ransomware attacks will become the nasty second jab of what really are one-two punch attacks.

Possible cyber-terrorist attacks against newly networked medical devices coming onto the market could cause significant disruptions, some even fatal. Life-sustaining devices once isolated away from public networks are now exposed to them. Medical equipment is now part of the mix of databases and hard drives once thought impervious to hackers.

There's also a lack of urgency within the healthcare industry. The idea that medical data had value to criminals is novel, and it took significant healthcare data breaches to convince the industry to get serious about committing resources to secure itself against cyberattacks.

RECOMMENDATIONS

INCENTIVIZE HEALTHCARE TO IMPLEMENT BEST CYBERSECURITY PRACTICES

Healthcare needs a shift in focus away from prescriptive regulation toward regulation that encourages security best practices. An incentive-focused regulatory approach would encourage more healthcare companies to invest in necessary protections to information assets, possibly even driving broad adoption of controls necessary to solve the aforementioned data problems. What's needed is a sliding scale of liability protection on the basis of company's progress toward implementing an objective set of practices. The NIST Cybersecurity Framework, and the process used to develop it, could provide a good starting point for determining those practices.

The system should allow a company to accrue credits tied to its investments in security that it could use against future audits and fines in the event of a breach. This could be taken further by also offering modest tax incentives for certain high-value, but often-overlooked, security best practices, such as employee awareness training.

REDUCE REGULATORY COMPLEXITY

Congress should pursue legislation that harmonizes privacy, security, and information-risk-management requirements to eliminate the complex patchwork of regulations. Streamlining HIPAA audit requirements put into place by the HITECH Act. Audits drain resources from security budgets. Passing an audit, combined with proof of ongoing investment into cyber-security, should result in a less strenuous audit the next time around—a HIPAA-Lite version, as it were—or increased time interval between audits.

REPLACE SOCIAL SECURITY NUMBERS AS A PATIENT IDENTIFIER

Congress should remove language placed annually in federal spending bills that prohibits the Department of Health and Human Services from using any federal funds to promulgate or adopt any such standard. Technology has provided for alternatives to a numeric or alphanumeric identifier as a solution, and the government does not need to be the arbiter of the identification solution.

USE SECURITY AS A FACTOR OF REIMBURSEMENT

Congress should allow the Centers for Medicare and Medicaid to use security as a factor in reimbursement. Similarly, improving an organization's cybersecurity readiness should be considered a recognized activity under the clinical practice improvement performance category under the Medicare Access and CHIP Reauthorization Act Merit-based Incentive Payment System reimbursement scheme.

Five

Cybersecurity in the Banking and Financial Sector

Daniel Crisp, chief Information Risk Officer and Head of Technology
Compliance, BNY Mellon
Larry Trittschuh, Threat and Vulnerability Leader, Synchrony Financial
Gary McAlum, Chief Security Officer and Senior Vice President, USAA

WHAT MAKES THE FINANCIAL SERVICES SECTOR UNIQUE

Banks and other financial institutions remain a top target for cyberattacks, whether for financial gain, data theft, or retaliation. Today's consumers have higher expectations about service, given the proliferation of technologies available to them. Consumers are more likely to shop around for products and be more interested in direct and mobile channels. However, while the use of innovations such as mobile devices and applications for consumer banking has exploded, the exploitation of these devices has increased significantly.

Commercial banking, too, has seen tremendous benefits from technology and is poised to reap even more as the new distributed ledger system, known as blockchain, enters the mainstream. More than half of exchanges surveyed by the International Organization of Securities Commissions and the World Federation of Exchanges in 2013 reported experiencing a cyberattack during the previous twelve months. Neither is the insurance industry is immune to the changes in how business is conducted in today's contemporary and interconnected society. Insurers are prime targets to be victimized, given the richness of data—credit-card information, medical information, and other underwriting information.

CHALLENGES FACING THE NEW ADMINISTRATION

The current regulatory model for cybersecurity does not work. Cyber technology and attack methods change constantly, and the regulatory process is inherently time consuming and cumbersome.

The financial services sector continues to see an increase in disparate and fragmented cybersecurity regulation. For many institutions, it began with the Federal Financial Institutions Examination Council releasing in June 2015 a Cybersecurity Assessment Tool incorporating concepts from the voluntary NIST Cybersecurity Framework. Member agencies use the tool in regulatory inquiries. As a result, many large financial institutions expend immense amounts of time and resources determining how to demonstrate compliance.

Complicating matters further, financial institutions receive similar cybersecurity inquiries from different regulators, even from different offices of the same regulator. These duplicative reporting requirements ask largely the same questions but require exhaustive tailoring for each regulator. And the SEC is becoming ever more assertive in monitoring the cybersecurity of broker-dealers and registered investment advisers, even testing firms' implementation of cybersecurity controls.

Technology innovations have eliminated borders for criminal enterprises. Attackers can exploit vulnerabilities from anywhere and impact entire networks in a matter of seconds. This poses a tremendous risk of cascading failure across the sector. Phishing is a main pathway for cyber theft, and spear-phishing is even more pernicious. The use of phishing is widespread, unrelenting, and a low-cost, high-payoff technique for attackers.

Mobile banking is a boon for consumers but opens up a new front for attackers to exploit. Cyber thieves craft malicious apps targeting banking data, but it's not just banking apps that pose a cybersecurity challenge.

RECOMMENDATIONS

GOVERNMENT SHOULD RETHINK ITS APPROACH TO CYBERSECURITY

The federal government's credibility in educating, let alone regulating and mandating, cybersecurity practices is severely undermined by its track record of inefficiency. Agencies have yet to adjust to the interconnected nature of cybersecurity, approach it as if it were a static problem addressable through existing formulations. Punitive checklist compliance is a waste of resources. The number of regulatory agency examiners with specialized information technology training is low, and much of government's shared cyber-threat data are out of date and stripped of context as to be useless.

HARMONIZE, STREAMLINE, AND IMPROVE REGULATIONS

Regulatory and legislative mandates and compliance frameworks that address information security for the financial sector, such as Sarbanes-Oxley, Gramm-Leach-Bliley, the Fair and Accurate Credit Transactions Act, as well as state compliance regimes, must be consolidated and streamlined.

Regulations should encourage banks to take a risk-based approach, which is customized to the threats they face and takes into account the bank's business model and resources available. Utilizing a standard mechanism such as the NIST Cybersecurity Framework to align the proliferation of different legal and regulatory cybersecurity requirements enables harmonization and adopts unified fundamental guidance for developing cybersecurity policies and practices within the industry.

OPERATIONAL IMPROVEMENTS

Toss the Password into the Dustbin of History

"Killing the password" has been a long-standing Obama administration priority, one that it reiterated in the National Cyber Action Plan unveiled in February 2016. The new administration should accelerate the work of the National Strategy for Trusted Identities in Cyberspace, a program charged in 2011 with creating market conditions favorable to a wholesale replacement of passwords. Today, it's clear the effort has stalled.

Incentivize ISPs to Become More Active in Cybersecurity

ISPs are critical players in improving cybersecurity across the Internet but are not incentivized to implement well-established security protocols, such as DNS Security Extension and BGPSec, that would make launching cyberattacks harder for hackers. We are not advocating for heavy-handed regulation but a common set of strong security standards that ISPs can be evaluated against in the market place, much like the "5-star safety rating" system developed years ago by the National Highway Traffic Safety Administration.

Adopt Antiphishing Technology

The existing Internet technology standard known as DMARC (domain-based message authentication, reporting, and conformance) should be implemented by the federal government and even further in the private sector.

ENCOURAGE DEVELOPMENT OF MORE CYBERSECURITY EXPERTS

The new administration should consider leveraging the federal science, technology, engineering, and mathematics program to promote wider interest among students in technology jobs. The current national goal of graduating an additional one million students with STEM majors should be reassessed with an eye toward increasing both that number as well as the number of technology graduates represented within it.

Six

Cybersecurity in the Power Utility Sector

Scott DePasquale, Chairman and CEO, Utilidata

WHAT MAKES THE UTILITIES SECTOR UNIQUE

Over the past decade, the bulk power system has seen improvements and increased investment in resiliency and cybersecurity. However, local power-distribution assets are not only more vulnerable to cyberattack but also more critical to national electricity delivery than previously contemplated.

MARKETPLACE INNOVATION IS LAGGING

While products to protect information technology infrastructure are readily available and mature, there are far fewer products in the marketplace that provide security for the highly connected operational technologies that control physical assets on the power grid.

To add complexity, many power utility executives struggle with the uncertainties associated with recovery of security-related costs and overhead on the basis of traditional state rate making procedures. Even if there were adequate funding by utilities to address their normal (i.e., "commercial") cybersecurity risk, there will inevitably be a gap between vulnerabilities that can be cost-effectively mitigated and the residual risk posed by sophisticated nation-state powers seeking to disrupt the grid. Even utilities, duty-bound by public-good considerations, are still private-sector businesses that are unlikely to invest far beyond the thresholds of normal commercial risk.

LIMITED INFORMATION TO INFORM CYBERSECURITY DECISIONS

Exacerbating the situation is how utility asset vendors sell closed-source devices and software solutions, which typically come bundled with significant contractual prohibitions against tampering or reverse engineering. This results in a difficult situation, preventing utilities from processes that might allow them to verify the integrity of hardware and software they purchase.

CHALLENGES FACING THE NEW ADMINISTRATION

A GRID THAT IS BECOMING INCREASINGLY DIFFICULT AND COSTLY TO DEFEND

For the past fifteen years, the electric power industry, with significant support from government, has invested heavily in making the distribution system smarter, more efficient, and more connected. Smart grid technologies have been incentivized and implemented with little regard for the increased cyber risk. Equally concerning is that utilities are sourcing advanced technologies and products from multiple vendors with little or no ability to properly assess supply-chain risks.

CREEPING POSSIBILITY OF A TERRORIST ATTACK

The possibility of terrorist attacks will grow. The level of sophistication required to effect widespread damage to the grid has typically suggested that only nation-states will be effective. However, a growing community of postnational actors are being contracted by states as an extension of their offensive capabilities, which is creating an international marketplace for sophisticated disruption capabilities.

RECOMMENDATIONS

ENHANCE INFORMATION SHARING BETWEEN UTILITIES AND THE FEDERAL GOVERNMENT

Greater federal government transparency in managing data will foster trust and confidence in relationship building and communication. The next president should instruct the existing utility industry sector coordinating council and the corresponding government coordinating council established under the National Infrastructure Protection Plan to engage on these information-sharing issues and report back to the administration within three months on their plan to create greater clarity and transparency regarding information sharing within the sector, including any legislative adjustments that may be needed.

REFORM THE CLEARANCE ATTAINMENT PROCESS FOR PRIVATE SECTOR EXECUTIVES

Long processing times and an insufficient number of security clearances being made available are significantly hindering the utility industry's ability to support the US cybersecurity mission. The next president should instruct DHS to coordinate among security clearance granting agencies and develop an expedited "TSA precheck" style system to enable already cleared individuals to maintain their clearances more easily and generally modernize the clearance process to include the use of transferable clearances from department to department.

ENSURE DOE REMAINS THE PRIMARY LIAISON BETWEEN UTILITIES AND THE FEDERAL GOVERNMENT

While DHS plays a critical role as utilities face cybersecurity challenges, the Department of Energy remains best suited as the main point of contact due to decades of working to provide meaningful, contextual, and actionable analysis. The next president and Congress should consider amending the Cybersecurity Act of 2015 to expand the benefits currently granted for sharing information with DHS to other appropriate agencies such as Energy.

CATALYZE AND ACCELERATE THE DEVELOPMENT OF THE PRIVATE CYBERSECURITY INSURANCE MARKET

Cybersecurity insurance is an undervalued tool and critical to the future safeguarding of utilities, but to date the market has focused on data-breach fallout. To expand coverage, the administration and Congress should replicate the success of the Terrorism Risk Insurance Act to create a similar reinsurance backstop for cyberattack-caused real-world damage to utilities and their customers.

PROMOTE INNOVATION THROUGH GOVERNMENT GRANTS

Initiatives such as Rapid Attack Detection, Isolation and Characterization Systems at DARPA and Cybersecurity for Energy Delivery Systems at Energy encourage investment in commercial products by appropriately reducing risk for potential vendors and helping bring together all relevant stakeholders. These programs should be continued and expanded.

INCREASE CYBERSECURITY FOCUS OF STATE-LEVEL REGULATORS AND LEGISLATURES

The federal government should pass a cybersecurity "states-must-consider" law so that states must demonstrate they have considered appropriate cost-effective cybersecurity standards for their electric utility ratemaking proceedings. Doing so will effectively increase the focus on distribution cybersecurity at the state level without imposing new regulations on distribution utilities.

ENCOURAGE PUBLIC-PRIVATE COLLABORATION TO MANAGE VENDOR RISKS

Vendors must play their part in the security of the grid. A new balance needs to be struck between the commercial needs of vendors, who would prefer not to reveal the workings of their products, and the needs of electric utilities to both ensure assets are not prepackaged with malware and understand better how assets would behave if they were to be controlled maliciously. Solving this requires a dialogue between utilities, vendors, and the government to evaluate possible solutions that cost-effectively increase confidence in US grid assets and help utilities prepare for cyberattacks. The Obama administration's proposal for a National Center for Cybersecurity Resilience, where companies could test the security of systems under controlled conditions, is a good start in this direction. So is the Federal Energy Regulatory Commission's proposed rule regarding supply-chain risk management. The government and utilities themselves could play a valuable role in incentivizing vendors to adopt the Underwriter's Laboratories model—this would ensure that all vendor products are rigorously and transparently inspected to ensure they meet baseline cybersecurity standards.

Seven

Cybersecurity and the Information Technology Industry

Art Coviello Jr., Executive Chairman (Retired), RSA

WHAT MAKES THE IT SECTOR UNIQUE

In the digital age, virtually all sectors rely on the IT sector, and no industry has escaped transformation because of IT innovations. The Internet changed virtually every aspect of modern life. Approximately 12 percent of global trade is conducted via international e-commerce. Even the political process has changed because of social-media interactions.

Computing power doubles every two years, and interconnected devices communicate and deliver instructions and intelligence to machinery, creating the Internet of Things and amassing huge amounts of data. However, this increase in surface creates ample opportunities for security breaches and the misuse of privacy information that will be felt by all sectors, not just IT.

These same innovations also create ample opportunities for advances in cybersecurity technologies. Development of products with artificial intelligence and the use of machine learning gives us the ability to prevent, predict, detect, and respond to attacks as never before.

However, do not mistake improved technical abilities for a true solution to the bad state of computer security. The challenges are imbedded in policy and management. The IT industry has flourished in a generally unregulated environment, which has been essential to its historic growth and productivity. An unhappy by-product of this growth is a system prone to outside attacks. The sector must find a mechanism to sustainably secure it without killing innovation.

CHALLENGES FACING THE NEW ADMINISTRATION

INTERNET OF THINGS
In the IoT, humans are the ultimate thing and will generate multitudes of personal data. We know better than to create this world without securing it first, yet we continue to do so.

CYBER WAR AND TERRORISM
Even absent direct escalation into a shooting war, cyberattacks will cross the plane from bits to atoms and become kinetic in the damage they cause.

COMMERCIAL ESPIONAGE
Intellectual property theft is an act of economic war and harms drivers of global economic growth.

PROPOSALS FOR BACKDOORS
Adoption of proposals to build encryption backdoors into IT products for law-enforcement and intelligence communities would benefit adversaries, provoke legitimate privacy concerns among citizens, and further deteriorate trust between the United States and world community.

GOVERNMENT CYBERSECURITY
Government systems repeatedly fail at security. Federal information technology infrastructure is obsolete, yet government continues to spend resources on legacy systems rather than funding upgrades.

INFORMATION SHARING
We cannot seem to navigate the legitimate concerns of privacy groups around information that can be shared and the business community around

legal liability. Moreover, liability protections are available only for sharing through DHS and no other preferred entities such as the FBI.

PUBLIC-PRIVATE PARTNERSHIP
Trust and cooperation between IT and government is at an all-time low. This will persist so long as government continues to threaten industry.

DATA-BREACH NOTIFICATION
Forty-seven states plus the District of Columbia maintain separate laws for data-breach notification, creating an undue burden on industry and increasing costs for notification of breaches.

RECOMMENDATIONS

CREATE A CABINET-LIKE POSITION TO UPGRADE CIVILIAN IT AND SECURITY INFRASTRUCTURE
Given the importance of IT in the running of our government, the need to manage and secure critical infrastructure, and the ongoing productivity benefits of continued innovation, appointing a cabinet-level position to manage an IT transformation should be one of the highest priorities for the next administration. The position needs full authority and funding.

WORKFORCE DEVELOPMENT
Government should work with colleges and universities across the country to obtain a steady flow of recruits for cybersecurity positions by providing scholarships to students willing to commit a specified number of years in government cybersecurity positions.

INCREASE AND IMPROVE INTERNATIONAL LAW ENFORCEMENT AND COOPERATION TO PREVENT CYBER WAR AND TERRORISM
This should start with the president instituting a full review of national law-enforcement spending to assure that fighting digital crime is far better resourced. The commander-in-chief should also initiate a concerted process

to modernize international law and procedures with respect to clarifying criminal laws internationally.

INCREASE GOVERNMENT RESEARCH AND DEVELOPMENT FUNDING FOR RISKY TECHNOLOGY RESEARCH

Rather than routinely cut research and development funding, the United States should emulate what our competitors are doing in other countries by providing increased government support for basic IT research and general-purpose digital programs.

PUBLIC-PRIVATE PARTNERSHIP

Collaboration between the public and private sectors to test the effectiveness of the NIST Cybersecurity Framework is needed to define what using the framework entails. By testing the framework, cost-effective aspects will be discovered. Cooperation would also allow the Enduring Security Framework to be reenergized and expanded to include allies.

LAW ENFORCEMENT SHOULD STOP PUSHING THE "GOING DARK" NARRATIVE

New enabling capabilities for the IoT and advancements in computer power and storage capacity for big-data applications can be used by law-enforcement, defense, and intelligence communities in lawful ways. Law enforcement should spend more energy in adjusting their investigative techniques to this new world than fighting the inevitable onset of encryption, which is good for cybersecurity by preventing data theft and cyber espionage.

Eight

Cybersecurity in
Telecommunications

Richard Spearman, Group Corporate Security Director, Vodafone

WHAT MAKES THE TELECOMMUNICATIONS SECTOR UNIQUE

T he global telecommunications sector is a mix of government, former
government, and commercial operators. The networks are a critical
part of the business infrastructure and increasingly seen as part of the critical national infrastructure. They deliver services for customers but also wider benefits for society.

The telecommunications industry stores, manages, and transports a
vast amount of valuable data for individuals and society, digital commerce,
and critical national infrastructure.

The threat from cyber actors is increasing in sophistication, persistence,
and variety—and the risks posed are not easily mitigated. Cybersecurity needs
to be multidimensional, transcending the risk management and response capabilities of any single enterprise, industry, or government. The damage inflicted by successful cyberattacks is not just financial and commercial but can
also lead to long-term reputational damage and regulatory action.

Customer confidence is crucial. Customers need to know that their data
are safe and to understand how companies will use these data and the basis on which the government can secure access to these data. Customers
need to trust service providers to behave responsibly in this regard.
Telecommunications is a regulated business. Service providers are required

to give government's access to customer traffic and data in accordance with licensing regulations and the laws of the jurisdictions in which they operate. Our policy is clear: telecommunications companies should not hand over customer data unless they are lawfully required to do so.

CHALLENGES FACING THE NEW ADMINISTRATION

MAINTAINING TRUST BETWEEN BUSINESS, GOVERNMENT, AND SOCIETY

We need to align the interests of customers with those of business and government. The experience of Apple versus the FBI might suggest that the interests of industry, government, and society are divergent. We would argue absolutely not. It is about reaching an agreed compromise, a question of balance not absolute choices. Crucially it is about trust and transparency.

REGULATION LAGS BEHIND GLOBALIZATION AND THE PACE OF CHANGE

In a globalized information economy, telecommunications companies will often deliver products and services using centralized platforms and infrastructure located across multiple jurisdictions. Regulations that unduly restrict the cross-border transfer of personal and machine-generated data are likely to impede service delivery and distort investment decisions.

The speed of technology change challenges existing regulation. Services come and go rapidly and the development cycle is shortening. Legislation should clearly outline the purpose and offer clarity about the types of government agency who can require access to customer data, along with the process by which that data can be secured. The process should be auditable, and it should be possible, through that audit, to verify that the lawful system is being used.

THE NEED TO KEEP UP WITH THOSE WHO THREATEN OUR NETWORKS

The scale and changing nature of the challenge are disrupting industry attempts to build internationally compatible safeguards and making it more difficult to have a mature debate with customers about privacy and security.

RECOMMENDATIONS

INCIDENT REPORTING AND INFORMATION SHARING

Following an incident, everyone needs to be clear and precise about what has happened, but government decisions about incident notification and public disclosure of major incidents (or audits) should not be allowed to disrupt or undermine industry attempts to mount an appropriate and proportionate response.

For the industry to make meaningful headway on standards and standardization, we need to see more intergovernment coordination on standards work to deliver globally accepted outcomes that strike at the heart of the issues.

The telecommunications industry also requires a legal and regulatory framework to promote and uphold technology neutrality and provide a legal framework to encourage investment in future-capable networks that will carry exponentially growing data in virtualized cloud-based environments.

TAKE A LIGHT HAND WITH REGULATION

Government needs to lead and support national and international conversations required to find the appropriate balance between the need to protect the privacy of the individual and the need to ensure the collective security of society. Policy and regulation must be developed with the specific needs of the enterprise sector in mind rather than as a by-product of regulation designed for consumer needs.

BROADEN THE VISION OF THE PUBLIC-PRIVATE PARTNERSHIP BETWEEN TELECOMMUNICATIONS AND GOVERNMENT

In the digital age, private companies are on the frontline of defense when it comes to cyber threats. Many attacks are not launched at telecommunications companies but through them, in some cases against government or national-security targets. Third parties may struggle to manage the impact of high-level attacks if their prevailing business models don't allow for further investment in cybersecurity. In these situations it might be cost effective for government to use telecommunications companies to provide enhanced security in situations where further investment is needed to reduce the impact of high-level threats and provide a broader common level of defense that it beyond the reach of some organizations but ultimately in the national interest.

Nine

Winning the Cyber-Talent War: Strategies to Enhance Cybersecurity Workforce Development

Dr. David Brumley, Professor of Electrical and Computer Engineering and Director of Carnegie Mellon's CyLab Security and Privacy Institute

EXAMINING PROGRESS TO DATE IN EFFORTS TO STRENGTHEN THE CYBERSECURITY WORKFORCE

A PARTNERSHIP FOR BUILDING THE FUTURE PUBLIC-SECTOR WORKFORCE—THE SCHOLARSHIP FOR SERVICE PROGRAM

Funded by the National Science Foundation and operated in partnership with DHS, the Cyber Corps of the Scholarship for Service program has demonstrated significant impact in encouraging students to pursue cybersecurity careers and creating a pipeline of talent for the public sector.

NATIONAL CENTERS OF ACADEMIC EXCELLENCE IN CYBER DEFENSE

This program sets criteria and mapping curricula to assist institutions in building effective cybersecurity education and research programs—helping to establish a national framework for cybersecurity education. All four-year baccalaureate, graduate education, and two-year institutions are eligible.

PRESIDENTIAL INNOVATION FELLOWS

The fellows program is designed to engage early career IT professionals and engage them in short stints in government. While not focused exclusively or even predominantly on cybersecurity, the Presidential Innovation Fellows program provides a window on a future where an improved flow of critical cybersecurity talent could be a vital resource for meeting major short-term challenges and raising the overall level of skills in the cyber workforce.

NATIONAL GUARD AND MILITARY RESERVE CYBER OPERATIONS

Regional centers being developed by the National Guard and Reserve are creating a nexus of talent within states and cities that draws on professionals engaged in industry and academia who can be mobilized to support government needs in the case of major incidents.

ENGAGING VETERANS IN CYBERSECURITY CAREERS

A number of promising initiatives have also been launched in the last few years to focus cybersecurity education on veterans. These efforts include specific outreach and degree programs—including those launched by the state of Virginia and boot camp programs launched by companies such as PricewaterhouseCoopers, among others.

INITIAL STEPS TO NURTURE CYBERSECURITY CAREER PATHS FOR YOUNG AMERICANS

As part of the National Initiative for Cybersecurity Education (more often known as NICE), federal agencies collaborate to strengthen K–12 student and teacher engagement. One of the leading examples of this effort is the GenCyber initiative supported by NSF and the NSA. GenCyber supports collaborations with academic institutions to conduct cybersecurity summer camps for students and teachers.

SHAPING AN AGENDA FOR THE NEW ADMINISTRATION: PRINCIPLE BUILDING BLOCKS OF AN EFFECTIVE NATIONAL CYBER WORKFORCE STRATEGY

FOCUS A NATIONAL INITIATIVE ON BUILDING THE TALENT PIPELINE

Attracting students into the federal government must be augmented by an aggressive strategy to build the pipeline of interest in earlier grade levels. This will require a broad range of engagement with K–12 education that includes classroom initiatives, expanded teacher education, and after-school competitions to spark interest.

EMBRACE THE POSITIVE ELEMENTS OF THE HACKER DYNAMIC

Hackers are ultracurious, highly imaginative professionals who are able to spot even the most hidden vulnerabilities in systems. Meeting the nation's cybersecurity talent needs will require nurturing the natural curiosity and imaginative creativity that defines the hacker experience.

CREATE NEW VEHICLES FOR INDUSTRY, GOVERNMENT, EDUCATION COLLABORATION

While policies to date have focused on the needs of the federal government, the national cybersecurity workforce is a challenge for the private sector as well. Opportunities must be explored to foster closer coordination among government, industry, and the higher-education community as the nature of the cybersecurity challenge evolves.

POLICY RECOMMENDATIONS FOR NEW NATIONAL FEDERAL CYBERSECURITY WORKFORCE

INTENSIFY INITIATIVES TO CREATE A CYBER-AWARE GENERATION

Incorporating basic cybersecurity education into curricula at all education levels and work experiences would enhance this first line of defense. Along with this effort, we need to invest in research and applied development of innovations that continue to make security and privacy easier for consumers.

DEVELOP A CORE CYBERSECURITY CURRICULUM THAT CAN BE ADAPTED AND APPLIED AT ALL EDUCATION LEVELS AND START BUILDING CYBERSECURITY INTO STEM PROGRAMS

Recognizing the importance of cybersecurity as a fundamental element of STEM education will also enhance the growth of programs and stronger student interest.

ENGAGE INDUSTRY AND THE HIGHER-EDUCATION COMMUNITY IN COMMITMENT TO TRAIN ONE HUNDRED THOUSAND HIGH-SCHOOL AND MIDDLE-SCHOOL TEACHERS IN BASIC CYBERSECURITY EDUCATION IN THE NEXT FIVE YEARS

This component can tap the development of new online and gamification tools that have the potential to significantly impact the ability to bring cost-effective education resources to schools throughout the nation. Carnegie Mellon experienced the success with picoCTF, and nationwide adoption of this model, specifically aimed at educators who can run their own versions of the contest, could have an exponential impact.

USING THE FIRST ROBOTICS LEAGUE AS A MODEL, ADVANCE A NATIONAL STRATEGY FOR MIDDLE-SCHOOL AND HIGH-SCHOOL HACKING CONTESTS TO EXCITE THE NEXT GENERATION OF CYBERSECURITY PROFESSIONALS

Now in its twenty-fifth year, FIRST reaches seventy-five thousand students around the world each year and provides a broader portal to STEM careers. A national hacking contest initiative can have a similar impact.

EXPAND THE SCHOLARSHIP FOR SERVICE PROGRAM AND FOSTER EVEN DEEPER CROSS-INSTITUTIONAL COLLABORATION

The proposal to increase the number of institutions in the program is a valuable component of a talent initiative. One model for such an effort is the Cyber Stakes program, which has fostered collaborative education and exercises between Carnegie Mellon and service academies.

EXPLORE CREATION OF A CYBERSECURITY ROTC PROGRAM

A cyber-specific ROTC-like initiative would underscore the sense of national mission that is vital to addressing the environment for strengthening the cybersecurity talent pipeline. A key to this effort would be to create a strong network among institutions operating this program to ensure that the development of these students included both deep technical and operational experiences.

Additionally, consideration should be given to development a "2+2" model for this effort, where a student who has a potential interest in cybersecurity can receive a modest financial-aid supplement in their first and second year. At the end of the second year, these students (and any other students in the program) can choose to apply for acceptance into a program fully funding their tuition during the third and fourth year, if they commit to a cybersecurity minor in addition to their computer science or electrical and computer engineering major. In return, the student would be required to sign up for three years of service in a government cybersecurity position.

CREATE NEW MECHANISMS FOR INDUSTRY, GOVERNMENT, HIGHER EDUCATION COLLABORATION

One strategic approach to fostering these new mechanisms would be to support the development of regional test beds for collaboration on the emerging Internet of Things. These test beds could focus both on innovation in cyber applications and advancing opportunities for formal education programs as well as ongoing training initiatives.

Ten

Cybersecurity in the Manufacturing Sector

Brian Raymond, Director of Innovation Policy,
National Association of Manufacturers

WHAT MAKES THE MANUFACTURING SECTOR UNIQUE

Manufacturers are the creators, users, servicers, and installers of the Internet of Things. This technology is creating enormous opportunity and driving transformative change. It has made all manufacturers into technology companies.

The days of interacting with the customer only during a single transaction are over. Connected technology enables manufacturers to provide real-time performance monitoring and usage patterns for their customers throughout the entire lifespan of a product. A tire manufacturer won't just sell tires but a package to reduce costs through sensors that collect data on fuel consumption and tire pressure.

While connected technology drives innovation in the manufacturing sector, it also creates new challenges. Manufacturers are now the first line of defense in securing our nation's most critical online assets. They place cybersecurity at the highest priority level.

One of the primary targets for cyberattack inside the manufacturing ecosystem is industrial control systems. This is the class of computers that help manage the shop floor. ICS are configured in growing numbers to be reachable through the Internet, including systems retrofitted with modern networking capabilities.

Even when companies take measures to secure their Internet-addressable ICS, they often link their factory production and enterprise information technology networks. That connection results in benefits such as increased productivity, but a new class of malware is exploiting those links to target ICS, likely for espionage.

CHALLENGES FACING THE NEW ADMINISTRATION

THE IOT IS GOING FASTER THAN SECURITY CAN KEEP UP

Many IoT devices will possess minimal processing power. That is the nature of the thing—ubiquitous and cheap devices everywhere whose power comes through networking. As a result, many devices may not have capability for basic cybersecurity best practices, such as encryption and operating system updates. Even where capacity exists, manufacturers might not find it economical to patch devices made on a slim margin in a market relentlessly focused on the next generation of products.

CYBER ESPIONAGE

Only the government tops the manufacturing sector as a victim of cyber espionage. Espionage isn't just a matter of lost revenue. It's a threat to economic security with implications for national security.

INDUSTRIAL CONTROL SYSTEM SECURITY IS UNDERRATED

Attackers seeking to disrupt industrial processes don't need to exploit an underlying software vulnerability, the way that sophisticated hackers do when attacking enterprise IT systems. They simply need to gain access to the ICS (perhaps through the corporate IT network) and use the exposed digital controls to manipulate the system into failure. No further hacking required.

The Department of Homeland Security stood up in 2009 the Industrial Control Systems Cyber Emergency Response Team in recognition of this challenge, but the years since have proved disappointing. Its main output is further transmitting alerts already widely available to industry.

RECOMMENDATIONS

INCENTIVES FOR IMPROVING CYBERSECURITY

Small- and medium-sized manufacturers in particular face bad economics when it comes to achieving a level of cybersecurity robust enough to stand up to nation-states, manufacturing's main cyber threat. This gap between commercially sustainable levels of cybersecurity and what's necessary to counteract foreign adversaries isn't just a market failure. It's the space that federal government was designed to fill by dint of its constitutional charge to provide for the common defense.

What's necessary is a public-private partnership that uses economic tools to encourage investment beyond ordinary levels of commercial cybersecurity spending. Specifically, the government should complete the task begun with creation of the National Institute of Standards and Technology Cybersecurity Framework in determining what the most cost-effective elements of cyber defense are.

FUND IOT SECURITY RESEARCH

No amount of incentives can overcome a key characteristic of the Internet of Things: ubiquity of cheap computers with minimal computing power. The ability to seed the environment with cheap computers is what makes the IoT possible.

This is an irreducible problem that requires a different approach to cybersecurity, one premised on building secure systems from insecure components. This isn't a new notion, but it's one that's needs urgent revitalization. The National Science Foundation, the Defense Advanced Research Projects Agency, and the research arm of the Department of Homeland Security should make funding research into this a priority.

ICS-CERT SHOULD BE STRENGTHENED

The Industrial Controls Systems Cyber Emergency Response Team performance needs to enhance its focus on development of best practices and on research. The organization's outreach to the manufacturing sector should also be improved.

"We tend to count things—how many alerts, how many advisories, how many incidents do you respond to," said ICS-CERT director Marty Edwards in May 2016. "I think we have to get to the point of measuring what impact did we make inside of a company, or how is a sector improving or degrading over time in the cybersecurity area," he added. The manufacturing sector concurs.

Eleven

Cybersecurity in the Food and Agriculture Sector

Dr. Robert Zandoli, Global Chief Information
Security Officer, Bunge Limited

WHAT MAKES THE AGRICULTURE SECTOR UNIQUE

Whether it's wired-up off-road equipment and machinery, high-tech food and grain processing, radio frequency ID-tagged livestock, or global-positioning-system tracking, the agriculture sector depends on information systems to sustain and improve operations, competiveness, and profitability.

Wringing out even more efficient yields is a global and domestic necessity. Population growth and rising living standards will increase future demands for agricultural products. Breadbasket countries like the United States need to find sustained growth in yields and more efficient ways to farm to meet these demands. Without making use of remote sensing and computer science, significant increases in agricultural yields will be impossible.

Embracing technology comes with risks, and the sector finds itself targeted as never before, thanks to its intellectual property being coveted by foreign competitors and hacktivists. Until recently, most food and agriculture companies did not invest in cybersecurity defense and were lax in fortifying their infrastructure and developing sound cybersecurity practices. That's beginning to change.

The delay in grasping the threat wasn't limited to the private sector. In 2010, two federal oversight agencies, USDA and FDA, classified cybersecurity as a low priority. However, in 2015, the agencies reversed course.

This past lack of urgency in the agriculture sector was a mistake, as it missed its chance to get ahead of the threats. All sectors of critical infrastructure are interlaced with dependencies, but the biological requirement of food is arguably at the root of them all. An extreme, coordinated cyberattack on agricultural companies would have human and financial consequences.

CHALLENGES FACING THE NEW ADMINISTRATION

Between the seed seller and the supermarket shopper lies a huge, complex, and volatile supply chain, one of the most complex worldwide. Its components are vastly different in size and sophistication and compete in an economy that optimizes for the lowest possible cost. This level of diversity and size, combined with small budgets for overhead, isn't the best recipe for robust cybersecurity since it results in huge disparities among individual components. As a result, the agriculture sector will be confronted with the same weakest-link problem facing other sectors.

Agricultural production and operations will only increase dependency on software and hardware applications vulnerable to cyberattacks. Smart farm machinery will handle many of the labor-intensive and repetitive jobs still requiring manual work. Smarter, more robust automation will expand into food processing as machines become more apt to deal with irregular size, shape, and quality-control problems.

This new level of connectivity creates vulnerabilities that the sector hasn't fully contended with, especially not in the operational environment. Foreign nations are trying to illegally get ahold of American agricultural technology, particularly data on genetic engineering, improved seeds and fertilizer as well as information related to organic insecticide and irrigation equipment. While most recent cases of intellectual property espionage were done the old-fashioned way, it's naive to assume cyber espionage will not become a major element of commercial espionage.

Prospects of agroterrorism also concern the sector. A sophisticated terrorist attack could wreck America's status as a trusted food exporter and undermine domestic confidence in the food supply chain. The sector's growing digitization brings with it new opportunities for terrorists to attack places that previously have been too remote or difficult to strike. Cyber terrorism is a relatively low-cost venture with high payoff potential, making the risks of agroterrorism too large to ignore.

RECOMMENDATIONS

INCREASE AWARENESS

Neither branch of government gives food and agriculture cybersecurity the attention it demands. While new regulations from the federal government are not necessary, agencies that interact with the sector should recognize cybersecurity for the priority issues it has. The FDA and USDA should start educational programs promoting good cybersecurity practices among sector industries.

There is no congressional subcommittee charged with food and agriculture cybersecurity oversight or deals with communication technology's new dominant role in the sector's growth. Committees within the full House and Senate agricultural committees must be assigned this task.

DEFINE WHAT CONSTITUTES A NATION-STATE ATTACK AGAINST THE AGRICULTURE SECTOR

Despite widespread attacks by foreign powers, the federal government has yet to define at what point a cyberattack constitutes an act of war or what type of defense it will offer against such attacks. Nor has it updated and adjusted its defense spending in light of this modern threat.

INCENTIVES

Increasing cybersecurity will cost money, and finding the additional funding will not be simple for the sector since it is governed by tight margins and faces a highly competitive world market. Federal involvement in correcting food and agriculture market failures goes back to the New Deal, and this is a new market failure that need correction. Loan forgiveness or grants tied to cybersecurity practices measured against benchmarks such as the NIST Cybersecurity Framework should be implemented, as should new or modified incentive programs for standards, practices, and technologies that are not cost effective but necessary for national security.

IMPROVE INFORMATION SHARING

Agricultural cybersecurity information sharing lacks a center. The sector needs a dedicated cyber-threat information-sharing mechanism, designed for chief information security officers at large corporations, industry associations, and agricultural cooperatives. For smaller, individual enterprises, this mechanism should provide the option of automated updates to threat-protection software. There are plenty of data exchanges dedicated to various threats, such as food-borne illnesses or crop diseases, but cyber gets lost.

Twelve

The Evolving Role of Boards in Cyber-Risk Oversight

Ken Daly, CEO, National Association of Corporate Directors
Larry Clinton, President and CEO, Internet Security Alliance

One of the core roles of a board of directors in any organization is to oversee risk. This oversight has always encompassed physical assets, human capital, and the like. Over the last two decades, the nature of enterprise asset value has shifted away from the physical to into the digital sphere. In the private sector, for example, up to 80 percent of total value of the Fortune 500 now consists of intellectual property and other intangibles.

In 2014 the National Association of Corporate Directors, in conjunction with AIG and the Internet Security Alliance, published the *NACD Director's Handbook on Cyber-Risk Oversight*. The handbook was unique in that it shifted focus away from the operational information technology issues that had traditionally dominated cybersecurity discussions and instead placed cyber risk in the strategic context that directors were most familiar with—including mergers and acquisitions, new product and service launches, strategic partnerships, and so on.

In the 2016 edition of its *Global State of Information Security Survey*, PricewaterhouseCoopers credited the handbook, by name, with contributing to significant improvements in how corporations were understanding, managing, and overseeing cyber risk.

UNDERSTANDING THE SPECIFIC CYBER THREATS THAT ARE MOST MATERIAL TO THE ORGANIZATION

Members of management and the board of directors must treat cybersecurity as an enterprise-wide risk issue, not a "technology issue" that can be relegated to an IT department.

The implications for boards of directors are twofold. First, directors should ask members of management to translate "cyber risks" into business and strategy risks and assess them in the context of the company's overall risk appetite. Aspects of those risks will likely be very different among consumer retailers, biotech companies, traditional manufacturers, high-tech startups, utilities, law firms, and banks. Second, boards need to set the expectation with management that success is defined by how quickly the organization can detect—and respond to—cyberattacks and data breaches. When it comes to cyber threats, protection is essential, but total prevention is unrealistic.

ESTABLISHING BOARD PROCESSES THAT SUPPORT HIGH-QUALITY DIALOGUE ON CYBER MATTERS

The *Report of the NACD Blue Ribbon Commission on Risk Governance: Balancing Risk and Reward* recommended that risk oversight ought to be part of the duties of the full board. The full board should be briefed at least semiannually or as situations warrant. The allocation of cyber-risk-oversight responsibilities should be clearly outlined in the board's governance guidelines and committee charters to avoid either duplication of activities or gaps in oversight.

MAINTAINING ACCESS TO CURRENT INFORMATION AND EXPERTISE ABOUT CYBER RISKS

Depending on their industry circumstances and threat profile (among other things), some organizations will choose to include a board member with specific cyber-related experience, and others will not. All boards can and should take steps to bring cutting-edge cyber expertise into boardroom discussions, by requesting briefings on a regular basis from independent advisors such as external audit firms and outside counsel, third-party consultants, or law enforcement. This information should be viewed as complementary to—not a replacement for or a signal of mistrust in—reports from management.

COORDINATION WITH GOVERNMENT
Individually and together, NACD and ISA have conducted a large number of roundtable dialogues with directors, senior executives, and leaders from government and law enforcement. Several themes have emerged from these discussions.

ONE-SIZE-FITS-ALL MANDATES FOR BOARD-LEVEL CYBER OVERSIGHT ARE NOT HELPFUL
Proposals aimed at requiring all boards to have a director who is a "cybersecurity expert"—even setting aside the fact that the severe shortage of senior-level cybersecurity talent, with hundreds of thousands of positions vacant in the United States alone, making such proposals impossible to implement—would take the important responsibility for board composition and director recruitment out of the hands of the only group with firsthand knowledge about a specific board's current and future skill requirements.

INFORMATION SHARING BETWEEN THE PUBLIC AND PRIVATE SECTORS IS HIGHLY BENEFICIAL
Directors and senior executives alike are interested in gaining a clearer understanding of what government agencies such as the departments of Homeland Security and Justice, the FBI, and the Secret Service do—and what they don't do—for companies in the cyber-risk arena, both in general and in the aftermath of a specific breach or attack. Because relationships with government and law enforcement are in management's domain, NACD has encouraged directors to ask the CIO, CISO, CEO, and other executives to provide the board with updates about those relationships and corresponding public sector–private sector communication activities related to cybersecurity. Expanding safe-harbor provisions related to information sharing is also important.

IDENTIFY OPPORTUNITIES TO COORDINATE AND STREAMLINE REGULATORY REQUIREMENTS

Current cyber regulations differ and in some cases contradict one another on multiple dimensions: from state to state, state versus federal, and domestic versus foreign jurisdictions, to name just a few. Industry-specific requirements add another layer of complexity. The associated cost burden is significant, especially for emerging-growth companies. More uniformity would enable management teams and boards to provide better information more efficiently. Another point of difficulty is that companies and boards are frequently faced with conflicting demands after a cyber breach: on the one hand, demand for prompt disclosure to satisfy requirements from the Securities and Exchange Commission and regulators for investor and consumer protection, and on the other hand, requests from law enforcement to refrain from going public in order to help an active investigation.

Thirteen

Cybersecurity Assurance: A Comprehensive Approach

Center for Audit Quality

T he Center for Audit Quality's members are audit and consulting firms that perform financial-statement audits of public companies. Because these firms provide a wide range of audit and consulting services across all industry sectors, they have the opportunity to observe cyber readiness in a variety of situations. We also describe our thoughts on a more comprehensive approach to assess and provide assurance over internal controls related to cybersecurity risk management. Work is currently being undertaken by the American Institute of CPAs and the CAQ to operationalize this new approach.

KEY CONSIDERATIONS FROM THE AUDITOR'S VANTAGE POINT

Initially, all things "cyber" were relegated to the information technology department in most companies. Today, the trend has shifted and the C-suite and boards of directors are increasingly taking ownership of cyber risk. While there continues to be considerable discussion of what management and board responsibilities are related to cybersecurity and corporate cyber readiness, many organizations are still working to find the most comprehensive structure. There are a few leading frameworks but numerous standards, methodologies, and processes that have been put forth by federal and state governments, industry-specific groups, independent agencies, and other stakeholders. We believe the options available to better manage cyber risks would benefit greatly from enhanced consistency across these myriad approaches.

DEVELOPING A MORE COMPREHENSIVE APPROACH

We see a need for organizations to conduct ongoing, strategic, enterprise-wide assessments of their cyber risk and the adequacy of their programs and internal controls. Existing financial-statement audit process and related internal control assessments do not extend to controls specifically related to cybersecurity procedures and controls unless they impact the financial statements.

The profession is proposing a new, comprehensive approach driven by the internal control structure of the company and that can be delivered with independence and objectivity. The American Institute of CPAs has begun to development of a new and comprehensive process to examine internal controls related specifically to cybersecurity risk management. This cybersecurity examination would be separate and apart from the existing financial-statement audit process.

The objective of a process would be to provide the user with three key pieces of information about the entity's cybersecurity-risk-management program: (1) a description of the entity's cybersecurity-risk-management program, (2) management's assertion about whether that description is fairly presented and whether the controls are suitably designed and operating effectively, and (3) the practitioner's opinion on fair presentation of the description and on the suitability of design and operating effectiveness of the controls.

The examination that the AICPA is contemplating would be entirely voluntary on the part of companies and audit firms. The criteria that are being developed are a customized version of the AICPA Trust Services Criteria that have been enhanced for cybersecurity considerations and closely aligned with the seventeen principles in the Internal Control-Integrated Framework, an internal control framework issued in 2013 by the Committee of Sponsoring Organizations of the Treadway Commission, known as COSO.

The criteria will be mapped to the existing National Institute of Standards and Technology Cybersecurity Framework and the International Organization for Standardization Information Security Management standard (ISO/IEC 27001). In this way, companies can choose from among multiple cybersecurity internal control frameworks for their cybersecurity-risk-management programs and not be required to move to different standards to avail themselves of an independent and objective assessment of their cybersecurity internal control environment. However, reports issued under this new approach would benefit from the consistency, rigor, independence, and objectivity of the practitioners.

THE AUDIT PROFESSION: A STRONG FOUNDATION TO BUILD ON

One of the cornerstones of such a new approach would be the application of the core elements of services from an independent auditor: independence and objectivity.

The audit profession, through performing internal control over financial reporting audits, has further honed existing expertise in evaluating the design and implementation of internal controls. As part of the ICFR audit, auditors look at a flow of transactions and ask, "What could go wrong?" They critically assess whether management has a control in place that is sufficiently designed to timely prevent or detect a potential material misstatement. The auditor then tests those controls to determine whether they operate effectively to address the assessed risk of misstatement.

Auditors also have experience in performing independent, objective assessments of an entity's privacy and security practices through other attest engagements that are already trusted in the capital market. The audit profession brings a multidisciplinary skill set and approach to these engagements, involving subject-matter expertise in cybersecurity and information technology. The proposed service would be an extension of this existing knowledge and experience.

PRINCIPLES FOR BETTER CYBERSECURITY OUTCOMES

We believe there are several overall principles that must support all efforts at improving cybersecurity:

341

- Avoid blaming the victim. To date, the prevailing attitude when a breach has been discovered and disclosed is to see the customers and shareholders as the only victims.
- The regulatory systems that come into play in breach situations should allow for an appropriate assessment of cyber defenses deployed by management, including the timeliness of remediation and the resiliency of the company.
- Improvements driven by the private sector significantly increase the opportunity to produce meaningful and timely improvements in current practice.

Fourteen

The Role of Cyber Insurance in Promoting Cybersecurity

Tracie Grella, Head of Cyber Risk Insurance, AIG

MARKET OVERVIEW

Insurance exists to help companies and individuals manage the financial impact of unexpected events. Demand for cyber insurance is rapidly increasing, but take-up rates vary on the basis of company size, industry sector, value of data assets, and regulatory requirements. Companies that purchase cyber insurance generally are buying modest limits. A recent survey of risk managers suggests that nearly 60 percent buy less than $20 million of coverage.

CYBER INSURANCE—PRODUCT AND SERVICE

The insurance industry has created a system to help companies plan, prepare for and respond to incidents. Insurers frequently conduct in-depth reviews of company cybersecurity frameworks during the underwriting process. Insurers also offer a suite of ex-ante and ex-post services that minimize the likelihood and impact of a breach.

MARKET CHALLENGES

While the market is advancing quickly, there are several inhibiting factors that constrain its full capacity:

- Disparate company preparedness and investment.
- Lack of suitable data for modeling.
- Challenges of risk aggregation and correlation.
- Weak public understanding of cyberattack importance.
- Competing priorities and opportunity costs of insurance purchases.
- Shortage of qualified talent to address the risk.
- Rapid growth of the Internet of Things and resultant risks.

RECOMMENDATIONS

TAX INCENTIVES FOR CYBERSECURITY INVESTMENT
This could take the form of tax incentives for such investments or the purchase of cyber insurance. The latter would ensure that more companies are subjected to an independent review of their cybersecurity framework. Companies that partner with cyber insurers also have strong economic incentives to continually improve security practices that raise the overall level of national preparedness.

GOVERNMENT INTELLIGENCE SHARING
Some Information and Security Analysis Centers are more effective than others, and it would be beneficial to enhance all of them to ensure a consistent level of information and engagement across industry sectors. While participation in such groups is voluntary, the federal government can incentivize strong participation by using these forums to deliver timely and highly valuable intelligence on emerging cybersecurity threats.

SCENARIO PLANNING WORKSHOPS
The insurance industry is prepared to facilitate cross-industry cyber scenario workshops. These would involve federal government agencies, universities, corporations, and other participants. The workshops would focus on designing and implementing scenario analysis to better understand the types of attacks that could impact the private and public sector.

CYBERSECURITY EDUCATION

The government's program to certify universities and provide loan forgiveness to students who major in cybersecurity and work for the government is a very good start. We recommend continuing to invest in such programs to ensure that a suitable pool of talent is filled and that companies can draw on this pool. Federal funding for research at nonprofits and universities would also dramatically improve the level of knowledge in the field.

PUBLIC SERVICE CAMPAIGN

We also recommend creating a public campaign similar to the "Say No to Drugs" campaign. Additionally, educational materials should be developed and delivered to midsized and small businesses through various channels such as the Small Business Administration and other governmental programs.

GEOPOLITICAL RISK MANAGEMENT

Companies are incapable of protecting against sophisticated, well-funded nation-state attacks. As such, the DHS, FBI, and NSA need to take the lead in protecting the country against such attacks through appropriate offensive and defensive means. Further, intelligence gained from such actions should be shared openly with the private sector to enhance understanding of threats and allow for preparedness.

CLARIFY THE TERRORISM RISK INSURANCE ACT

Large-scale terrorist attacks launched by cyber means should qualify as certified acts of terrorism and trigger TRIA for covered lines. Additionally, greater clarity on what constitutes an act of cyber war would be helpful to ensure that all parties are clear if, and when, an event occurs.

LEGAL AND REGULATORY IMMUNITY

The federal government should consider legal or regulatory immunity for companies that develop products to prevent and address cyberattacks. The federal government should also consider extending the SAFETY Act to include liability limitations for certified products and services that are designed to prevent or mitigate loss from cyber terrorism and cyber-criminal activity.

SOFTWARE AND HARDWARE SECURITY STANDARDS

The insurance industry also supports the creation of an independent organization that would be tasked with certifying the security of commonly used software and hardware devices. This initiative would be equivalent to standards developed under the Underwriter Laboratories for the introduction of new electronic devices and components.

Fifteen

Deploying a Voluntary Cyber-Resilience Program: A Strategic Imperative

Andrea Bonime-Blanc, JD/PhD, CEO, GEC Risk Advisory

A HOLISTIC APPROACH TO CORPORATE CYBER RESILIENCE

This chapter makes the case that to be cyber resilient, businesses of any kind, shape, or form should design, develop, and implement a voluntary internal cyber governance, risk, and compliance/culture program ("Cyber-GRC program"). Developing and adopting such a program allows companies to gain better and more sustainable cyber resilience. The cyber-resilient company will have the following three general categories of Cyber-GRC in place: cyber governance, cyber-risk management, and cyber culture.

A ROBUST CYBER-RESILIENT CULTURE TRUMPS THE LAW

By building internal resilience into the governance, risk, and culture of a company, the need for additional and potentially costly and ineffective laws and regulations will be obviated.

A PARADIGM FROM ANOTHER TIME: THE DEFENSE INDUSTRY INITIATIVE AND THE RISE OF THE EFFECTIVE E&C PROGRAM

The paradigm is the result of decades of collaboration between companies, professional associations, and research and academic sources, as well

347

as lessons learned from challenging examples, mistakes, and scandals. However, cyber risk is different from the average ethics and compliance challenge. Cyber events occur mainly because of the barrage of technological, geopolitical, and economic changes that have evolved. Companies do not fully control cyber challenges.

The Defense Industry Initiative emerged in the wake of several waves of corruption and fraud involving the defense industry. It calls for five key components of defense contractor self-governance:

1. Creating well-defined risk-based codes of conduct.
2. Developing a system that tracks and vets conflicts of interest.
3. Developing an employee instructional and communications system.
4. A system to monitor compliance and internal controls.
5. An independent audit committee.

The DII was the principal precursor to a key governmental initiative: Chapter Eight of the United States Sentencing Guidelines. The USSG provides a series of guidelines for prosecutors and judges to help them determine whether a company has an effective E&C program, which could lead to substantial financial and reputational benefits.

THE EMERGENCE OF THE USSG
Chapter Eight of the sentencing guidelines provided the first cross-industry set of government incentives for corporate wrongdoers to create an internal system of business conduct and compliance. In essence, Chapter Eight mimics many of the tenets of the DII principles.

THE EMERGENCE OF A GLOBAL E&C PARADIGM
The most recent salvo of an effective E&C program was issued in mid-2016 by the Ethics and Compliance Initiative, consisting of a series of principles:

- Principle 1: ethics and compliance is central to business strategy.
- Principle 2: ethics and compliance risks are identified, owned, managed, and mitigated.

- Principle 3: leaders at all levels across the organization build and sustain a culture of integrity.
- Principle 4: the organization encourages, protects, and values the reporting of concerns and suspected wrongdoing.
- Principle 5: the organization takes action and holds itself accountable when wrongdoing occurs.

BUILDING AND DEPLOYING A VOLUNTARY AND EFFECTIVE CYBER-GRC PROGRAM: A ROADMAP

There are three basic elements of a strong cyber resilience or GRC Program: governance, risk management, and culture.

GOVERNANCE

This means that the company board, C-suite and top enterprise risk and technology managers are all on the same page about how strategic risk, including cyber risk, is handled at the company. Integrate cyber-risk management into enterprise risk management.

RISK MANAGEMENT

Understand that cyber risk is more often than not a strategic risk: not every risk is a strategic risk. Many are operational, financial, technological, legal, environmental, and the like. Cyber risk can be a strategic risk under two circumstances: instantaneously, when it seriously and deleteriously affects business strategy, or over time, when a situation affecting a company's and its stakeholders' well-being has been brewing slowly and eventually surfaces with high impact and strategic consequences.

Understand cyber-reputation risk as it relates to your company: reputation risk has become one of the top five to ten strategic risks that concern boards and C-suites. Any risk, including cyber risk, qualifies as an underlying risk onto which reputation risk may layer and attach itself.

Know your cyber stakeholders and their crown jewels: companies have stakeholders, and each stakeholder has one or more "stakes" in the company. Companies should focus on how to manage their risks in a manner that builds resilience, sustainability, and protection of stakeholder interests.

Knowledge of stakeholders and their crown jewels goes a long way in understanding what the top cyber-risk priorities are.

CULTURE

Create a robust cyber culture: integrate cyber-risk learning and teachable moments into ethics and compliance or human resources or learning center scheduled and unscheduled training and take it all the way up to the boardroom on a regular and periodic basis.

CYBER RESILIENCE BEGINS AT HOME

If companies build it, regulators should respect it. The key is to create cyber resilience through the deployment of an appropriate Cyber-GRC program that is customized to the needs and profile of a company and that both private and public sectors alike can recognize as such.

Sixteen

The Digital Equilibrium Project: Balancing Cybersecurity and Privacy

James Kaplan, Partner, McKinsey & Co
Salim Hasham, Partner, McKinsey & Co
Chris Rezek, Senior Expert, McKinsey & Co

C oncerned that today's polarized approaches to privacy and security are resulting in the erosion of both, a group of cybersecurity, government, and privacy experts banded together as part of the "Digital Equilibrium Project" to foster a new, productive dialogue on balancing security and privacy in the connected world. This chapter contains our foundational thoughts on how to advance the discussion past simple binary propositions about security and privacy.

WHAT WE PROPOSE

- A new balanced approach, not based on creating detailed polices or legislation but a framework for creating those instruments. A constitution, not a book of laws.
- A set of structures for continued dialogue and problem solving, so that continued rapid changes can be understood and incorporated into policy, law, and public discourse.

- A framework that builds on successes and finds and leverages analogies to today's world in free trade, diplomacy, law enforcement, and social norms, while embracing the unique characteristics of speed, scale, and change that mark our new digital age.

QUESTION 1: WHAT PRIVACY MANAGEMENT PRACTICES SHOULD ORGANIZATIONS ADOPT TO ACHIEVE THEIR GOALS WHILE PROTECTING THEIR CUSTOMERS?

In an open market, consumers could choose to do business with providers who managed personal information in ways the consumer could accept. However, those market forces can only work when there is transparency, when both sides know what they are trading, and open communication can enable the market to settle on its "natural" level.

STARTING HYPOTHESIS

While perfect transparency is impossible, organizations could make significant progress by clarifying and simplifying privacy statements. Consumers who understood information collection practices could make informed choices, even automatically if privacy policies are machine-readable, and help establish a more market-based approach to establishing norms. Machine-readable parameters set by consumers, if made practical, could enable a more fluid transaction-based approach to negotiating privacy between these parties.

QUESTION 2: HOW CAN ORGANIZATIONS CONTINUE TO IMPROVE THE PROTECTION OF THEIR DIGITAL INFRASTRUCTURES AND ADOPT PRIVACY MANAGEMENT PRACTICES THAT PROTECT THEIR EMPLOYEES?

Employees work for their companies, and companies have a right and obligation to protect their assets and reputations, including gaining information about their employees. As digital infrastructures become more fluid and software based, organizations will be left with only two constants upon which they can focus: their users and their users' applications. Those challenges cannot be addressed at a technical level alone. Boards of directors could play a far larger role in developing policies for privacy and security.

STARTING HYPOTHESIS

Employees in privacy-oriented nations could recognize that they have more to lose by not empowering their security professionals than they do to gain through inflexible postures on privacy. Enterprises could do a better job of providing transparency so their employees know how their information is being collected and protected in the workplace. Boards of directors could add new members who offer the new skills they need and can collaborate to create more shared knowledge and perspectives.

Governments could borrow from the nuclear (or other) industry to create and clarify a government role to help corporations protect their critical infrastructure from attack while managing privacy and security interests. We need to find a way to rework the compliance versus cyber balance so that companies spend more time on value-added cybersecurity strategy and less on compliance-related work.

QUESTION 3: WHAT PRACTICES SHOULD GOVERNMENTS ADOPT TO MAINTAIN CIVIL LIBERTIES AND EXPECTATIONS OF PRIVACY, WHILE ENSURING SAFETY AND SECURITY OF ITS CITIZENS AND CRITICAL INFRASTRUCTURE?

In terms of our collective physical safety, this question is the most pressing to make progress on, but perhaps the most difficult. As individuals, corporations, nations, criminals, and terrorists all increasingly roam the Internet together, enabling governments to protect their citizens without compromising the privacy and trust of those citizens is increasingly difficult.

STARTING HYPOTHESIS

Government could play a bigger role in helping define the "how," not just the "why," of protecting critical infrastructure, building on the NIST Cybersecurity Framework. Government could provide proper incentives for corporations to invest in cybersecurity for critical infrastructure. Governments could develop and enforce safety standards for software used in critical infrastructures. Governance and transparency could be strengthened for intelligence agencies, so that citizens can have confidence that those agencies are working within the existing laws and guidelines.

Government could communicate more clearly both the intentions and realities of intelligence gathering efforts.

Legal limits to domestic military involvement can be rethought: digital tools can now create kinetic actions to cause real physical harm to our infrastructure. Governments need to find an approach for attribution and retribution to find and punish culprits of cybercrime, even across national borders. At the same time, private companies may need to be allowed to "hack back" and retrieve their stolen information before it's gone for good.

QUESTION 4: WHAT NORMS SHOULD COUNTRIES ADOPT TO PROTECT THEIR SOVEREIGNTY WHILE ENABLING GLOBAL COMMERCE AND COLLABORATION AGAINST CRIMINAL AND TERRORIST THREATS?

Spying on communications has never been easier for governments with the proper skills, and as more information of every form has become digital, more governments have gotten into the business of spying on behalf of their local corporations, in the form of intellectual property theft and communications intercepts.

STARTING HYPOTHESIS

Just as nations finally concluded that the long-term benefits of free trade outweighed the short-term benefits of capturing or sinking each other's ships on the high seas, nations will eventually come together to create digital rules of engagement. We need to limit cyber espionage, the targeting of individual corporations or organizations for economic or political motives. We need to create "arms control" mechanisms to limit the spread of increasingly sophisticated malware tools. Unlike traditional weapons, cyber weapons spread rapidly, are quickly reproduced and modified, and are cheap. We need to address the issues of nonstate actors who often have multiple roles, working for their own goals as well as providing services to governments. We need to ensure that digital tools can be created free from nation-state interference either overt or covert so that these tools can be trusted by users globally.

Seventeen

Best Practices for Cybersecurity Public-Private Partnerships

Larry Clinton, President and CEO, Internet Security Alliance

INTRODUCTION

President Barack Obama has said,

> The federal government cannot succeed in securing cyberspace if it works in isolation. The public and private sectors interests are intertwined with a shared responsibility for ensuring a secure, reliable infrastructure upon which businesses and government depend...Only through such partnerships will the United States be able to enhance cybersecurity and reap the full benefits of the digital revolution.

However, despite years of attempting to conduct cybersecurity programs in partnership, it's become apparent that not only were most partnership programs unsatisfying to both parties but even the definition of partnership is also unclear. This confusion and frustration was seen as endangering the partnership model or redefining it in such a way as to rob it of its novel approach to security.

This chapter identifies a set of best practices for operating cybersecurity public-private partnerships on the basis of a collaborative research project conducted jointly by the IT Sector Coordinating Council and DHS staff.

METHOD

The government and industry investigators used a modified critical-incident methodology to examine a range of joint programs ostensibly run under the partnership model as identified in the National Infrastructure Protection Plan.

Acting separately, the government and industry groups independently evaluated the various projects on a success scale. Both government and industry evaluators determined that same projects to be successful and less successful.

The groups then undependably identified a set of practices that in their expert opinion as practitioners in the field made the programs successful or not. Consensus was reached as to what practices accounted for the success of the projects.

The case studies that were used for this analysis included

- the 2006 development of the National Infrastructure Protection Plan,
- the IT Sector Baseline Risk Assessment,
- the construction of the "Cyberspace Policy Review,"
- industry integration into the National Infrastructure Coordination Center,
- the IT Supply-Chain–Risk-Management Collaboration, and
- the development of the "Blueprint for a Secure Cyber Future."

RESULTS

Both industry and government evaluators agreed on a dozen best practices that tended to generate successful partnership programs in cybersecurity. These are as follows:

- Senior-level commitment to the partnership process communicated to staff and upper echelons.

- Involvement at the priority, goal, and objective phases of projects, not just implementation.
- Use of the process identified in the NIPP for involving industry.
- Reaching out to stakeholders early on, ideally at the "blank page" stage.
- Continuous and regular interaction between government and industry stakeholders.
- Providing adequate time for stakeholder review (equivalent to government review).
- Establishing coleadership of programs.
- Consensus partnership decision making.
- Communicating genuine interest in stakeholder input (e.g., via codrafting).
- Adequate engagement from federal agencies beyond DHS.
- Government follow-through on partnership-related decisions.
- Adequate and competent support services.

EXAMPLES OF USE OF THESE BEST PRACTICES
Chapter 17 concludes with two examples of partnership programs, the development of the NIST Cybersecurity Framework and the CSRIC Working Group 4 program conducted by the FCC and the Telecommunications Sector Coordinating Council.

Both programs follow most if not all of the best practices identified in the previous study and were publically judged to be successful by both industry and government.